A–Z OF BRITISH
BUS BODIES

A–Z OF BRITISH BUS BODIES

James Taylor

THE CROWOOD PRESS

First published in 2013 by
The Crowood Press Ltd
Ramsbury, Marlborough
Wiltshire SN8 2HR

www.crowood.com

British Library Cataloguing-in-Publication Data
A catalogue record for this book is available from the British Library.

ISBN 978 1 84797 530 0

Typeset by Jean Cussons Typesetting, Diss, Norfolk

Printed and bound in Singapore by Craft Print International Ltd

CONTENTS

LIST OF ABBREVIATIONS

It is standard practice to use abbreviations to describe bus-body configurations. The abbreviations were developed in the 1950s and have been continuously adapted since to meet changing circumstances. Some of them will be found in this book and so, for readers not familiar with them, they are listed below.

A typical abbreviation breaks down into three main groups. For example, in the abbreviation H56R, the figure in the centre is the seating capacity and the letters on either side indicate other features of the bodywork. (Note that on double-deck bodies, the figure may be subdivided, for example H30/26R, which would indicate thirty seats on the upper deck and twenty-six on the lower deck.)

Before the seating capacity figure:

B   Single-deck bus (stage-carriage type)
C   Coach
Ch   Charabanc
DP   Dual-purpose single-deck (suitable for bus or coach operation)
F   Full-front where not normally fitted, such as on vertical-engined models; this letter may precede others, as in FC35F
H   Highbridge-type double-deck, with centre upper-deck gangway
HD   Half-deck or 'observation coach' type, with rear seats on a higher level than front seats
L   Lowbridge-type double-deck, with sunken side gangway on upper deck to permit lower overall height
O   Open top; this is used for both double-deckers and single-deck saloons
T   Toastrack (open-sided single-deck type)
U   Utility type, built to 1942–5 Ministry of Supply specifications; this letter may precede others, as in UH56R. This abbreviation has largely fallen out of use today

After the seating capacity figure:

C   Centre entrance
D   Dual entrance
F   Forward entrance (front-engined types) or Front entrance (underfloor-engined types)
R   Rear entrance
RD   Rear entrance with platform doors
RO   Rear entrance with open rear staircase
T   Toilet compartment fitted; this letter may follow others, as in C28FT

Part 1
INTRODUCTION

THE SCOPE OF THIS BOOK

This is the sort of book I wish I had been able to find when I was first interested in buses in the late 1950s. Enthralled by references in the pages of *Buses Illustrated* and by the sight of unusual bodies while on holiday trips around Britain, I wanted to know more about the companies who had built these buses and coaches. It was not hard to find out more about the chassis makers, even defunct ones such as Crossley or Gilford, but there seemed to be no source of reference to tell me about Heaver, Samlesbury, Waveney, Welsh Metal Industries and the like. In fact, only the most basic information about the big names such as Duple, Harrington, MCW and Park Royal seemed to be available in those days.

When I came to prepare this book, I discovered that there were far greater numbers of public service vehicle (PSV) bodybuilders in Britain than I had imagined. That made the task of writing it harder, but more interesting as well. Since I first became interested in buses, of course, a great deal more information has become available both in print and on the web, and it would be wrong of me not to acknowledge how important that has been in putting this book together. Somebody once said that we only think we are tall because we stand on the shoulders of giants and that is a particularly good way of explaining how I feel after preparing this book. The legendary names in the bus enthusiast's world are too many to list here, but they have definitely been the giants.

Right from the start, I should explain that this book is in no way intended to be the definitive reference source to its subject. Such a book would require another lifetime or two to prepare and would run to many volumes. The aim of this book is to make the entry for each coachbuilder into a succinct summary of what is known, that is, enough to satisfy the merely curious, but also a starting point for those interested in discovering more. And there is more – much more – to be discovered. There are still many constructors of PSV bodies who have been only imperfectly identified, or not identified at all. This is particularly true of the 1920s period, but frustratingly true also of a favourite period of mine, which is the late 1940s and early 1950s.

There are very many companies who are known by little more than their name and a date, and I debated long and hard about whether to include them or not. In the end, I thought that I should – discovering that some trace of a company has been recorded is better than finding it absent from these lists, even if the information recorded is not very enlightening. Where information is extremely limited, however, I have wielded an editorial pencil. So I hope that readers will understand that where an entry simply indicates that a company 'constructed single-deck bodies in the late 1920s', it is an invitation to further research on the subject. On that score, if any readers are able to add information or corrections to what is in this book, I would be delighted to hear via Crowood. I will add any new information of substance to a second edition, if one is published.

As the book's title implies, it covers bus and coach bodybuilders who were active between 1919 and 1975. Some of these may only just have crept into the period, so a company that had been active before World War I, but closed down in 1919, would be included. Many companies listed continued in business after 1975; their entries acknowledge this, but generally give only a brief mention of their later activities.

In order to keep the lists within manageable proportions, I have deliberately restricted their scope in some areas. Companies responsible only for minibuses or minibus conversions have been excluded and those that built only welfare-type or works bus bodies are also not listed. Several operators constructed bodywork for their own use in their own workshops; these have also been excluded, unless they also built bodies for other operators as well. However, there is a list of them in the Appendix at the back of the book. Finally, I have included companies based in the Republic of Ireland where information has been available, even though many of them did not sell their products outside their own country.

A book like this cannot provide fully detailed histories of every single PSV bodybuilder within its chosen limits. However, it can offer a first port of call for anybody who wants to know a little more about a company, as well as an encouragement, perhaps, to pursue further research. There are many excellent books on individual coachbuilders to be had, most of them compiled by dedicated enthusiasts. Though they tend to have small print runs and are not always easy to find, typing the name of a coachbuilder of interest into one of the online book specialist sites will very often uncover a copy for sale.

SOURCES

I have put this book together from a huge variety of sources, beginning with my own observations going back to the late 1950s and early 1960s. I have of course drawn on very many books, many written by highly respected PSV authors and some written as one-off labours of love by dedicated enthusiasts. There are so many of these that it would be impossible to list them all; I would not claim to have read all those available, either, and of course there are new ones appearing all the time. However, it is important to make quite clear here that this book relies heavily on the wonderful research that has gone into so many of them and in that respect I make no claims to originality.

I have also gained information from a large number of magazines, most notably *Commercial Motor*, *Bus and Coach*, *Buses* (and its forerunner, *Buses Illustrated*). Particularly useful have been the *Commercial Motor* online archive at www.archive.commercialmotor.com and some of the PSV Circle publications devoted to bodybuilders. I have made extensive use of archives held by the Omnibus Society, the Kithead Trust and the British Commercial Vehicle Museum (BCVM), although I would not claim

by any means to have gleaned every scrap of information that may be available there. The internet has been a further source and information has turned up in some of the wonderful sites fed by reminiscences (such as Old Bus Photos), in some of the more serious sites dedicated to recording fleets (Ian's Bus Stop and the Peter Gould material at www.petergould.co.uk), and even in local history sites not otherwise interested in anything to do with the PSV world.

Photographs have come from a number of sources, including the BCVM, the R.C. Davis Collection (now held by the Omnibus Society), the Kithead Trust, Nick Larkin, Roy Marshall, the Omnibus Society, Ron Phillips, the late Brian Smith (via the Canvey Island Transport Museum), the Peter Davis collection (now held by the Omnibus Society) and my own collection. In a small number of cases, it has not been possible to discover the identity of the original photographer despite best efforts; sincere apologies here if any reader feels slighted and I would aim to put the matter right if this book goes to a second edition.

About halfway through turning my mass of notes into a book, I also discovered in the Omnibus Society archives a wonderful typewritten document that listed bus and coach bodybuilders. I have since learned that this was put together by Derek Roy of the PSV Circle, as an aid to the Circle's sub-editors. His painstaking work has contributed a great deal of detail to my own book and if I had discovered the document earlier, I would have had to put in a lot less effort!

Finally, thanks go to Nigel Furness for reading through the manuscript at an early stage and providing constructive criticism; to Tom Clarke, who provided last-minute help on his speciality, Gurney Nutting; and to the Omnibus Society itself, whose members' formidable knowledge has made this book far more accurate than it otherwise might have been.

CONTEXT AND BACKGROUND

In Britain as elsewhere, the business of building bodies for public service vehicles (PSVs) grew up separately from the business of building chassis for those vehicles. The reasons were simple. Many of the bodybuilders had started life in the days of the horse-drawn vehicle and their specialism was in constructing sound and attractive bodies, to which the addition of axles was a mere accessory. The chassis makers, on the other hand, mostly had very different backgrounds. Their expertise was in things mechanical, notably in engines and gearboxes; mounting these on a ladder-frame chassis was a secondary part of their activity. The two types of manufacturer needed one another, but there was no pressure in the beginning for them to amalgamate and thereby produce complete vehicles. Although some of the chassis makers did turn to making complete vehicles, they were in the minority.

The early years of the twentieth century saw some quite fierce competition, with chassis imported from continental Europe vying for custom with home-built types. Yet the bodies were almost invariably made in Britain to suit local requirements. The Great War of 1914–18 brought some great strides in the technology of road vehicles, with body makers and chassis manufacturers subsequently enjoying a period of peaceful co-existence for half a century or more.

However, things were changing. As the market for buses and coaches began to contract during the 1950s, a battle for survival began. At first, it was characterized by mergers and by the failures of the smaller companies. Then, as the pressures became more intense, the move towards integral construction (bodies that carried their own running units and had no separate chassis frame) gathered momentum. The major steps were made at the end of the 1960s, with those body makers who had not joined the trend finding themselves in difficulties.

By the middle of the 1970s, the integral bus and coach had become the norm and the old distinction between body maker and chassis manufacturer had largely disappeared. At the same time, continental European manufacturers had begun to exploit the gaps that were developing in the British market. By the later 1970s, the bus bodybuilding scene in Britain had changed forever and it is at that point – actually a period rather than a clearly defined date – that this book closes its coverage. For the sake of convenience, the cut-off date chosen is 1975.

CONSTRUCTING A BODY

A 1938 publication issued by Duple shows the bodybuilding process of the time from start to finish and helps in understanding what happened at this major coachbuilder. Obviously, smaller companies operating from less spacious premises had less sophisticated methods, but the essential principles would have been the same. In 1938, all Duple bodies were of composite construction and the company prided itself on invariably delivering completed vehicles on time.

When a customer's chassis reached the Hendon works from its manufacturer, the first job was to strip it of all electrical and loose equipment. Once the chassis had reached Duple, it would not move again under its own power until it had been completed; tractors were used to move unfinished vehicles from one department to the next.

The Drawing Office prepared a full-size drawing of the agreed body design. This drawing then went with the vehicle through the various stages of manufacture, to avoid the need for departmental foremen to make constant visits to a central Drawing Office. The completed drawing was accompanied by full workshop schedules, itemized with instructions for each department involved in the construction of the body. When the job was completed, all the information was recorded so that a repeat order or a request for replacement sections could be dealt with immediately. Amendments to the original instructions were also recorded, on special coloured amendment sheets.

The sections of the wooden framework were roughly prepared in the Mill, before passing to the adjacent

Setting-Out Department. It was here that jigs were formed, wood was shaped and the mortises and tenons required to join one section to the next were prepared. Meanwhile, the metal and metal-reinforced elements of the composite bodywork – bulkheads, wheel arches, cross-members, skirt rails, and so on – were fabricated in the Smithy and Fitters' Shop.

The elements of each body were then taken to the Body Assembly bays, where the new body began to take shape. Each body was assembled on a jig, or on body trestles. The base, bulkhead, sides, rear end, roof, cab and doors were all put together to form the body frame or skeleton.

The body frame then moved to the Erection Shop for mounting to the chassis. Here, it was clothed with sheet metal panels formed and beaten in the Sheet Metal Section. Once fully panelled, each vehicle moved on to the Paint Bay. This was essentially a large workshop where the air was changed every three minutes to prevent contamination and to reduce the presence of dust particles. Some panels, such as mudguards, would be sprayed off the vehicle.

Meanwhile, the vehicle's interior trim and seats were being prepared in the Trimming Department and Seat-Making Section. The customer would have specified a particular style of seating and upholstery, choosing a moquette from stock patterns that were kept in books.

Each completed vehicle then moved to the Finishing Bays. Here, any remaining loose parts or electrical items removed when the chassis had been delivered were refitted. The vehicle then passed over an inspection pit where it would be examined by a Certifying Officer from the

A full-size body drawing is prepared in the Duple Drawing Office. The date is 3 March 1937; the body is for an Albion chassis.

Ministry of Transport, who would issue a Certificate of Fitness if he was satisfied. Clients were also invited to inspect their new vehicles at this stage if they so wished. From there, the completed vehicle was passed to the Delivery Department and on to the customer.

THE 1920s

The decade following the end of the Great War in 1918 was one of expansion in the bus business, and in the coach business too. Municipal authorities began to see the advantage of the motor bus (and also the trolleybus) as a more flexible alternative to the tram. In rural districts, demand for small service buses increased as these became a popular alternative to the train. And as the nation gained a taste for day trips and longer tours, demand also rose for more comfortable vehicles, the distant forerunners of today's coaches.

Chassis builders responded as best they could, but there was a shortage initially, so many military lorries that had survived war service were refurbished mechanically and fitted with bus or coach bodywork to meet demand. From the middle of the 1920s, imported American chassis helped meet demand, too. All this created an additional demand for bodywork and after 1919 many small local businesses turned their hand to bus and coach body construction, often combining it with building van and lorry bodywork, and even car bodies as well. Others were established from nothing, often by men returning from service in the Great War and eager to set themselves up in business.

Chassis arriving at the Duple works in Hendon, 1938. They would have been driven there by road from their manufacturers. An AEC Regal and a Dennis Lance are seen here.

Timber preparation was carried out in the Mill, where wood was cut to size.

The major national bodybuilders had not yet become established and it was common practice for operators of all kinds to patronize local companies if they could. There was good business to be had by securing orders from municipal authorities, which tended to want large batches of buses to the same design in order to simplify servicing and spares. However, there was also a reasonable living to be made by supplying bodywork for local independent operators and, as a result, dozens of small companies turned to this. There were also as yet no nationally agreed standards governing bus construction and, as local authorities had the last say on what was and was not permitted, the firms who constructed bus bodies found it easier to keep to a fairly local clientele.

Some of the small companies, inevitably, built no more than a handful of bodies, in some cases perhaps

This was the Setting-Out Department, where timber sections were shaped and joints were cut.

no more than one. Records in many cases are sketchy or non-existent and, despite the diligent research that has been done in this area, the picture we have today is far from complete. That explains why, in this book, some of the smaller companies from this period are recorded in no more than a few lines.

At the start of the 1920s, chassis typically stood high off the ground, with the result that most bodies seemed very tall. Designs were mostly functionally boxy, with little to distinguish one maker's products from another's. By the middle of the decade, lower single-deck chassis (such as the 1925 Leyland Lion) began to bring overall heights down.

Most new buses – and, of course, coaches – in the 1920s were single-deck types. Double-deckers were relatively uncommon in rural areas. Height and safety concerns were an issue; even though many large towns and cities were used to double-deck trams, the thinking was that a bus could swerve or manoeuvre quickly in the way that a tram could not and so risk overturning. Even in London, enclosed top decks were not permitted before the mid-1920s, the thinking in this case being that the weight of a fixed roof added to the potential instability of the vehicle.

Then from 1927, a new generation of lower double-deck chassis came on to the market. Spearheaded by the Leyland Titan and followed two years later by the AEC Regent, these allowed further development of the double-decker in ways that had simply been impossible before. Leyland in particular pioneered an ultra-low height design of body, for which there was a ready market because of the large number of low railway bridges in Britain. This had the upper-deck gangway on one side instead of in the centre, so that it impinged on headroom above the downstairs seats rather than the downstairs gangway. The design was known as the lowbridge type, for obvious reasons, and was widely copied after Leyland chose not to renew its original patent. At the start of the period, single-deck service buses tended to be tall and boxy, with fixed roofs. Independent coach operators meanwhile favoured charabanc bodies for day trips and tours in the summer. Like many cars of the period, these were roofless vehicles with no weather protection. However, the great British weather was rarely predictable, even in the summer, and many charabancs were fitted with canvas roofs that could be erected over the passengers when the rain came. There were also 'all-weather' types, which benefited from side windows, front and rear domes, plus a folding roof.

More or less in parallel with similar developments in

The metal elements of the body – mostly steel – were prepared in the Smithy and the Fitters' Shop.

the car bodywork field, the fully enclosed coach body followed, typically with a folding or sliding 'sunshine roof' that could rapidly be opened or closed to suit the weather conditions. Forward entrances became popular on coaches, although rear entrances were more common on service buses. Some service-bus operators ordered bodies with both forward and rear entrances, to improve the flow of passengers through the bus at stops.

The later 1920s also saw new features on coaches, intended to afford greater luxury and so attract custom from rival operators whose vehicles were less well equipped. As early as 1925 there were toilet compartments on some long-distance coaches; the luxury elements came from such things as plush furnishings, veneered wood, quilted roof linings and curtained windows. Some coaches had kitchens; some were equipped as 'sleepers', with reclining seats; others were 'radio coaches', allowing passengers to listen to radio broadcasts – which in those days of course all came from the BBC.

THE 1930s

During the 1930s, bus and coach bodybuilding became a more specialized business. Many of the small firms that had been established in the flush of enthusiasm that accompanied the 1920s had not lasted the distance and many of those that had survived had done so by attracting business nationally rather than only locally. Even so, many operators, both municipal and private, still tended to patronize local suppliers when they could. Now, the introduction of national Construction and Use Regulations in January 1931 ensured that bodies built in one part of the country would meet requirements in others, thus encouraging more bodybuilders to seek new business further from home.

Two photographs showing the Body Assembly Department, where the frames were put together.

Body frame subassemblies are seen nearest the camera and behind them body frames are mounted to chassis in the Erection Shop.

Body design generally made great advances after the late 1920s. As chassis became lower, so bodybuilders finished the job off by extending the lower panelling downwards to conceal the chassis frame, exhaust system, fuel tank, battery box and other mechanical items. Buses and coaches looked more of a unit and less like a body perched on top of a frame with axles.

Body construction methods began to change, too. In the 1920s, bodies had mainly consisted of a wooden framework to which metal panels were attached by nails or screws (the Weymann system used fabric panels, but was relatively uncommon on PSVs). Now, several firms began to offer metal-framed bodies, which brought considerable advantages in durability. However, the victory of the all-metal body over the composite type was far from complete at this stage and it would not become so until the early 1950s.

Double-deck bodies became very much more popular, as some municipal operators began to replace their tram fleets. On double-deck bodies, the staircase moved inside the main bodywork at the start of the decade and full-length top decks superseded the type that stopped short behind the driver's cab. Some operators evolved their own distinctive styles – for example, those operators affiliated to the BEF (British Electric Federation) had their favourite styles constructed by more than one maker. So companies like Brush, Roe and Weymann often built bodies to their individual interpretations of particular styles. These individual interpretations made many manufacturers' bodies instantly recognizable. In the early years of the decade, six-bay construction (with six windows on each side downstairs) was the norm

BUS OPERATIONS IN IRELAND

The Irish Republic

After the establishment of the Irish Free State in 1922, a number of bus service networks sprang up all over the country. There was intense competition at this stage and the railways, seeing a threat to their own service networks, rushed to set up bus services in competition.

Legislation was needed to bring the situation under control, with the Road Transport and Road Traffic Acts of 1932 and 1933 being designed to do just that. By the middle of the decade, the vast majority of services were run by four statutory operators: the Dublin United Tramways Company, the Great Northern Railway (GNR), the Great Southern Railways and the Londonderry & Lough Swilly Railway. The number of independent operators was reduced to around thirty and their business was almost exclusively local.

The next major change came on 1 January 1945, when Córas Iompair Éireann (CIÉ, the Irish Transport Company) was established under the 1944 Transport Act. The Great Southern Railways and the Dublin United Transport Company (as it now was) amalgamated, remaining a private company until nationalized under the 1950 Transport Act.

Meanwhile, the GNR ran into profitability problems and was jointly nationalized by the Governments of the Republic and of Northern Ireland. In 1958, the Great Northern Railway Act then divided the GNR into two. CIÉ took the services south of the border, while those north of the border went to the Ulster Transport Authority. CIÉ remained responsible for all bus, coach, railway and canal operations until 1987.

Northern Ireland

During the 1920s, there were many small independent operators in Northern Ireland, plus a small number of larger ones. The situation was controlled by the November 1926 Motor Vehicles (Traffic and Regulations) Act, which introduced minimum standards. Meanwhile, the railway companies had begun operating bus services in order to protect their market and in 1932 three of them (the Belfast & County Down Railway, the Great Northern Railway and the Northern Counties Committee) asked the Government to grant them a monopoly of road services in Northern Ireland.

Their wish was granted, with a small number of exceptions and exemptions, by the Road and Railway Transport Act in July 1935. From October 1935, the new Northern Irish Transport Board (NIRTB) gradually absorbed most other operators, with the situation remaining like that until 1948, when the NIRTB was merged with the railways as the Ulster Transport Authority. The road services were then passed to a new holding company in 1966, before coming under the control of Ulsterbus in April 1967.

Two scenes from the Sheet Metal Section, showing panels being prepared and fitted to vehicle frames.

on two-axle chassis; by the middle of the 1930s, most makers had moved to less fussy-looking five-bay designs.

Single-deck bus bodies were generally quite functional in appearance, although also more resolved as designs than those of the previous decade. But by the late 1930s, economic necessity had led to the development of dual-purpose single-deckers. These had enough seats to work as service buses during the week and enough luxury to act as coaches on summer weekends; they were often regularly used on the longer stage-carriage services as well. That way, a vehicle could be kept in service all year round rather than simply being mothballed for the winter when demand for coach tours was low.

Coach bodies were initially based on the bus designs, simply offering more comfortable seats with more leg room, but special coach shapes soon began to appear. Bodybuilders tended to have a basic standard design, but were more than willing to make variations to suit an operator's tastes. As the idea of the luxury coach developed, there were some quite remarkably individual designs on display at the annual Commercial Motor Show. Some were designed as much to show the maker's skill as anything else and remained unique.

One way or another, the design of coach bodies in the 1930s became far more varied; fashions also changed as the decade progressed. From about 1934, the vogue was for body trim details that reflected the latest public interest in streamlining. Shortly after that, there was a vogue for stepped waist rails. The luxury features pioneered at the end of the 1920s were still in evidence and some new designs also appeared. Notable was the 'observation coach', with the rear half of the seating set above the front half in order to give their occupants a better view forwards. Underneath, the body space vacated was made available for luggage, which helped to explain why these designs were often used on airport duties.

The vogue for streamlining did not only affect single-deck coaches. Several municipal authorities adapted the trimmings of streamlining to create very attractive liveries for their vehicles and some had double-deckers specially built to incorporate some of the principles of streamlining. Although sloping fronts hardly improved a vehicle's aerodynamics, they did look the part, especially when combined with full-fronts, where the space alongside the driver's cab was covered in to become part of the bodywork. Blackpool Corporation developed a very distinctive style with all these features, plus an unusual central entrance, and had it made by their local body-builder, H.V. Burlingham.

Double-decker capacity increased in this period, too. At the start of the 1930s, the typical double-decker had forty-eight to fifty-one seats; fifty-four seats soon became common, with fifty-six the norm by 1940. During 1939, Coventry Corporation took some sixty-seaters built locally by Metro-Cammell; their lightweight all-metal bodies allowed the extra passengers to be accommodated within the weight regulations governing bus manufacture at the time.

THE 1940s

During 1940, all bus production in Britain was halted as the Government redeployed factories and resources in

The Paint Shop: some panels are being sprayed off the vehicles.

support of the war effort. Bus bodybuilders were sources of skilled labour and that skilled labour – and the factories where it worked – typically found itself building or repairing aircraft and aircraft components.

None of that diminished the demand for new buses, of course. Older examples continued to wear out just as quickly as before; indeed, often more quickly because skilled maintenance staff had been thinned out by the demand for soldiers, sailors and airmen. There soon arose an urgent need for replacements. The Government's first response was to permit buses to be built from parts in stock and from part-completed vehicles on which work had been stopped. These 'unfrozen' vehicles were all to pre-war designs and were completed in 1941.

The next stage was the design of a stripped-out 'utility' specification, which would impose a common design on multiple manufacturers. Bodies used wooden frames to conserve metal for military machinery (although there were exceptions) and their simplified shapes did not require skills such as panel beating. Steel panels were used to conserve precious aluminium for aircraft, so making these bodies both heavy and rust-prone.

The prototype utility double-decker was built in October 1941 on an 'unfrozen' Leyland Titan TD7 chassis for London, but Park Royal built the first volume-produced example in 1942, on a Guy Arab chassis. Other bodybuilders gained permission to follow suit. Nevertheless, there was room for some individual interpretation within the standard outline and the bodies were far from standardized. Brush, BBW, Croft, Duple, Massey, Northern Counties, Park Royal, Pickering, Roe and Strachans were the permitted builders, with each adding their individual touches. There were 'utility' trolleybuses as well as motor buses, and both lowbridge (L27/28R) and highbridge (H30/26R) bodies. Seats were thinly upholstered into 1943, when wooden slatted seats took over. Upholstery was permitted again from mid-1945. Most 'utility' bodies had only one opening window on each side for each deck and the early ones had no window in the top-deck emergency exit.

These two scenes from the Trim Shop show work progressing on the seats and interior trimming.

As for single-deckers, a standardized service bus design was built by Duple, Mulliner, Roe and SMT on the only chassis available – the Bedford OWB. There were no new coach bodies at all between 1940 and 1946. Many older chassis were also rebodied to 'utility' specification during the war. Beadle, Burlingham, Croft, East Lancs, Eastern Coach Works (ECW), Northern Coachbuilders and Reading all took part in this area of activity.

In all, around 6,700 'utility' bodies were built between 1942 and 1945. Part of the deal had been that builders were allowed to use up stocks of parts before switching to utility construction and both East Lancs and ECW managed to get through the whole war without building utility designs; Beadle only ran out of old-stock parts towards the end. But the return of peace did not mark a return to the pre-war status quo in the bus manufacturing industry, which for the rest of the decade went through one of its toughest – and most interesting – times.

There had obviously not been anywhere near enough utility buses to go round and in any case the combination of their simplified construction and minimal maintenance was already indicating that they would need early replacement. The use of unseasoned timber in their construction had not helped, as this deteriorated rapidly. So there was a huge pent-up demand for new buses. To compound that, the Government was pushing manufacturers of all kinds to build for export, in order to earn the revenue needed to rebuild the economy. So there was no chance that the old-established manufacturers would keep up with demand from the domestic market. The whole situation was further compounded by erratic supplies of raw materials as Britain gradually returned to normality.

With a booming market and an industry that could not meet demand, a multitude of new bus-body manufacturers started up. Many were small engineering companies that had built up most of the necessary skills from wartime work on aircraft. Others were builders of luxury car bodywork, for which there was very little demand in the difficult economy of the late 1940s. Some seem to have specialized in refurbishing existing bodies rather than building new ones; many such rebuilds were done by local firms not otherwise involved in PSV manufacture, while others were carried out in Corporation workshops.

In *The British Bus Story – The Fifties*, Alan Townsin listed thirty-nine new bus-body makers that had been set up between 1945 and 1950. But demand soon levelled out and by 1952 the market was saturated. Bus operators tended to return to the established makers, whose products they knew they could trust. Tellingly, just two of those companies that had entered the market between 1945 and 1950 were still in business ten years later. The others mostly faded into obscurity in the first half of the decade.

Ready for delivery: a selection of completed vehicles outside the Duple works at Hendon.

Although bus bodies in the immediate post-war period picked up where their counterparts of the late 1930s had left off, there were signs of change. Metal-framed bodies returned and familiarity with aluminium alloys in aircraft construction led to a willingness to experiment with these in bus bodies. There was a trend towards jig-building, again resulting from wartime aircraft practice that had aimed for standardization and ease of repair. There were no major new design trends for double-deckers yet, but single-deck design did begin to change – and very noticeably.

There was a marked swing towards forward entrances on single-deckers rather than the centre or rear entrances of the 1930s. In the interests of 'modernity', full-fronts became increasingly popular, often concealing the traditional vertical radiator behind a styled panel, although this was more noticeable on coaches than on service buses, which generally retained half-cab designs. Five-bay construction on double-deckers gradually gave way to four-bay designs. Some coach bodybuilders (mainly the smaller, newer ones) experimented with swoopy, aircraft-inspired styles and shapes as they tried to make their names. Many of these designs, which continued into the early 1950s, were excessive, bizarre, or both.

But the major change for single-deckers was the arrival of underfloor-engined chassis. The real challenges did not begin until AEC (with the Regal IV) and Leyland (with the Royal Tiger) entered the market in 1950, but the arrival of the first underfloor-engined designs from operator Birmingham & Midland Motor Bus Company (BMMO) in 1946 and chassis maker Sentinel in 1948 certainly made the designers of single-deck bodies sit up

and think very hard about the way things would go in the future.

THE 1950s

The 1950s was another decade of change and not least among the factors driving that change was the increasing popularity of the private car. Car owners used their vehicles for local journeys and holidays alike, so reducing the need for bus services and coach tours. The railways suffered similarly. Costs became more important to operators than ever before, as they tried to maintain profits in a dwindling market. Bus bodybuilders altered their designs to suit, squeezing more fare-paying seats into the footprint of the newly permitted 30ft (9m) long and 8ft (2.4m) wide chassis that came on to the market. By the end of the 1950s, double-deckers were seating as many as seventy-two passengers and single-deck buses were carrying forty-four or even forty-five, while even coaches typically had forty-one seats.

The full-size vertical-engined chassis lasted only until 1952–3, although the new lightweight Bedford SB chassis still had its engine at the front. The early 1950s saw a flowering of full-front designs and the new SB was always intended to have them. Coach designs in the early 1950s were a direct continuation of shapes pioneered in the 1930s, with curving waistlines and roof contours, and usually sloping window pillars as well. Generally speaking, the smaller concerns were happier working on vertical-engined chassis and many of them failed quite spectacularly to create pleasing designs for the new underfloor-engined types. As the demand for coach travel began to diminish and the bigger manufacturers came up with better designs at keener prices, so the order books of the smaller companies dried up and many of them passed into history. By the mid-1950s, coach bodybuilding was mainly carried out by a handful of the big names: Burlingham, Duple, Harrington and Plaxton. Duple was the most prolific, largely thanks to the special relationship it had developed with Bedford through designs for the SB chassis.

Atkinson, Daimler, Dennis and Guy all followed the lead set by Sentinel, AEC and Leyland, and even Bristol came up with an underfloor-engined chassis, although it was available only to the nationalized British Transport Commission (BTC) operators. This relentless move away from vertical-engined types forced the bodybuilders to come up with new designs very quickly and their indecent haste was evident in some of the results.

Service bus bodies were mostly square-rigged, box-like and heavy in appearance, with thick window pillars. The need for driver supervision of the entrance resulting from the move towards one-man operation meant that front entrances were almost universal by 1955. These were usually equipped with power-operated folding doors, which demanded a rectangular doorway that in turn contributed to this boxiness. For coaches, Duple and Harrington adapted existing designs for vertical-engined chassis with sometimes disappointing results. Many of the smaller bodybuilders came up with coach designs that were awkward or downright ugly, while others did their best to be imaginative but were often guilty of excess, or at least of style for style's sake.

Among the early entrants to the market, by far the most successful was the Seagull coach body by Burlingham, so named after the Blackpool operator for whom the first example was built. It became a design classic of its time. Designs of major importance from the later 1950s were the Plaxton Panorama, which featured the large windows its name suggested, and the Harrington Cavalier, which combined front and rear body peaks with a curved-glass windscreen made possible by new rules permitting fixed screens and new toughened glass technology delivering three-dimensional curves. The earliest underfloor-engined coaches mostly had centre entrances, but by the end of the decade front entrances were the norm.

Double-deck bodies in the first half of the 1950s evolved mainly to meet demands for lighter weight and higher seating capacities. Metal-framed construction was universal. Only the strong survived: Leyland closed its body department in 1954 and Crossley became an out-station of Park Royal after the company had been absorbed by the ACV group. Companies such as Brush, Cravens and Roberts were among the casualties. The need to reduce costs led to a period of rather austere designs at the end of the decade, coinciding with the arrival of the pioneer rear-engined chassis, the Leyland Atlantean. It would be the mid-1960s before really attractive designs were available for that chassis and its imitators, as all the first ones were adapted from existing designs for front-engined chassis.

THE 1960s

Compared to earlier times, only a handful of British body-builders remained active in the 1960s. Their numbers thinned out as the decade wore on, too: Burlingham and Willowbrook, for example, were engulfed by Duple. At the end of the decade, the fully standardized Leyland National bus arrived, and several older chassis from the Leyland group of companies disappeared. Without those chassis on which to work, the independent bodybuilders saw their custom disappearing fast.

Nevertheless, the 1960s were notable for some formidably attractive new coach designs. The spread of the motorways and of the express coach services that used them, plus the contraction of the railways network, added up to a demand for designs that were as good-looking as they were functional. The increasing use of glass-reinforced plastic (GRP) mouldings allowed designers to experiment with some interesting designs that would have been too complex, too expensive, or both, if made of traditional metal. Meanwhile, the newly permitted 36ft (11m) maximum length demanded different designs to achieve a harmonious balance of line; permitted width also increased by 2½in (64mm) to 8ft 2½in (2.5m).

On the service bus front, however, the standardization represented by the Leyland National was in many ways a watchword of the times. Variety was no longer seen as the spice of life. As they had been doing for many years, the BET (British Electric Traction) companies developed their own standard single-deck service bus style in the early years of the decade. This had modern-looking wrap-around front and rear screens and the bodybuilders who wanted BET orders had to build to this standardized design or lose the contract.

There was similar pressure from operators in other ways. A desperate need for attractive designs on the new

This scene from Shorts' factory shows how upper and lower decks were assembled separately before being fitted together. An upper deck is being transported across the body assembly shop by overhead crane.

Single-decker

Upper saloon of double-decker

Double-decker lower saloon

Three-axle trolley bus

These pictures show the jig-built metal frames of Leyland bodies from the 1930s. Wood was used only for the floors and as a medium for securing panels and brackets.

rear-engined double-deck chassis led several municipalities to take matters into their own hands. Bolton, Liverpool, Manchester and Oldham all drew up the designs they wanted. It was then down to the bodybuilders they approached to put them into production. From 1968, Park Royal and Roe had a new standard body design for the Leyland Atlantean and Daimler Fleetline chassis that then dominated the market, and the same design, with some modifications, was subsequently made by Metro-Cammell, Northern Counties and Willowbrook as well.

Anxious to maintain market share and to deliver a standardized design, Metro-Cammell moved into integral construction in 1969, buying in mechanical units from Scania in Sweden. Although the original Metro-Scania was less successful than its makers had hoped, it was important in showing the way forwards for bus construction in Britain.

Then, just as the 1960s were drawing to a close, more new legislation was introduced to affect the design of coaches. This was a relaxation of the maximum permitted length from 36ft (11m) to 39.4ft (12m). Operators and bodybuilders alike were slow to take advantage of the new regulations, which were announced in 1967 but took effect from 1968. Their main impact would be on the designs of the 1970s.

THE 1970s

The gradual shrinkage of the PSV market in Britain during the 1960s had taken its toll among the smaller builders of bus and coach bodywork, and even some of the bigger ones had huddled together for comfort. There was no future in increasing prices to compensate for lower sales volumes, because operators were being ever more tightly squeezed by social changes that did not favour public transport. Continuing the trend of the 1960s, more and more homes now owned a car, and more and more families stayed indoors to watch television in the evenings instead of going out and travelling to cinemas, theatres and other places of entertainment.

All this left the market ripe for continental European bus builders to move in. With their larger markets and consequently higher sales volumes, they could keep costs lower and compete very effectively with British products on their home ground. So it was that some British coach dealers – Moseley was the first – began to offer vehicles bodied by continental European coachbuilders. From 1968 Caetano bodies from Portugal had been available under the Moseley Continental brand;

though unfashionably rectangular in appearance, with garish grilles for decoration, they soon made their mark. By 1970, Caetano was an important player on the British coach market. Moseley looked into the possibilities of selling Van Hool coachwork from Belgium in 1969, but it was Arlington that eventually handled these bodies, which were available for both lightweight and heavyweight chassis as the 1970s got under way. Before the decade was out, there were others: Berkhof (from the Netherlands), Beulas (from Spain), Ikarus (from Hungary), Irizar (from Spain) and Jonckheere (from Belgium).

The 1970s also saw a greater willingness by operators to accept integral construction, not least because many of the products coming in from the European continent depended upon it. That it reduced flexibility in body design was no longer an issue; what mattered was whether the end result was affordable, while also being sufficiently attractive and comfortable to earn customer approval.

The need to deal with lower passenger numbers generally also led to the rise of a new type of bus in the early 1970s. While minibuses gradually gained in popularity for stage-carriage services, the midibus became popular where more room was needed. Based on underfloor-engined PSV chassis, these more or less matched such vehicles as the Bedford OB of the 1940s in size, but the real problem for bus bodybuilders was getting the proportions right. Too many looked like truncated toy editions of their full-size brethren.

Otherwise, single-deck service buses in the 1970s were broadly similar in configuration to their 1960s counterparts, while few operators of double-deckers bothered to take advantage of the dispensation that allowed them to be longer than 30ft (9m). As for coaches, the gradual increase in the popularity of continental European types forced the remaining British builders to offer new designs, but the first of the British-built high-floor types (with luggage room under the floor) was not introduced until 1976. It was, of course, by leading builder Plaxton, but even then it took some time to become accepted by UK buyers.

OPERATORS

Throughout this book there are references to the different types of bus and coach operators who bought the products of the companies it lists. These deserve some explanation. There were three categories of bus operating company for most of the 1919–75 period. These

More modern times: this was the body shell of a Duple Dominant coach, an all-metal design from the early 1970s.

were municipalities, independents and the operators who belonged to one of the big groups. The situation was quite fluid, as was only to be expected.

The municipalities need little explanation. They were bus fleets owned and operated by a city or town council or corporation, and were generally used on stage-carriage services in the local area. Examples were Lancaster City Transport, Sheffield Corporation or Eastbourne Corporation. The independents were privately owned companies, often operating no more than a handful of buses on local stage-carriage services, on excursions and tours, or on private-hire contracts. Nevertheless, they generally met local needs extremely well and commanded a loyalty from users that the larger concerns could not match. An example of a smaller independent was White Bus Services of Winkfield in Berkshire. There were also larger operators, such as Timpson's Coaches of Catford in London (who were later jointly owned by the BET and BTC), Barton Transport of Chilwell in Nottinghamshire and West Riding Automobile of Wakefield in Yorkshire.

The big groupings have a more complex story. Essentially, they were alliances of operators, intended not only to provide mutual support, but also to squeeze out weaker competitors. In the 1920s, the two main groupings were Tilling (centred on London operator Thomas Tilling) and British Electric Traction (dominated by BMMO). British Electric Traction had been formed in 1895 with interests in electric power and transport, inevitably forming or acquiring bus operating companies as well. In the early days, the name BEF (British Electric Federation) was sometimes used.

The BET also had a subsidiary, British Automobile Traction, which was partly owned by Tilling, and from 1928 the situation was simplified when a new Tilling &

Most builders of PSV bodies 'signed' their work, although some of the smaller ones did not. The Harrington plate is on the entrance step of a coach, while Plaxton sometimes displayed the model name on the outside as well.

British Automobile Traction grouping was set up. Yet another group, albeit a small one, was the National Electric Construction Group. This joined forces with BET in 1931.

The 1930s saw a number of changes. First, the SMT (Scottish Motor Traction) group came together in the early 1930s as Scottish operators saw the advantages of mutual support. Second, several of the larger independents joined either the Tilling or the BET groups. These groups were swelled still further after the Tilling & British Automobile Traction group was dissolved in 1942 and its member companies divided themselves between the Tilling and BET groups, which thus became the only major group survivors along with the SMT in Scotland.

After World War II, there were further changes. The 1947 Transport Act created the British Transport Commission (BTC) group, which came into being in 1948 and was set up initially to bring British Railways and London Transport under national control. The formerly independent railway companies had shareholdings in many bus operators as well, so the creation of the BTC meant that these shares now passed to the Government. In 1948, the twenty-strong Tilling group of bus operators realized that it had effectively lost control of its own constituent companies and decided to sell out to the BTC. A year later, the Scottish Motor Traction group reached the same decision. Among the companies of the nationalized BTC group were large regional operators such as Crosville, Eastern Counties, Southern Vectis and West Yorkshire.

BET's electric power interests were compulsorily nationalized in 1947, so its bus operating companies became the main focus of its activities for a time. The group did diversify into other fields, but retained its bus interests until the 1980s. Among its operators were the regional giants such as Ribble, BMMO (Midland Red), Maidstone & District, East Kent and Southdown.

The 1960s saw some more major changes to this breakdown, in that the BTC was wound up in 1962 and became the Transport Holding Company (THC), its Scottish SMT Group holdings were renamed the Scottish Bus Group (SBG) in 1961 and sold to the THC a year later, while BET sold its bus operating interests to the THC in 1968. This latter was in response to national transport changes previewed in a 1966 Government White Paper and brought into effect by the 1968 Transport Act.

This act led in 1969 to the formation of the National Bus Company (effectively the old THC) in England and Wales and the Scottish Bus Group in Scotland. These operators took over the long-distance and rural bus services. Also provided for, in the interests of centralization and efficiency, were five regional Passenger Transport Authorities – in Birmingham, Glasgow, Liverpool, Manchester and Newcastle. These policy-forming bodies lay behind Passenger Transport Executives (PTEs) that actually operated the buses and the first half of the 1970s saw these becoming established and taking over from both municipal and company-owned operations. They assumed new names and, of course, new liveries, and these first five PTEs were West Midlands, Greater Glasgow (renamed Strathclyde in 1975), Merseyside, Selnec (South-East Lancashire, North-East Cheshire) and Tyneside. There have been many changes since, especially those resulting from the deregulation of bus services in the 1980s, but these are beyond the period covered in this book.

Part 2

THE A–Z OF
BRITISH BUS BODIES

ABBOTT (1)

Abbott's was active as a bus bodybuilder in the early 1930s, but its mainstream work was always with car bodies. The company was often known as Abbott's of Farnham. It was formed in 1929 out of the ashes of car bodybuilders Page and Hunt. A leading former employee took over the premises and equipment at Wrecclesham near Farnham, and formed a new company under his own name of E.D. Abbott. The new company also took over Phoenix Coachworks of Farnham (*q.v.*), a trading name of Arnold & Comben (*q.v.*), and some early Abbott advertisements used the Phoenix name.

Abbott's secured some contracts for bus bodies, but continued as a car bodybuilder and retailer. Most of the buses (and some coaches) were single-deckers for chassis such as Gilfords and Dennis Aces, for local operators including Aldershot & District and King Alfred of Winchester. The bus-body contracts died away in the mid-1930s, but Abbott's remained in business until 1972.

ABBOTT (2)

A second company called Abbott operated from Leicester and built coach bodywork in the early 1930s.

ABURNSON

Aburnsons (Coachbuilders) Ltd of Lancing in Sussex was briefly involved in coach bodybuilding in 1949. The company used aluminium panels on ash frames for a full-front Seddon coach destined for Sargents of East Grinstead and offered similar bodies with between twenty-eight and thirty-two seats. It was also briefly involved in car bodybuilding, constructing a 'woody' estate for a Bentley MkVI chassis in 1948.

ACB

See Associated Coachbuilders.

ACCLES & POLLOCK

Accles & Pollock Ltd was formed in 1901 at Oldbury from a general engineering company that had been

In 1929, it made sense for Abbott to use the name of one of the companies it had bought. The sloping front window to the saloon above the bonnet is interesting on this 28-seat coach, built probably in 1929 on a Commer Avenger chassis.

founded in 1896. Much of its work focused on tube sections and from 1932 it acquired Metal Sections Ltd (which in 1948 became a separate company known as Metsec). Between 1932 and 1945, Accles & Pollock produced metal body frames, possibly from premises at 20 Cannon Street, Manchester. In the 1930s, several of these went to Manchester Corporation on Crossley Mancunian chassis. (*See* Metal Sections.)

ACTON

Acton & Co. was based at Greencroft Street, Salisbury, Wiltshire. In 1921 the company constructed some open-top double-deck bodywork.

ADC

The Associated Daimler Co. Ltd was a short-lived association between chassis manufacturers AEC (initially at Walthamstow in London) and Daimler in Coventry. It was partly a marketing arrangement and partly a genuine attempt to develop joint designs, of which there were several PSV types. Some of these received bodies that have been ascribed to ADC, although were most probably built at the London General Omnibus Company (LGOC) works. In 1927, AEC moved from Walthamstow to Southall in Middlesex, but in 1928 the ADC experiment came to an end and the two partners went their separate ways.

ADDIE & MEADOWS

This company was based at Airbles Road in Motherwell, Lanarkshire, and was active by 1922 and until at least 1928. Only one body is known for certain, built in 1922 on an ex-War Department Daimler Y chassis for Lanarkshire Tramways of Motherwell.

AEC

Chassis-builder AEC of Southall in Middlesex was more of a dabbler in the bodybuilding business than a full-time body maker, using for this purpose the workshops at Black Horse Lane, Walthamstow, that it had taken over from the LGOC. An example of its work was two thirty-seat dual-entrance buses on AEC 401 chassis for Glasgow. Nevertheless, the company's lack of a full-time bodybuilding department did not stop Chief Engineer John Rackham from having some body styles drawn up and getting them built onto AEC demonstrators to show 'approved' styles. The body on the first AEC Regent chassis in 1929 was built by Shorts (*q.v.*) to a detailed specification from AEC, while the Brush and Park Royal (*q.q.v.*) bodies on the 1931 Regent demonstrators had similar origins.

Built to an East Lancs design, the body on this 1948 Eastbourne Leyland PD2/1 was actually constructed by Air Dispatch.

In Alan Townsin's words, 'the overall concept [*of the 1931 bodies*] was altogether more sleek and considerably in advance of typical designs of that period, acting as a foretaste of common practice in the mid 'thirties – indeed the frontal profile was still being echoed in some new buses nearly twenty years later.' The bodies had 'a then new front-end profile, with continuous unbroken slope from the windscreen pillars to the upper-deck front dome, but with a prominent rounded projecting cab front panel. Brush built only a very few examples, but Park Royal was to adopt the basic design as standard and continued producing very similar bodywork until 1940 for certain customers.'

AEROCRAFT

See Aero-Engineering.

AERO-ENGINEERING

Aero-Engineering and Marine (Merseyside) Ltd was founded at the former RAF airfield in Hooton on the Wirral in 1935, as Martin Hearn Ltd, to service aircraft. The company was renamed in 1947 and took on overhaul work for armoured cars, manufacture of gliders and bus repair work. In the period around 1949–51, it undertook a number of bus-body rebuilds for Midland Red.

This company has sometimes been identified as Aerocraft, notably in connection with bodies on Albion chassis for independent operators on the Isle of Man.

AGNEW

The Agnew company was a Northern Irish company active in 1968 that built single-deck bus bodies.

AIR DISPATCH

Air Dispatch built bus bodies only very briefly in the period immediately after the end of the Second World War. The company was founded as Air Dispatch Ltd in July 1934 by the Hon. Mrs Victor Bruce, an early aviation pioneer. Its purpose was to fly weekend freight services from Croydon Airport in Surrey to French airports. On the outbreak of war, Air Dispatch Ltd and its sister company Commercial Air Hire Ltd moved to

Cardiff Airport, where they became involved in rebuilding war-damaged aircraft.

When the dominance of the nationalized airlines prevented a return to commercial air services in 1945, Air Dispatch Ltd turned to other business. Attracted by the demand for bus bodywork, the company refurbished some older bodies for St Helens Corporation and assembled new bodies designed by East Lancs of Blackburn. In 1947 it changed its name to Air Dispatch (Coachbuilders) Ltd, but this name was short-lived and the company was wound up after a failed attempt to sell the parent aviation company as a going concern. The final bodies were delivered to Eastbourne Corporation in 1948 and the business of Air Dispatch (Coachbuilders) Ltd was carried on under the Bruce Coach Works name (*q.v.*). The Bruce of that company was the Hon. Mrs Victor Bruce's son, Anthony Easter Bruce.

ALBANY

The Albany Carriage Co. operated from a former tram depot in Hanwell, London W7, from 1924. The company was best known for car bodywork, but appears to have done some bus bodies as well in the 1920s. It closed at the end of the decade.

ALEXANDER

The Alexander name first appeared on bus and coach bodies in the mid-1920s and the company was still active at the turn of the new century, although it has since been absorbed into newer combines. Its products were always associated with Scottish operators, although in the 1960s Alexander coach bodies became popular with members of the BET group all over Great Britain. The company was more properly known as Walter Alexander & Co. Ltd.

Walter Alexander established Alexander's Motor Service in 1913 to fill a gap in the services of the local tramways company between Falkirk and Grangemouth. By 1928 he had decided on expansion, and that he should also build the bodies on the buses that the expanded company would need. Several of the major British railway companies bought into the new Scottish Motor Traction Company Ltd (SMT) and just a year later Alexander decided to sell his bodybuilding business to the SMT group. During the 1930s, Alexander's provided the majority of the bodies needed by the SMT companies and during the war built a number of utility double-deck bodies.

The transport nationalization schemes of the 1940s led to the severance of the bodybuilding activities from the operating company, with the result that from

This handsome lowbridge Alexander body dates from 1949, although the Leyland TD5 chassis on which it is mounted is ten years older. It was rebodied as part of a major post-war programme by Ribble.

The Alexander J-type double-deck body for rear-engined chassis used panoramic front screens to break away from the boxiness of earlier designs. Trent's two-tone livery on this Daimler Fleetline made it look most attractive.

MARTIN LLEWELLYN/OMNICOLOUR

1948 the body side was renamed Walter Alexander & Co. (Coachbuilders) Ltd. Some double-deck bodies in this period were supplied in CKD form ('Completely Knocked Down', i.e. in kit form for local assembly) for assembly in Derry by the Londonderry & Lough Swilly Railway Co. Over the next half-century, the coachbuilding business at Falkirk continued to expand. Alexander's secured a strong export business and developed a number of designs specifically for overseas operators.

During the 1950s, Alexander's was mainly a builder of bus bodies, although it also developed some distinctive designs for underfloor-engined chassis. First came elegant centre-entrance types for Leyland Royal Tiger and Guy Arab chassis. A visor over the windscreen distinguished the second-generation or Coronation body in 1952. A front-entrance design with curved waist rail followed in 1953 and lasted until 1959; a straight-waisted design survived into the 36ft (11m) era of the 1960s. Alexander's also bodied a number of Bristol chassis as coaches for members of the Scottish bus group – a privilege reserved for ECW (q.v.) in other parts of the country. In 1958, Alexander's moved from its original premises in Stirling to a brand-new factory in Falkirk.

The company's most successful design from the 1960s was the Y-type, introduced in 1961 and, in many ways, the epitome of the 36ft motorway coach. In coach form with long side windows, it was a masterpiece, beautifully balanced with double-curvature glazing front and rear; the small-windowed bus and dual-purpose version were unfortunately more fussy. Both types were initially steel-framed to suit the conservative policies of the BET group operators, switching to alloy frames and an AY designation from about 1972. Y-types were seen on all the major British-built coach chassis of the period, including the AEC Reliance, Bristol RE and Leyland Leopard, and during the 1960s were even adapted to suit the Albion Viking and Bedford VAM.

Other single-deck designs of note included the M-type of 1969, for the latest 39.4ft (12m) chassis such as the Bristol RE; this featured double-glazed windows to reduce noise on overnight services. Despite the compromise of a tall front peak caused by re-employing the Y-type windscreen, the M-type was a handsome body and ninety-eight examples were built. On the service bus front, the big-windowed W-type found favour with London Country Bus Services and the Tyneside PTE in the early 1970s.

Alexander's also developed some attractive double-deck designs for rear-engined chassis in the later 1960s, with wrap-around screens on both decks at the front and at the top rear. The A-type and J-type were built up to 1972, along with low-height D-types (and alloy-framed AD-types) and K-types. These were succeeded by redesigned L- and AL-types, which were also suitable for the Bristol VR chassis. The 1981 and later bodies were R-types, and there were also ALX series double-deck bodies designed as low-floor types.

Alexander's also became involved with integral construction in the 1970s, building its AV-type double-decker for the Volvo Ailsa B55 from 1973 and S-type midibuses with Ford running gear from 1974, although the latter were not a great success. Minibuses, midibuses and motorway coaches all figured among Alexander's output as the century drew to a close and the ALX series also included low-floor single-deck designs of various sizes.

In 1990 the company was sold to Spotlaunch plc, but within two years changed ownership again in a management buyout. From 1995, it was owned by the Mayflower Corporation plc, but in 2001 became part of TransBus International. It continues as a part of Alexander Dennis.

ALEXANDER (BELFAST)

Alexander (Belfast) was a highly successful subsidiary of the parent Walter Alexander & Co. (Coachbuilders) Ltd that was active between 1969 and 2005. The company had started life as Potter of Belfast (q.v.). As Alexander (Belfast), it supplied bodies not only to Northern Irish but also to mainland British operators and went on to build up a substantial export business from the mid-1970s.

Spats and running boards over the rear wheels accentuate the length of this 1926 six-wheeler.

Dating from 1925, this Allen bus body was fairly typical of the times, but within two years or so would look very old-fashioned.

ALEXANDER MOTORS

Separate from the better known Walter Alexander concern, this company was based at Semple Street in Edinburgh and traded as Alexander's of Edinburgh Ltd. The company was active between 1929 and 1935, building single-deck bus and coach bodies for Scottish operators. The list of larger operators included Alexander's of Falkirk, Edinburgh Corporation and Scottish Motor Traction.

In 1937, the company was merged into Alexander's of Edinburgh Ltd, a business that focused on Ford sales and service.

ALLDAYS

Alldays Commercial Motors Ltd had offices at 78 Jermyn Street, London SW1, by 1923 and works in Farm Lane, Fulham SW6. The company was active in the 1920s building both bus and coach bodies on chassis such as ADC, Daimler CB, Dennis, Fiat, Lancia and Leyland. Its special 'parlour-type' bodies had twenty-four seats and were designed for 30cwt lorry chassis; the company also bodied some RAF Leylands. Both new and reconstructed bodies came with a six-month guarantee.

ALLEN

Frank Allen Ltd was at Bridge Street in Brigg, Lincolnshire, and active from about 1914 until 1930, although the company had been founded in 1817. By 1925 it was offering 'Allen Saloon' bodies with aluminium panelling and fourteen seats for Ford, Chevrolet, Morris, Overland, and Reo 1-ton chassis. In 1928 there was a six-wheel

Gilford restaurant car for Russell's Motor Service, with a toilet at the rear. By 1931 the company was working with full-size half-cab chassis, but was also building goods bodies. It was taken over by Slater Bros, who operated from the same address, but who appear not to have continued the PSV bodying business.

ALLSOPP

Thomas Allsopp Ltd was a builder of commercial bodywork with premises at Penistone Road North, Sheffield 6. Between 1926 and 1949, the company also built some coach bodywork.

ALL-WEATHER

All-weather Motor Bodies Ltd was a minor bus bodybuilder active between 1932 and 1955. The company was formed as a subsidiary of the car bodybuilder Gill, which had acquired a reputation for the all-weather type of body. It was based at Canterbury Road in Kilburn, London NW6.

On both cars and buses, all-weather bodies were out of fashion by the early 1930s, but the company did not confine itself exclusively to the type. Of interest in 1949, for example, was a streamlined single-deck coach built on AEC Regal III chassis. Work in the late 1940s included rebodying of 1930s vehicles, some with full-fronts.

AMMANFORD COACH BUILDING

The Ammanford Coach Building Co. was a Carmarthenshire company in the town of the same name that had an involvement with coach bodywork in 1949. The company also seems to have been known as Ammanford Manufacturing.

AMOS BROTHERS

Andrew, James and Willie Amos had set up in business as motor engineers at Victoria Garage, Selkirk, by June 1920. They built charabanc and lorry bodies for their own hire fleet and for others, merging with a bus operating company to become Brook & Amos Ltd. This company was absorbed by SMT in 1926.

ANDERSON (1)

The firm of G.H. Anderson is recorded as having some involvement with PSV bodywork in 1925. Its premises were at Whitburn, probably the one near Sunderland rather than the West Lothian town.

ANDERSON (2)

Sam Anderson was a haulage contractor with premises at Beechwood, Newhouse, Motherwell in Lanarkshire. The company built two coach bodies for local operators in 1947 and 1949.

ANDREWS (1)

Arthur Andrews of Newbury in Berkshire converted a Talbot car to a bus for local operator Denhams, later rebodying it as a fourteen-seater bus.

ANDREWS (2)

C.K. Andrews Ltd was at Uplands Garage in Swansea's Fisher Street and acted mainly as a dealer. The company built both bus and coach bodies between 1928 and 1936, some of them for its own PSV operations.

ANGUS

In 1924, a Lanarkshire operator took one fourteen-seat body on a Reo chassis from an Airdrie firm called Angus.

The company was probably R. Angus & Sons of Mill Street, which was trading as a coachbuilder by 1929, but this was its only known PSV body.

APPLEWHITE

The Applewhite business was active in the 1920s building bus and coach bodies for operators primarily in Lincolnshire. In 1919, Fred Applewhite took over the engineering business of which he was works manager. This was in St Rumbold Street, Lincoln (and may once have belonged to Rainforth's, another Lincoln bodybuilder (*q.v.*)), and he renamed it F. Applewhite & Sons. The premises were known as the Central Coach and Motor Bodyworks.

Fred Applewhite & Sons built this twenty-seater on an extended Chevrolet chassis for a local hotelier in Lincoln, in 1926.

Applewhite's built bodies for cars and lorries, as well as buses. The bus bodies seem to have been exclusively single-deck types and there are thought to have been no more than six of them. They included toastrack types for use at Skegness, twenty-seaters on Chevrolet chassis and a six-wheeler for a local hotelier. Lincoln Corporation Transport also took a small batch of Applewhite-bodied Leyland Lions in 1929 with reinforced red concrete floors, which were known as the Leyland 'Fireproofs'. One survives in the Lincoln Vintage Vehicle Society Collection, in its later condition with conventional wooden floor. The Applewhite business closed in 1932.

28-32 SEATER A.E.C. REGAL COACH
AS EXHIBITED AT —— OLYMPIA

WRITE— FOR FULL PARTICULARS
US   OF THE GREATEST
NOW   ATTRACTION OF THE
               OLYMPIA SHOW
Arlington Coachwork !

Best known as a dealer, Arlington also built some bodies and advertised this coach on an AEC Regal chassis as if it were of its own manufacture.

APPLEYARD

Appleyard was and remains a well-known car dealer chain with its headquarters in Leeds. It turned out a small number of single-deck PSV bodies from its own workshops around 1950, examples being a full-front body on Morris-Commercial chassis and at least one body for an AEC Regal III chassis.

ARCHER & TAYLOR

Archer & Taylor Ltd was a small bodybuilding concern located at 28 Portman Road in Ipswich. The company built some coach bodywork in the 1930s.

ARLINGTON

Arlington Bodybuilders Ltd was best known for its commercial-vehicle bodywork, but also put its name to some bus bodies and acted as a coach dealer. It may be that the bus bodies were not actually built on the Arlington premises, but were subcontracted to other companies. From 1928 to 1937, the company traded in London W5 as the Arlington Motor Co. Ltd, subsequently moving to High Road, Ponders End, Middlesex.

ARMOURY

Almost nothing is known about Armoury, which built

the 29-seat coach body on a Bedford OL lorry chassis for an Isle of Man operator in 1949. The location of this operator suggests that Armoury was also based on the Isle of Man.

ARMSTRONG

During the 1920s, Armstrong & Co. built coach bodies from premises at Leysfield Road in Shepherd's Bush, London W12. The company was registered in December 1924 and was later known as Armstrong & Co. (Coachbuilders) Ltd.

ARMSTRONG & BRICE

Armstrong & Brice are believed to have built some coach bodywork around 1930, but nothing further is known about the company.

ARNOLD

The Manchester firm of William Arnold Ltd was best known as a car bodybuilder. It had started in that business in 1910 and by the 1920s was associated with many of the more prestigious makes of chassis. Between 1928 and 1931, the company also turned its hand to both single-deck and double-deck bus bodies. The Arnold addresses were 101–115 Upper Brook Street, Chorlton-cum-Medlock, Manchester 13, and 24–26 St Ann's Square in Manchester city centre.

ARNOLD & COMBEN

The Arnold & Comben company was active at East Street, Farnham, Surrey, between 1922 and 1934, building single-deck bodies for Aldershot & District, among others. Among these were several rebodies on earlier chassis. Luxury buses, restaurant and sleeping coaches were among the types offered. The company also used the name of Phoenix Coachworks (q.v.).

The company had its origins in the business of Sturt & Goatcher, which built bodies for 'horseless carriages' in Farnham. George Sturt, whose family were wheelwrights, sold the business to his manager, William Arnold, in 1920. Mr Comben, otherwise unidentified, had certainly joined by 1923 and the company both built

Aldershot & District favoured local makers and this was part of its 1929 intake from the Farnham coachbuilder Arnold & Comben.

bus bodies and sold cars. Today, the company features on the family tree of Farnham Jaguar dealership Swain & Jones.

ASCOUGH (ASCO)

Ascough Ltd was formed out of Cars & Commercials (*q.v.*) with offices and a factory at Blessington, County Wicklow, in the Republic of Ireland, and began trading in 1973. It continued to build the Clubman 19- to 21-seat coach developed by the earlier company. A few examples reached the mainland through Eurobus Ltd, a dealer with headquarters in Dublin and a branch at Whitchurch in Shropshire. Eurobus literature usually had the name as Asco. The design continued into the early 1980s, but Ascough had become Eurovan Conversions by the middle of the decade.

Wearing Austin-Morris badges, this is a Leyland EA440 chassis dating from 1973 with the Irish builder's Clubman coach body.

ASHBY

There were some single-deck bus bodies bearing the Ashby name in the 1930s, but nothing more is known of the company responsible.

ASHCROFT

Ashcroft Bros Ltd had premises at Valley Road, Bidston, Birkenhead, and its earliest bus bodies included some twenty-seaters on Renault JX1 and JX2 chassis in 1924 for Altrincham & District. The company also built double-deck bodywork in the second half of the 1920s and first half of the 1930s. Much later, in 1954, the same company built five double-deck bodies on Leyland Titan PD2 chassis for Birkenhead Corporation, probably using frames by Metal Sections (*q.v.*).

ASHWOOD

The Ashwood Motor Bodyworks Ltd seems to have started out as a timber works at Cranmer Street in Long Eaton, Nottinghamshire. By 1931, it was at Inglehurst, Derby Road in Long Eaton. It was active as a builder of single-deck bus bodies in 1930–1 and there is some suspicion that it was connected with the operator Barton of nearby Chilwell.

ASSOCIATED COACHBUILDERS

Associated Coachbuilders, sometimes known as ACB, was a Sunderland company active between 1946 and 1954. Its premises were at Thirwell Street in Southwick. The company's origins may lie in a takeover of the Sunderland coachbuilder Blagg (*q.v.*) in 1946.

Early bodies were mainly coach types for independent operators on chassis such as the AEC Regal, Albion Valiant, Foden PVSC and Leyland Tiger PS1, but there were single-deck buses as well. The company even built a 'woody' estate car body on the rare Invicta Black Prince chassis. By 1950 ACB was building full-front single-deck designs as well as half-cabs. The company made use of Perspex roof panels on some of these bodies. In 1948, ACB bodied a Jensen lorry. Then for underfloor-engined chassis, the company came up with the Land Cruiser coach body, later renamed the Coronation Land Cruiser in honour of the Queen's coronation year in

1953. Some of these, on Sentinel underframes, were distinguished by rear wheel spats.

ASSOCIATED DELIVERIES

Associated Deliveries Ltd was a Reading company, probably more involved with commercial bodywork than with PSVs. However, in the late 1940s it joined what appears to have been a consortium of smaller coachbuilders that had banded together to attract work and perhaps also to spread design costs. The others were Dutfield, Hogger, Longford and Theale (*q.q.v.*). Associated Deliveries may have put its name to some coach bodies in 1949–50, but then faded from the scene. Its primary address was at 119 Kings Road, but by 1952 it also seems to have been operating from the aerodrome at Theale.

AS-U-DRYV

As-u-dryv Sunshine Saloons Ltd was a supplier of fabric roofs for all-weather coaches, similar in principle to the winding-head designs offered by Tickford for cars. The company had offices at 90 Cannon Street in central London in the late 1920s. It is not clear if the company also built complete PSV bodies or not.

AUSTIN

Beginning in 1914, chassis-maker Austin built PSV bodywork for a number of its own chassis. Most seem to have been small station buses and hotel buses, but there were also some charabancs.

AUTO-CELLULOSE

Auto-Cellulose Ltd was based at Spon Lane in Smethwick. The company was active as early as August 1924, when it was offering fourteen- to sixteen-seat bodies for Chevrolet chassis. In the 1930s it built coach bodies, mostly for small operators in the Midlands. There is a story that Duple threatened the company with legal action for infringement of design rights and there is no doubt that some Auto-Cellulose bodies of the period did resemble the Duple designs very closely.

The company remained active right through until 1963, when it built its last body. Another story claims that when the company closed, the former works manager bought the remaining stock and bodied three coaches in his garden at home over the following five years.

AUTOMOBILE SERVICES

The name of Automobile Services Ltd is believed to be associated with coach bodywork around 1928, but nothing else is known about the company. The name may be no more than a misprint for United Automobile Services (*q.v.*).

AYLESBURY

Aylesbury was a coachbuilder from the Republic of Ireland that built single-deck bus bodies in the 1920s. Among the buyers was the Great Southern Railway, which took some on Leyland Lion chassis.

Auto-Cellulose's early efforts on Chevrolet chassis in the mid-1920s (right) were predictable enough and later coach designs, like the 1937 example illustrated here on a Leyland Tiger chassis (left), followed the lead of Duple.

BAICO

Baico Patents Ltd made what the company called 'chars-a-bancs de luxe' and in 1924 advertised twenty-seater all-weather bus bodies among its offerings. The company had premises at 115 Fulham Road, London SW3.

BAIN

Magnus Bain was a bodybuilder at Keiss in Caithness. It built one known body in 1926, on a Chevrolet chassis for a Keiss operator.

BAKER

A company called Baker was offering PSV bodywork in 1927 and seems to have been operating from premises in Hove, Sussex. Nothing more definite is known.

BAKER & JEFFERIES

Baker & Jefferies is another PSV bodybuilder about whom almost nothing is known. That the company built some bus bodywork in 1920 on AEC YC chassis for Reading Corporation is more or less the extent of today's knowledge. Even whether it operated from Berkshire or Hampshire is unclear.

BAKERS OF TONBRIDGE

Bakers of Tonbridge only just merit inclusion in these lists, because the company built only one known bus body – and that was a converted lorry.

Chas Baker & Co. of Tonbridge was a car dealer in Tonbridge and in 1921 modified a Ford TT (the long-wheelbase version of the Ford T) to carry a local village cricket team to its away matches. The vehicle had a conventional enclosed lorry cab with an open back into which were fitted a pair of inward-facing garden-type bench seats. Bakers was absorbed by the Caffyns dealership chain in 1935 (*see* Caffyns).

BAMBER

Bamber & Co. Ltd was a Southport company best known

Dating from the mid-1920s, this twenty-seater body was typical of those turned out by small coachbuilders such as this London company.

as a dealer. However, it is also thought to have built some coach bodywork in 1928–9. The company was at 33 Liverpool Road in Birkdale.

BANKFIELD

Bankfield Engineering Ltd of Southport became involved with the refurbishment of worn-out bodies for St Helens Corporation in 1947–50.

BANKS

George Banks, from Rattar, Scarfskerry, in Caithness, built at least one mail bus on a 1-ton Ford chassis in 1924.

BARKING

The Barking Garage & Engineering Co. Ltd was based at 16 Wakering Road, Barking, Essex. It was incorporated in 1941, but its involvement with PSV bodywork seems to have been limited to the construction of one or more coach bodies in 1951.

BARKUS

The Barkus name is associated with some bus bodywork around 1924; the company responsible was probably the Barkus Light Engineering and Aircraft Company that was based at 67 Caversham Road in Reading. Its owner was W.J. Barkus and in 1939 he sold out to Bucklers, who were responsible from 1947 for the Buckler car.

BARNABY

The Hull firm of Barnaby was founded in 1870 as a blacksmith and wheelwright. It became B. Barnaby & Sons in 1926, but from 1937 was Barnaby's Motor Bodies (Hull) Ltd. Premises were at Neptune Street and Ropery Street. In 1960, the company was sold and, after a succession of owners, was finally wound up in 1974. In later years, it also built hearses.

Most of Barnaby's customers were in Yorkshire. Early bodies included charabancs and during the 1930s the company was building single-deck saloons for local operators on chassis such as the Leyland Cheetah and Leyland Tiger. The company was again active in the late 1940s building single-deck buses and coaches on both forward-

control chassis (Dennis Lancets and Leyland Tigers) and smaller normal-control types (Bedford OBs) and rebodying a number of earlier chassis. There were some double-deckers, too.

BARNARDS

Barnards Ltd was a major ironworks in Norwich, having been established in 1826 as Bishop & Barnards at Croslany Street. By the time of the 1939–45 war, it also had a factory on the Mousehold. Once war work was over, the company tried its hand in the bus and coach body business, attracting two former Northern Coachbuilders employees to help out; this was why there were similarities between Barnards bodies and NCB types. Most Barnards bodies were on Guy chassis and of the company's 100 or so bodies built, more than one-third were double-deck types. There were also small coaches such as 28-seaters on Austin CXB chassis. Barnards bodies were well made and had a reputation for durability. By 1955, the company had become part of Tinsley Wire Industries of Sheffield and has since closed down.

BARNES

Not every builder of bus bodywork in the early days was dedicated to that job alone. J. Barnes & Sons, of Private Lane, Helmshore, near Rossendale in Lancashire, was a wheelwright, but clearly responded to local demand by building some bus bodies in 1920.

BARNEY, SANDS & HARTRIDGE LTD

This Gravesend company was established in Maidstone in 1939 as a coachbuilding business by Ron Barney, Roy Sands and Peter Hartridge. Activities were soon suspended as the three principals were drafted to work on aircraft and military vehicles, but were re-established in 1946 at Glebe Road. The company built small numbers of bus and coach bodies. It was bought by local company West Brothers in 1976 and still trades under its original name as a crash repair workshop.

BARNSLEY

See Unity.

Bullock & Sons (B&S) of Featherstone in Yorkshire was the buyer of this 1932 Leyland Tiger TS2 with Barnaby C32R coachwork.

BARRASS

Almost nothing is known about this company, which was based at Stainforth in Doncaster. Only one body has been definitely confirmed – a coach built for a local company in the 1930s.

BARTLE

Bartle was a London coachbuilder active in the PSV world between 1919 and 1926. The company had been a well-regarded builder of car bodywork before World War I and had actually been founded as early as 1854. Its full name was James Bartle & Co. Ltd and it operated from the Notting Hill district. From 1924, the company

focused on making its Windsor car and on building bodies for commercial and PSV chassis.

By 1916, it was at the Western Iron Works in Lancaster Road, but in the 1920s it gave its address as Windsor Car Works in the same road. In 1924, it was advertising 14- to 28-seater charabanc bodies for any chassis, and by then had built at least one dual-entrance thirty-seater on a Dennis E-type chassis (for the Griffin Motor Co. of Brynmawr in South Wales, which traded as Western). In 1925 there were some bodies for Devon General and in 1926 the company was advertising its all-weather touring saloon and a Standard Bartle Service Bus. At least one of the latter had been built for Pritchard's Garage Co., of Stoke-on-Trent. The Windsor car business failed in 1927, apparently taking the rest of the company with it.

BARTON & DANSON

Henry Barton and Bill Danson were both employed by Massey Brothers (*q.v.*), but left after a disagreement. Trading as Barton & Danson, they set up their own coachbuilding business at Moor Road in Orrell, a mile west of the Massey works at Pemberton, near Wigan in Lancashire. There was a third partner, Joseph Coulshed, but the business ran into financial difficulties in 1925. It was dissolved, but reformed in 1926 using the original name of Barton & Danson, even though Danson was no longer a partner.

The company lasted until 1931. Danson's son George went on to be the joint founder of East Lancs (*q.v.*), while Barton had a controlling interest in the Orrell operator, Cadman's Services, from 1930.

BARTON TOWNLEY

This Lancaster company was active in the mid-1920s. It is believed to have subcontracted bodywork to other local firms, specifically G. Fox Ltd (*q.v.*). Barton Townley was a local businessman who established a chain of car dealerships that still survives in several towns across the north of England.

If 'world renowned' was pushing the bounds of credibility a little, Bartle at least managed to get its London-made product bought as far away as Devon. This is a 1925 example.

BATLEY

A company called Batley involved with PSV bodywork in the 1920s is thought to have come from the County Durham area, but nothing further is known.

BATTERSBY

Battersby built three 28-seat forward-entrance bus bodies for Blackpool Corporation in 1924 on Tilling-Stevens TS3 chassis. The company has not otherwise been identified, but is likely to have been based in the Blackpool area.

BAYLEYS

Bayleys Ltd was a London coachbuilder active in the PSV world between 1914 and 1927. The company was established by Edward Hobson Bayley in 1797, but by the time of its PSV work was at 42 Newington Causeway in Southwark. In 1919, it constructed some 26-seat bus bodies on ex-War Office Daimler chassis for Aldershot & District, while its other work included charabanc bodies.

BBW

The Bristol Tramways & Carriage Co. Ltd was formed in 1887 and bought its first motor buses in 1906. The following year, its tram depot at Brislington constructed three charabanc bodies for Thornycroft chassis. When Bristol began to build its own chassis in 1908, the Brislington works provided the bodies and by 1914 it was also building bodies for other operators. These were branded as being of BBW manufacture; the letters probably stood simply for Bodybuilding Works. After the Great War some bodies came from the Bristol company's Filton depot, but production was soon transferred to Brislington to allow Bristol aircraft production to start at Filton.

When Bristol passed into Tilling Group ownership in 1931, so did BBW. Although there was a continuing demand for bodies throughout the 1930s, the BBW designs often seemed old-fashioned and angular, the double-deckers having steeply sloping front panels. Most, but by no means all, were on Bristol chassis for the Bristol Tramways & Carriage Co. and for Tilling companies Southern and Western National.

BBW resumed body manufacture after the 1939–45 war, but using ECW designs and common parts such as Widney ventilators. ECW was, of course, the other body maker in the Tilling Group and, after nationalization in 1947, increasingly became the favoured body maker for what was now the BTC group of operators. BBW did some rebuilds for Tilling operators, including Red & White in 1950, and in 1952 it finished off outstanding

contracts for Lydney (q.v.) when that company closed down. However, in 1955 BBW built its last body, a bus for Southern National. The BBW works closed during the following year.

There is controversy over the words behind the BBW name. It seems to have started as internal Bristol-speak for Bodybuilding Works, but some commentators have argued that the letters stood for Brislington Bodyworks and others that it meant Bristol Bodyworks.

BEADLE

The Beadle company is probably best remembered for its pioneering integral-construction single-deckers of the late 1940s and early 1950s, but in fact the company history went back as far as 1894, when John Clayton Beadle began building horse-drawn vehicles at Spital Street in Dartford, Kent. He may have begun building commercial bodies for motor vehicles soon afterwards, but was certainly building car bodies by 1899. John C. Beadle, Ltd became a limited company in 1915.

During the 1920s, Beadle regularly exhibited bus and coach bodies at the Commercial Motor Show and after the Depression abandoned car bodybuilding to focus on the much healthier bus and coach market. At its peak in the 1930s, the company employed between 300 and 400 people. There were both double-deck and single-deck bodies, and among the coach bodies in 1939 was a batch for Royal Blue on earlier Leyland Tiger chassis, featuring that company's characteristic luggage rack at the rear of the roof.

During World War II, Beadle continued to build bodies from stocks of parts and only turned to utility-specification bodies right at the end. The company was also designated to rebody earlier chassis with utility-standard bodies during the war.

Experiments with integral construction began after the war ended in 1945. The company began with some buses using Commer running units for Eastern National and then worked closely with chassis-builder Sentinel. Beadle bodied all the early underfloor-engined STC and SLC single-deckers, but later Sentinel underframes were made available for other bodybuilders.

Between 1950 and 1954, Beadle became known for its semi-integral single-deckers, which were created from older chassis whose bodies had deteriorated beyond repair during the war years. The typical semi-integral Beadle depended on a pre-war chassis that had been cut into two sections to make front and rear subframes and

The Dartford company tended to cater for local operators in the early days. The East Kent bus was on a Tilling-Stevens chassis in 1928, and the six-wheeler was an all-weather design from the previous year.

these were then bolted up under a self-supporting body structure. Coaches always had full-front bodywork, but buses were sometimes half-cab designs. Most of the 206

After 1945, the company moved into integral construction, notably with this design for Sentinel.

Again with integral construction, this was the Beadle Rochester coach of the mid-1950s, built with a deliberate resemblance to the Duple Ambassador design.

built were bought by major BET Federation companies in the south-east, such as East Kent, Maidstone & District and Southdown.

From 1952, Beadle belonged to the Rootes Group and as a result used Commer running gear in its next generation of integral single-deck designs. By 1956, there were four of these: the 29-seat Canterbury coach and 32-seat Thanet bus, both 26ft (7.9m) long, and the 41-seat Rochester coach and 45-seat Chatham bus. The Rochester unashamedly borrowed the design of its windows from the Weymann Fanfare body, mainly to suit Southdown Motor Services, which bought twenty-five examples. Most of the others (there were seventy-eight in all) went to small independent operators, however. Beadle production ended in 1957 and the company was closed down, although the name has survived through its associated car dealership chain.

Maidstone & District took many Beadle-Leyland rebuilds. This 1952 example was sold to independent operator Thornes of Selby, who restored it to M&D colours after withdrawal from service.

BEALE

Beale's was another small company that turned its hand to PSV bodybuilding in the years immediately after the Second World War. Based at Southbourne Grove, Westcliff-on-Sea, in Essex, Charles W. Beale was a firm of joiners that rebuilt some trolleybuses for Southend Corporation and then built a few coach bodies for local operators on such chassis as the Austin CXB.

BEARDMORE

The Beardmore company is perhaps best known for its taxicabs, built from its Paisley premises after 1919. However, the company also built a handful of bodies for its own single-deck bus chassis in 1925. All went to Scottish operators.

BECCOLS

Beccols Ltd was formed in 1947 as a coachbuilding firm in Norris Road, Chequerbent, near Bolton in Lancashire. Its name derived from those of the Directors, Bert Becket and George Nicols. Nicols had been with Northern Counties (*q.v.*).

Early bodies were coach types on front-engined chassis, with either half-cabs or full-fronts, and featured decorative wheel-arch mouldings. In 1950 came a central-entrance coach body for underfloor-engined chassis, offering thirty-nine or forty-one seats. A few were built for independent operators on Leyland Royal Tiger and AEC Regal IV chassis, but Beccols went into liquidation in March 1952.

BEDFORDSHIRE AUTOCAR

Operating from premises at 8–10 The Broadway in Bedford, the Bedfordshire Autocar Co. Ltd built some bus bodywork in 1920. It later became a main dealer for Ford vehicles.

BELL (1)

T.G. Bell & Co. Ltd built both bus and coach bodywork between 1924 and 1930 from premises at Finningley in Yorkshire.

BELL (2)

Bell's Motor Bodyworks Ltd was at Scunthorpe in Lincolnshire and constructed some single-deck bus bodywork between 1928 and 1930.

BELLE

Belle Coachworks was a subsidiary of Shreeves Coaches of Lowestoft, operating from Horn Hill in the same town. Needing replacement vehicles after 1945, the company decided to bypass the waiting list by building its own bodies on ex-military chassis. These were mostly Bedford O and S series and all were built for Shreeves' own fleet or for associated bus fleets; it appears that much of the work was done by experienced bodybuilders 'moonlighting' from established local companies.

Belle Coach Works still trade in Lowestoft as commercial vehicle repairers and builders; BR Shreeve & Sons still trade as Belle Coaches.

BELLHOUSE HARTWELL

Bellhouse Higson was originally a dye works, founded in the nineteenth century. Around 1932, Director C.F. Bellhouse was joined by A.W. Hartwell and the company name changed to Bellhouse Hartwell & Co. Ltd. It was based at Leigh Road, Westhoughton, Bolton.

A prototype coach body appeared in the late 1930s, but World War II intervened and the company focused on aircraft fabrications and component manufacture. Like many other aircraft industry companies, it found additional work in the years immediately after the war by building PSV bodywork. There were both half-cab and underfloor-engine coach bodies, for customers including Hebble and Scout Motor Services of Preston.

However, Bellhouse Hartwell is probably best remembered for its 41-seat Landmaster coach body on underfloor-engined chassis. The 1951 version showed the way, with a striking design featuring roof windows and very ornate side mouldings; for the 1952 Commercial Motor Show this evolved into a design with the headlamps now in bulbous projections ahead of the front panel. Bellhouse Hartwell built its last PSV body in July 1955, subsequently becoming a military aerospace firm. It finally closed its doors in July 2002.

BENCE

William J. Bence and his descendants were behind many companies in the Bristol area, but the one of most relevance here had its origins in 1891. That was when Mr Bence, a wheelwright by trade, began operating a horse-drawn carrier business that connected Bristol with many of the outlying villages. He actively encouraged the carriage of passengers, especially on market days, and in 1919 established a motor-bus service from his main premises at Longwell Green, in Gloucestershire.

Among the Bence businesses were agencies for chassis manufacturers, including Ford, and of course the wheelwright's business soon came to build bodies for these, both for the company's own use and for others. The coachworks, W.J. Bence & Sons, was established at Longwell Green and also constructed delivery vans.

This arm of the company was active in the PSV field right through the 1930s and when war came the Bence group was asked to work on vehicle bodies. At this stage, its workshops became known as Bence Motor Bodies Ltd, being renamed as Longwell Green Coachworks (q.v.) from about 1944.

BENNETT (1)

F.T. Bennett was based at Rue du Pré, St Peter Port, Guernsey, and by 1926 was building all-metal charabanc bodies that it claimed cost about the same as a wooden body while saving weight. It continued until about 1934, manufacturing single-deck bus bodies from an address given as Park Street, Guernsey.

BENNETT (2)

J.C. Bennett & Co. (Coachbuilders) Ltd was a Glasgow company with premises at 31 South Annandale Road, Glasgow N1, and (by 1947) at 240 Petershill Road in Springburn. It may have been in business as early as 1930 at Bearsden in Dunbartonshre, but moved to Glasgow in 1940.

In the 1950s and 1960s the company built mainly school buses, but also rebuilt some bodies for David Macbrayne Ltd of Glasgow. It made its last-known PSV bodies in 1961, ceased trading in 1995 and was dissolved in 2000.

BENTON & CO.

The Benton & Co. responsible for some single-deck bus bodywork in the 1920s may well have been E. Benton & Co. (Nottingham) Ltd. This company was registered in June 1920 at Meadow Lane in Nottingham.

BERW

In October 1929, operator Imperial Motors of Abercynon formed a partnership with J.C. Morris to build bus bodies at the existing coach-building premises of Griffiths & Company, which were at Berw Road in Pontypridd. The new venture took the name of the Berw Carriage & Engineering Company and built most of the subsequent bodies for the bus and lorry fleets of Howell M. Davies, who traded as Imperial.

BEUKEN

John Beuken & Co. was a bus operator at East End Garage, Fauldhouse, West Lothian. Active in the 1920s, it built bodywork for its own fleet and at least one body, on a Bean chassis, for another operator.

BINNIE

A. Binnie (Coachbuilders) Ltd was best known as Scotland's leading manufacturer of mobile libraries in the 1970s and 1980s. The company had actually begun as a haulage business in 1929, but from 1947 moved into bodybuilding. Between 1947 and 1950, it capitalized on the demand for new coach bodies and for rebuilt PSV bodies, but thereafter focused on specialist commercial bodywork. The company's premises were at Woodhall Road, Wishaw in Lanarkshire.

BIRCH

Birch Brothers was an operator based in Cathcart Street in London's Kentish Town, NW5. It began building its own motor-bus bodies shortly after the start of the twentieth century and soon found its expertise in demand by other London operators. From 1912, it had a contract to maintain bus bodies for the British Automobile Traction concern, which lasted until BAT ceased activities in

The London coachbuilder promoted its all-weather designs in 1926 for the 1927 coaching season.

The full-front Airflo coach was certainly unusual when announced in May 1934. Luggage was carried in a compartment above the driver, as well as in longitudinal racks above the passengers. A redesign in 1935 bore witness to buyer resistance to this tall design.

London on the formation of the London Passenger Transport Board in 1933.

There were single-deckers on chassis such as Bean in the 1920s, but by 1926 the company was offering low-height modern bodies on older high-frame chassis. Advertisements that year variously claimed thirty or forty years of experience in bus bodywork. By 1925, there were 49-seat double-deckers for Leyland chassis, while single-deckers included all-weather types. Birch Bros had double-deck bodywork for the Leyland Titan before the end of the decade and by 1932 was building double-deckers with full-length top decks and enclosed staircases. By 1934, the company's coach bodies for Leyland Lion chassis incorporated the QT Easiway opening roof made by Quicktho in Wandsworth, SW18.

The last Birch Bros bodies were built in 1947. These were front-entrance lowbridge double-deckers on Leyland Titan PD1 chassis for its own fleet. The coaching operations were sold to the George Ewer group in 1971.

BLACKBURN AEROPLANE & MOTOR CO. LTD

The Blackburn Aeroplane & Motor Co. Ltd had been set up in 1914, going on to make its name as an aircraft manufacturer during World War I. However, demand for aircraft inevitably dried up when peace returned, with the result that the company turned to other things for a few years. Among these were car and bodywork manufacture, including for other chassis makers.

The Blackburn bodyworks was in Leeds and between 1920 and 1926 it also built some single-deck and double-deck bus bodies; Huddersfield Corporation was among the customers. When Government orders for aircraft began to pick up again, the company returned to its primary business.

BLACKMORE

Blackmore & Sons was a small boatyard at Bideford in Devon, noted for its construction of wooden vessels. The company built just one coach body, a 29-seater with a forward entrance on an Austin CXB chassis in 1950.

BLAGG

Blagg was a little-known coachbuilder based at Hendon in Sunderland, which built for various small operators in the north-east during the 1930s. In 1939, it supplied Sunderland Corporation with two forward-entrance 32-seater buses on Crossley Alpha chassis, one of which has been preserved.

Some sources say the company was absorbed by ACB (*q.v.*) in 1946.

BLAKE

J. Blake & Co. Ltd was founded in 1871 as a carriage builder in Liverpool. The company had car dealerships from early in the twentieth century and built car bodies in the 1920s, using the Weymann patents. It was also a commercial bodybuilder until well after the 1939–45 war. Blake's of Liverpool (as the company was known) built some coach bodywork around 1951, including on Crossley chassis.

BMMO

The Birmingham & Midland Motor Omnibus Co. Ltd was primarily an operator, but from the 1930s it had a policy of designing and building its own buses. These were primarily for its own use, but a good number were also sold to other operators.

The Carlyle Works in Birmingham built bodies for coaches and for both single-deck and double-deck buses with chassis by BMMO.

BOLTON

The Bolton company responsible for some charabanc bodywork in 1921 is thought to have been based in Coventry, but nothing further is known.

BONALLACK

The Bonallack company was an East London firm initially based at Cable Street, E1 and Romford Street in Forest Gate. By spring 1924 it was offering charabanc and fourteen- or twenty-seater bodies on 25cwt and 30cwt Gotfredson chassis. It later became Bonallack Vehicles Ltd, with premises at Manor Park, E12 and in Basildon, Essex.

The company is now better known for its commercial bodies under the name of Freight Bonallack.

BOND (1)

S.H. Bond, of Lesstone Road, Wythenshawe in Manchester, carried out a number of bus rebuilds for corporation fleets in the aftermath of World War II. In the early 1950s, it completed some one-and-a-half deck bodies on Burlingham frames for Manchester Corporation and in the middle of the decade built a batch of double-deck trolleybuses for Ashton-under-Lyne. The company also built hearses.

BOND (2)

In 1929, J.H. Woolliscroft (Silver Service) of Darley Dale took delivery of an AEC Reliance with Bond bodywork. The date suggests that this was not the same company as Bond of Wythenshawe (q.v.), which was active in the early 1950s, but no further details of this possible second Bond company have come to light.

BOOKER

Booker Motor Bodies (Western) Ltd was based at the Ford Road Industrial Estate, Brunel Road in Newton Abbott, and also had premises at Netherhampton, Salisbury. The company was best known for its horseboxes and mobile libraries, but also built some single-deck bus bodies between 1968 and 1978.

BOTWOODS

Botwoods was established as a carriage builder in Ipswich in 1875, but soon moved into the motor trade, selling cars and building bodies for them. From 1902 to 1910 Reggie Egerton worked in the business, but left after a disagreement. Botwoods then became Botwoods Ltd, with premises at Major's Corner, Ipswich.

From 1919, the company was absorbed by Mann Egerton, founded by Reggie Egerton's brother Hubert. However, it continued under its own name and built some single-deck bus bodies in the 1920s.

BRACEBRIDGE

Bracebridge Motor Bodyworks Ltd built single-deck bus bodies for many local operators from its premises at Bracebridge, Lincoln, between 1921 and 1934. The company still exists as a motor-body repair business and between 1981 and 1984 converted a number of minibuses.

BRANKSOME

The Branksome concern was active in the 1930s, but the scope of its PSV work is not clear. It seems to have been known as either Branksome Carriage Works or Branksome Carriage & Motor Works, and was initially

BIRMINGHAM
RAILWAY CARRIAGE & WAGON CO., LTD.,
SMETHWICK

Pioneers in the construction of Steel Passenger Stock. Specialists in the designing and building of all types of Coaches for Steam or Electric Traction; Diesel, Petrol or Steam driven Rail Cars; Air-Conditioned Cars, Tramcar Bodies, Omnibus Bodies, High Capacity Wagons and Freight Cars of every description; Containers, etc.

Telephone No.: Smethwick 1294. Telegrams: "Carriage, Smethwick."

One of the company's best-known bus-body contracts was for London trolleybuses in 1936.

at 1 Grosvenor Buildings, Seamoor Road, Bournemouth. Later addresses in the 1930s were in Poole Road, Branksome. The company also did some car bodywork in the mid-1920s.

BRCW

The Birmingham Railway Carriage and Wagon Company had been founded as the Birmingham Wagon Company in 1854. After building some of the London Underground railway stock, in the 1930s it fielded orders from London Transport for single-deckers on AEC Q chassis and for double-deck trolleybuses. By this time, its premises were in Smethwick.

A planned merger with Roberts of Wakefield, also involved in the railway carriage business, was not pursued. The company survived until 1963, but was not involved in bus bodying after the 1939–45 war.

BRECHIN

The Brechin company that built single-deck bus bodywork between 1924 and 1927 is thought to have had premises at Kilmarnock, but there is no further hard information.

BRIGGS

The Briggs company built some single-deck bus body-

work in 1927. It was based at Loughborough in Leicestershire.

BRIGHOUSE

Brighouse Motors built both bus and coach bodywork between 1928 and 1953, but probably not in great quantities. The company is thought to have been the Brighouse Motor Agency Ltd of Bradford Road, Bailiffe, in Brighouse, Yorkshire.

BRITISH ALUMINIUM

The British Aluminium Co. Ltd advertised single-deck bodywork for Vulcan chassis in 1929, but was almost certainly not responsible for assembling any. Instead, it supplied kits of parts for assembly in operators' own workshops, or by local coachbuilding companies. Its trading address was Adelaide House in London EC4.

BRITISH COMMERCIAL

The British Commercial Lorry & Engineering Co. Ltd had premises in Manchester. It seems to have been active only briefly in the PSV market, building single-deck bus bodies in 1919–20. Widnes Corporation was a customer.

BRITISH TRAILER COMPANY

As its name suggested, the British Trailer Company was primarily a maker of commercial trailers, although it did turn its hand to body construction during the war, when it built Field Marshal Montgomery's command caravan. It became involved in bus bodywork during the late 1940s, when it was based at Phoenix Works, Richmond Road, Trafford Park in Manchester, but bus bodybuilding ceased in the 1950s.

The company later moved to Graham Works on Liverpool's Kirkby Industrial Estate, but closed down in 1971.

BROCKHOUSE

Brockhouse was a Scottish bodybuilder with premises at Livingstone Street, Clydebank, in Glasgow. Originally

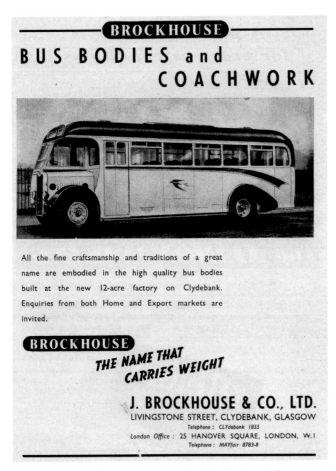

BROCKHOUSE

BUS BODIES and COACHWORK

All the fine craftsmanship and traditions of a great name are embodied in the high quality bus bodies built at the new 12-acre factory on Clydebank. Enquiries from both Home and Export markets are invited.

BROCKHOUSE

THE NAME THAT CARRIES WEIGHT

J. BROCKHOUSE & CO., LTD.

LIVINGSTONE STREET, CLYDEBANK, GLASGOW
Telephone : CLYdebank 1855
London Office : 25 HANOVER SQUARE, LONDON, W.I
Telephone : MAYfair 8783-8

The Glasgow coachbuilder catered mainly for Scottish operators, this coach being for the Bluebird fleet of W. Alexander & Sons.

founded as a blacksmith's business in West Bromwich in 1898, J. Brockhouse & Co. Ltd also had a controlling interest in the Sunbeam Trolleybus Company, until it was sold to Guy Motors in 1948.

Although Brockhouse had built a handful of bus bodies on Albion chassis for export in 1938, its Glasgow branch entered the bus-body business seriously in 1947, initially constructing a batch of coaches for Alexander's of Falkirk. In 1948, Brockhouse built a new factory on the Clydebank site to accommodate manufacture of double-deck bodies to Park Royal designs, but the venture never really became established when it proved difficult to find the skilled labour needed.

Brockhouse bus bodies were made until 1951, with most going to Scottish operators, but a number also being exported. From 1950, the company established J. Brockhouse (South Africa) Ltd to build bus bodies in that country.

BROMILOW & EDWARDS

Bromilow & Edwards Ltd was established at Foundry Street in Bolton when two older companies merged. It has always been better known for its lorry and, especially, tipper bodies, and now trades as Edbro.

However, between 1927 and 1934 the company built both coach and double-decker bodies for local operators. Among the former was a 29-seat full-front body on a TSM Express chassis for Holts of Rochdale (Yelloway) in 1931, while among the latter were some unique double-deckers for Bolton Corporation on Leyland Titan TD2 chassis in 1932.

BROOKES BROS

This was a Yorkshire bodybuilder active between 1937 and 1951 and based at Dinnington, near Sheffield. It is known to have rebodied some pre-war AEC Regal chassis with half-cab coach bodies in the boom years for the industry after 1945.

BROOKS

A Norwich company called Brooks is believed to have been involved with PSV bodywork in 1937.

BROOM

Victor Broom Ltd is better known as a builder of car bodywork than for its involvement in the PSV business. It is, in fact, not absolutely certain that the company built any bus bodywork, but the circumstances suggest that it might have done.

The company was based in Camden Town, north-west London, from at least 1924, but seems to have suffered from financial difficulties for most of its brief life. It may well have taken on some PSV bodying to help make ends meet before closing its doors in 1929.

BROWN

A company called Brown is known to have built single-deck bus bodies from premises in Gateshead in 1921–2. No more information is available at present.

BRUCE COACH WORKS LTD

Bruce Coach Works grew out of Air Dispatch (Coach-builders) Ltd (*q.v.*) in 1948. It was named after its owner, Anthony Easter Bruce, who was the son of the Hon. Mrs Victor Bruce, founder of Air Dispatch. Its premises were at the Pengam Moor Airport, near Cardiff.

Bruce Coach Works had a close association with East Lancs (*q.v.*), mostly assembling bodywork designed by that company. It took over some business from Air Dispatch, including a number of rebuilds for St Helens Corporation. Bruce built both single-deck and double-deck bodies for mainly Welsh operators, including some double-deck trolleybuses for Cardiff Corporation. Bruce's last eight bodies were for Eastbourne Corporation, a former Air Dispatch customer, before the company closed in December 1951.

BRUSH

Between the mid-1920s and 1951, Brush was a major builder of double-deck and single-deck bus bodies,

although few coaches were built. In that period, the company was based in Loughborough, although Brush had been founded in London in 1879 to manufacture lighting and associated electrical equipment. The move to Loughborough had been made in 1889, when business expansion demanded larger premises.

Those larger premises had belonged to the Falcon Engine and Car Works, which had been building horse buses since 1885, an activity that later resurfaced among Brush's activities. Brush began work on the electrification of tramways in 1880, then moved on to building complete trams, including bodywork. From here, it was a small step to building motor buses (about 100 were built between 1904 and 1907 and entered service in Birmingham and London, among other places). There were trolleybus bodies before the war, too, and the tram business continued to flourish.

Brush continued to build vehicle bodies during the Great War, although most of its work was concerned with munitions. Tram production resumed after the war, but the last big order was in 1925 and Brush built its last tram in 1936. The company built its first covered-top double-deck bus body in 1924 and in 1931 constructed

ABOVE: **Refusing to be beaten by the outbreak of war, Brush was still determined to carry on in November 1939. The vehicles illustrated are a Daimler double-decker for Derby and a Dennis single-decker for the Caledonian fleet.**

LEFT: **The Loughborough company constructed the body on this Karrier six-wheeler for the Portsmouth municipality in 1927.**

Brush built many bodies to British Electric Federation designs, this being a 1933 example.

This was a 1926 double-deck body (H26/26RO) by Buckingham for Birmingham, which had favoured its local coachbuilder. The chassis is an AEC 504.

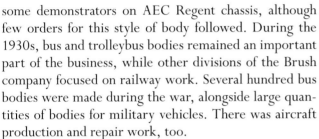

some demonstrators on AEC Regent chassis, although few orders for this style of body followed. During the 1930s, bus and trolleybus bodies remained an important part of the business, while other divisions of the Brush company focused on railway work. Several hundred bus bodies were made during the war, alongside large quantities of bodies for military vehicles. There was aircraft production and repair work, too.

After the war, Brush returned to bus bodybuilding and by 1949 was turning out around sixty bodies a month. However, this was a period of expansion in other areas of the business and bus bodies accounted for only about one-sixth of the group's turnover by the early 1950s. So Brush Coachworks Ltd built its last bodies in 1951 and was sold the following year to the neighbouring Willowbrook (*q.v.*) company. The rest of the Brush Group focused on railway work and electrical business until it was bought by the Hawker-Siddeley Group in 1957.

BRYSON

Bryson Bros was a Glasgow company that built single-deck bus bodywork between 1927 and 1929. The company may have been Bryson Bros (Motors) Ltd, which traded from 122 St Vincent Street and in 1929 was distributor for American De Soto cars.

BUCKINGHAM

Buckingham Motor Bodies was the trading name of John Buckingham Ltd, established in 1878 and based at 332–333 Bradford Street, Birmingham. The company's first new bus was a charabanc on a 30hp Scout chassis in 1915 and Buckingham built a quantity of Burfords for the

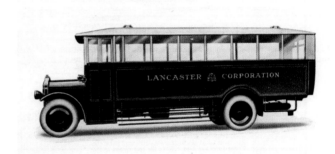

Nevertheless, Buckingham was also selling further afield in the 1920s. This single-decker – definitely by Buckingham and not Burlingham – was a 1926 Daimler for Lancaster.

Great Western Railway in 1924–5. There were double-deckers for the Birmingham municipality, too.

Buckingham also built the body for a Rolls-Royce 20hp car in 1925, but most of its business seems to have been hearse bodies. Some bodies attributed to Buckingham, especially some of those for Lancashire operators, are more likely to have been made by Burlingham (*q.v.*). By 1931 the company was in financial trouble, eventually closing down in August 1934.

BUNDY

H.E. Bundy (Coachbuilders) Ltd is thought to have made some coach bodywork in 1947. The company was based at Old Malt House, Poole Road, Wimborne, Dorset, but seems to have built no more PSV bodywork before closing in 1977.

BURLINGHAM

Burlingham was one of the leading British builders of bus and coach bodies between 1928 and 1960. Founded in Blackpool by Herbert Victor Burlingham initially as a general vehicle bodybuilder, the company became one of the four major suppliers of coach bodies during the 1950s and was building around 300 bodies a year when it sold out to Duple for £550,000 in 1960. Two years later, it was renamed Duple (Northern) Ltd.

Local demand around the seaside town of Blackpool was inevitably for coach bodies, so Burlingham quickly focused on these, initially building all-weather types but soon turning to closed saloons. Many had luggage racks on the rear of the roof and Burlingham was a pioneer of toilet compartments for long-distance coaches. The company's products sold as far afield as London and Scotland, although Burlingham bodywork was always more common in the northern parts of England. In 1929 the company moved into larger premises and in 1931 opened another new site.

In 1930, H.V. Burlingham sold the business to two local businessmen, then moved to Garstang to build caravans. The company's coach bodies pioneered new features, such as curved sightseeing windows in the roof sides, while Blackpool Corporation favoured Burlingham's with orders for single-deck buses from 1933 and double-deckers from 1935. These latter had an advanced design, with full-fronts and centre entrances, plus 'streamlined' features to the corporation's requirements. The company also built some bodies to Leyland design on Titan chassis, incorporating Leyland components.

When Ribble embarked on a major rebodying programme in the late 1940s, local builder Burlingham was a natural choice. This pre-war Leyland Tiger TS7 was rebodied as a bus.

Characteristic Burlingham coach features in the 1930s were ornately shaped window frames, while stained-glass window panels featured in double-deck stairwells and for toilet compartments. Some flamboyant designs appeared on the Maudslay SF40 chassis, but from the middle of the decade Burlingham and Duple borrowed from one another to meet customer requirements and the two firms' bodies became very similar. The 1937 and later Burlingham coach style followed Duple's 1936 style, with a graceful curve from front to rear, but deleted the canopy over the bonnet and incorporated a distinctive V-shaped rear panel. Particularly attractive was a four-bay half-cab coach body introduced in 1939, with slender polished metal pillars.

Wartime saw Burlingham building mobile canteen bodies and some utility single-deck bodies, along-

The Blackpool builder sold all over the north of England, this 1930 AEC Regal going to an operator on the opposite side of the country.

Ribble was a regular Burlingham customer, taking a large quantity of these Leyland PD2s with platform doors in the mid-1950s.

The Seagull name was carried over on to later designs, those seen here being a 1960 Seagull 60 on Ford Thames chassis (right) and a Seagull 70 on an AEC Reliance (left).

side airframe assemblies for Wellington bombers. The company also rebuilt a number of older vehicles with utility single-deck bodies.

The first post-war coach left the factory in January 1946, continuing the style announced in 1939, but now with an extra window pillar in each side for strength, as no seasoned timber was available. To suit Government calls for standardized designs, Burlingham introduced new single-deck and double-deck bodies later that year. There were few export orders, but business was brisk at home.

Government requirements gradually relaxed and 1948 brought some pioneering full-front lowbridge double-deck coach bodies on 8ft (2.4m) wide Titan PD1 chassis for Ribble, as that operator's first White Lady express coaches. The same basic design, with generously radiused windows, less its full-front and ornate detailing, was used for many ordinary service buses as well. From 1949, there were more streamlined central-entrance double-deckers for Blackpool, again on the new 8ft wide chassis. Full-fronts appeared on coach bodies, but most Burlingham bodies on heavyweight single-deck chassis still had half-cabs. There were also some bodies for independent operators on Leyland Comet chassis, the only normal-control models bodied at Blackpool in this period.

With the arrival of underfloor-engined single-deck chassis, Burlingham drew up two new designs for the 1950 Earls Court Show. They shared many features, but one had been given a curved waist rail and a curved moulding running from front to rear to create a side feature below the windows. This was known to the company as the 'tank panel', because of its resemblance to the appearance of tank tracks. This body, for local coach operator Woods, carried that company's seagull

logo on its side and, when the design proved a big hit, Burlingham's adopted the name of Seagull for it.

The Seagull went on to become Britain's most successful coach body on underfloor-engined chassis in the 1950s and variants were introduced for vertical-engined chassis as well. The design was modified every two years or so until 1959, although these redesigns gradually diminished its attractiveness and the late model for vertical-engined chassis had an ungainly front end which earned it the 'Pig' nickname.

Meanwhile, Burlingham had also introduced a straightforward single-deck service bus design for underfloor-engined chassis, created some one-and-a-half-deck airport coaches for Manchester Corporation and continued to build double-deck bodies. Notable was a large batch of full-front, forward-entrance bodies on Titan PD3/4 chassis for Ribble in 1957–8.

A new range of coach bodies appeared in 1959 – the Seagull 60 for front-engined lightweight chassis and the

The original Seagull coach body has become a much-loved classic. This is a 1951 example on Leyland Royal Tiger chassis, owned by Whittle of Highley. Passengers are standing on the seats to see the sights of London through the open sunroof.

Burlingham built the first 'White Lady' full-front double-deck coaches for Ribble, and the design caused quite a stir when new. This is the prototype when new in 1948; the grille design was later modified. Subsequent batches by East Lancs had an even more attractive four-bay layout.

Seagull 70 for underfloor-engined types. Despite the name, however, these had little in common with the classic Seagull of the 1950s. After the Duple takeover in 1960, the Burlingham designs continued in production under their own name until 1962, when the company was renamed Duple (Northern) Ltd.

BURTENSHAW

The Burtenshaw family of Reigate had a long association with carriage-building and by 1913 George Burtenshaw was in business at West Street in the town as 'the original Reigate carriage works'. He advertised 'carriages and motor bodies of every description built to order'. There seems to have been some rivalry between him and another Burtenshaw, this time Frank, whose premises were at Bell Street.

During 1936, George Burtenshaw's company built some coach bodies, including some on Leyland Tiger chassis for Western SMT.

BUSH & TWIDDY

Bush & Twiddy Ltd owned the East Anglian Highways fleet that was sold to Eastern Counties in 1932. Operating from Croft Coach Works, Sussex Street in Norwich, the company built bodies for its own use, mostly thirty-two seaters on AEC Regal chassis but also some fourteen-seater coaches on Chevrolet chassis in 1929–30. The company is later said to have become involved with rebuilding war-damaged buses, including at least one London Transport AEC Renown 'Scooter' single-decker during 1944.

CADOGAN

Cadogan (Perth) Ltd built bus and coach bodies from premises at St Catherines Road in the city, beginning in 1924. The company was not associated with the London car bodybuilder of the same name and Daniel Cadogan had learned his trade with Peter Crerar (*q.v.*) in Crieff.

Perth Corporation Transport became an early customer and the Cadogan company also had a contract to maintain the Perth fleet until its sale to W. Alexander & Son in 1934. Cadogan built single-deck bus and coach bodies on a variety of chassis for Scottish operators right through the 1930s. During World War II, it constructed some bodies on Austin chassis and carried out repair work. It built a handful of bodies on Bedford OB and Austin chassis in 1947–8, when the business was wound up and its assets passed to the Scottish Co-Operative Wholesale Society Ltd.

CAFFYNS

Caffyns Ltd is an Eastbourne company best known for its chain of car dealerships. However, in the 1920s it was an established coachbuilder, constructing car bodies on a wide variety of chassis. The company also built a pair of single-deck bus bodies on Morris Dictator chassis in 1931.

CAHILL

The company now known as Cahill Truck Bodies was

established in 1939 at Graignamanagh, County Kilkenny in the Republic of Ireland. The company built some bus bodywork on Bedford chassis in the late 1940s, but has always been better known for its commercial vehicles and horsebox bodywork.

CALEDONIAN

Just one charabanc body is known to have come from the Caledonian Motor Bodyworks Ltd, which was at Murray Street, Paisley, Renfrewshire by 1924. Nothing else is known about the company.

CAMERON

Cameron may have been a Scottish coachbuilder in the early 1930s, but nothing more is known for certain about the company.

CAMPBELL

The Campbell company built bus bodies from premises in Hastings in the early 1920s.

CAMPBELL BROTHERS

This was a coach operator from Whitburn in West Lothian. The company built a few coach bodies for its own fleet between 1947 and 1949, but also did repairs and rebuilds for other local operators and rebodied a pre-war Leyland Tiger for a local operator in 1949.

CANHAM

F.W. Canham & Sons was responsible for both single-deck bus and open-top double-deck bodies from 1919–23. It operated from Roslyn Stables in Ipswich, Suffolk.

CARLYLE

Between 1923 and 1969, operator BMMO (Midland Red) (q.v.) built most of the buses it needed for its own fleet and also sold a number to other operators within the British Electric Traction group. In the early days, the chassis carried SOS nameplates. Both bodies and chassis were constructed at the company's Carlyle Road Works in Edgbaston, Birmingham, and as a result the bodies are often referred to as Carlyle types.

This Carlyle has an indirect connection with the company of the same name that built minibuses and midibuses in Birmingham between 1983 and 1989. The later company was established by privatizing the engineering department of Midland Red.

CARS & COMMERCIALS

Cars & Commercials Ltd was a Dublin company established around 1971. It developed a 19- to 21-seat coach body for Austin-Morris chassis and branded it as the Clubman type. The company became Ascough (q.v.) in 1973, and continued the design.

CARTER

Carter was a coachbuilder from Macclesfield in Cheshire that built a number of charabanc bodies on 1923 AEC YC chassis owned by the North Western Road Car Co. Ltd. The company may have been active as early as 1919.

CASELLY

Caselly (or possibly Casseley) was a Belfast company responsible for a ten-seat toastrack body on Austin 20 chassis in 1925.

CAWOOD

T.W. Cawood & Son was a Doncaster company that carried out a number of body rebuilds towards the end of World War II and in the later 1940s. It may be connected with a later company, Cawood's Garage Ltd of Thorne Road.

CENTRAL

Central Garage (Bradford) Ltd built some sixteen-seater PSV bodies in the early 1960s. Its address was Civic Service Station, Otley Road, Shipley in Yorkshire.

CENTRAL AIRCRAFT COMPANY

This company was established in the London NW6 district of Kilburn, as a subsidiary of the joinery company, R. Cattle Ltd. It built aircraft and components under licence during the Great War and in 1921 built a sixteen-seater charabanc body on a Ford 1-ton chassis.

CHADWICK

Probably operating from Stoke-on-Trent in Staffordshire, the Chadwick company built charabanc, coach and single-deck bus bodies in the 1920s.

CHALLANDS ROSS

This company was initially registered as Challands, Jackson & Co. Ltd in 1914 at London Road, Nottingham. It was a vehicle bodybuilder from the start. In 1918, Robert H. Ross joined the company and set up a separate motor vehicle department; he also secured the local agency for Thornycroft chassis. In February 1919, the company name was changed to Challands, Ross & Co. Ltd, and new headquarters were established on Canal Street, although the workshops remained at London Road.

Challands Ross built bus and coach bodies in the second half of the 1920s, mainly on Thornycroft chassis, but also on other chassis for local operators, including Barton. Further afield, there was a twenty-seat forward-entrance bus on Thornycroft chassis for Isle of Man Road Services in 1927.

PSV work seems to have ceased during the 1930s, although the company remained in business as a commercial bodybuilder. It moved to Highbury Works on Highbury Avenue in Bulwell in 1955, while still retaining the Canal Street offices. The company ceased trading in June 1989.

CHALLENGERS

Challengers Coachbuilders was also known as Challengers Engineering Ltd and was owned by Jack Crabtree, who had been involved with Elite, Lewis & Crabtree, Shearing & Crabtree and Shearings (*q.q.v.*). Challengers operated from Moorhey Street in Oldham, and was involved with PSV bodywork between 1946 and 1949.

CHALMERS

John Chalmers & Sons Ltd built some single-deck bus bodies in the mid-1920s from its premises at 50–58 High Street in the Surrey town of Redhill.

CHAMBERLIN

Chamberlin & Sons Ltd constructed coach bodywork in the late 1920s from 52–56 Buckingham Street in Aylesbury, Buckinghamshire.

CHARLESWORTH

Charlesworth Motor Bodies Ltd was a Coventry coachbuilder best known for its car bodywork in the 1920s. Its premises were at 128 Much Park Road. As work dried up in the late 1920s, the company turned its hand to commercial and PSV bodies as well, with a 1929 advertisement advertising 'high class passenger coachwork' of all types on any chassis. There seem to have been some takers and Charlesworth put its name to some coach bodywork between 1929 and 1932.

The company was restructured as Charlesworth Bodies (1931) Ltd in November 1931 and enjoyed a new lease of life building car bodies under contract to various chassis makers, but was unable to revive its business after the 1939–45 war and in 1947 was bought out by the car maker Lea-Francis.

Better known as a builder of car bodies, Charlesworth constructed some PSV bodies as well, including this 1929 charabanc on a Daimler chassis.

CHARLTON

Charlton Coach & Motors was a Huddersfield company responsible for some bus bodywork around 1922–3.

CHARTERWAY

Charterway Coachcraft was founded by Philip Mardon in 1969 in Southport. From 1972 it was at Mayflower Works, Liverpool Road, Formby. The company built coach bodies on Mercedes-Benz chassis, plus welfare-type buses.

It also joined forces with James Cocker & Sons (Southport) Ltd (*q.v.*) in 1971–2 as Charterway-Cocker Coachcraft Ltd, offering the 25-seat Countryman and 45-seat Challenger coach bodies.

CHATHAM

The Chatham Motor Co. Ltd was based at Railway Street in Chatham and was founded in 1924. It was constructing bus bodies during 1930–1.

CHELSEA

The Chelsea Motor Building Co. Ltd had premises at 164 King's Road, London SW3. In 1923–4 it advertised its willingness to construct van and PSV bodies of all types and sizes.

CHISHOLM

Chisholm was the local joiner in Coldingham, Berwickshire, who constructed a fourteen-seat body on an Albion chassis for a Coldingham operator in 1928.

CHURCHILL

Churchill Constructors Ltd was established in 1946 as a general body and coachwork repairs business to fulfil contract work for the Government. It had premises on the Mousehold Estate, Salhouse Road in Norwich. As the repair contracts dried up, the company turned to the manufacture of complete bodies.

Early bodies during 1948 were a 35-seater coach on an AEC Regal chassis and a special service coach on a Bedford OB chassis for use in Egypt by the British airline BOAC.

Churchill was always associated with front-engined chassis, although it built a single coach body on underfloor-engined Leyland Royal Tiger chassis in November 1951. There were many bodies for Commer Avenger and Bedford SB chassis, as well as some of the last Tilling-Stevens Express models in 1952. The company closed down in 1953.

CITY CARRIAGE WORKS

The City Carriage Works Ltd was another company active in London during the 1920s, in this case from

Despite its London premises, Chelsea attracted business from this Nottinghamshire operator in 1923.

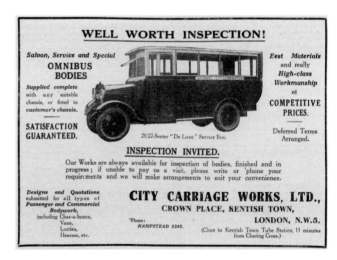

London-based City Carriage Works attracted custom from Sussex, as this 1925 advertisement demonstrates.

premises at Crown Place in Kentish Town, NW5. By 1924, it was advertising charabanc bodies with a light, detachable one-piece roof for Berliet, Chevrolet and Reo chassis; a 20- to 22-seat service bus body was on offer by November 1925; and in 1926 the company advertised the availability of 14- to 16-, 18- to 20- and 20- to 22-seater bodies.

CITY WHEEL WORKS

City Wheel Works was a Dublin bodybuilder active in the 1920s. Among its products were bus bodies for the Great Southern Railway on Leyland Lion chassis.

CLARK

Clark & Co. (Scunthorpe) Ltd was a dealer and operator with a branch in Doncaster, as well as the constructor of bus and coach bodies from the late 1920s. Its premises were at Oswald Road, Scunthorpe.

Clark's output included many bodies on ADC and AEC Regal chassis for local operator Enterprise & Silver Dawn; late creations were a pair of Bedfords in 1937.

CLYDE

The Clyde Shipping Co. – rather better known as a cruise ship and ferry operator based in Glasgow – was involved in building coach bodywork in 1939.

COACHES & COMPONENTS

Coaches & Components Ltd had premises at 469–471A Holloway Road, London N7. The company is known to have built just one coach body some time around 1946.

COCKER

James Cocker & Sons (Southport) Ltd was a coachbuilder at Manor Road in Southport and later at Kew Works, Meols Cop Road in the town. The company may have been founded in the 1930s and was best known for commercial bodies, but also built some coach bodywork after 1966.

In 1971–2, it was briefly involved in a joint venture

Many Commer Avengers were bodied by Churchill in the late 1940s and early 1950s. This 1949 petrol-engined example was for Newmans of Hythe in Kent.

with fellow Southport builder Charterway Coachcraft (*q.v.*).

COLLIER

Collier appears to have been a Suffolk coachbuilder active in the 1920s as a manufacturer of single-deck bus bodies.

COMMER

Commer was founded as the Commercial Car Company in London in 1905 and by 1909 was building bus chassis. It is known to have constructed its own charabanc bodies for its WP3 chassis by 1913.

Absorbed into the Rootes Group in 1926, Commer remained primarily a chassis maker, but during the 1930s also built some twenty-seater coach bodies on its own Centaur chassis. The brand had ceased to exist by 1979, although by then the coachwork activities had long since come to an end.

COMMERCIAL MOTORS

Commercial Motors (Harrow) Ltd was involved with single-deck bus bodywork from its premises at Harrow Coach Works in Sherwood Road, South Harrow, in 1956.

CONNAUGHT

Connaught Coachworks & Palmer Ltd built some charabanc bodywork in 1921. Connaught was an old-established coachbuilder with origins in the late eighteenth century, but by the 1920s it was well known for its bodywork on prestigious car chassis.

Palmers (*q.v.*) was a Dover coachworks that is thought to have done contract work for Connaught (there was a Connaught Coachworks in Dover) in the 1930s. Somewhere between the two lies the truth about who built the charabanc bodies.

CONSTABLE

Constable is thought to have built the fourteen-seat body on a Dearborn FX chassis in 1923 and to have built some coach bodies as well. The company may have been F.W. Constable of London Road in Gloucester.

COOK

Mr T. Cook was a wheelwright in Gaveley, Huntingdonshire. His claim to fame in the PSV world was his conversion of an ex-US Army Ford Model T ambulance to a bus in 1919 for local operator Whippet Coaches.

CORRIE

Thomas Corrie was a hotel and garage owner in Lockerbie in the 1920s. He was also a bodybuilder and is known to have built a fourteen-seat bus body on a Morris chassis for a local operator in 1926.

COUNTY MOTORS

County Motors (Leigh) Ltd had premises at Chapel Street in the Lancashire town and had some involvement with coach bodywork in 1949, building notably on Crossley chassis.

COWIESON

F.D. Cowieson was an architect who gave his name to a Glasgow firm established in about 1907 at 3 Charles Street in the St Rollox district of the city. F.D. Cowieson & Co. initially specialized in supplying prefabricated buildings and agricultural buildings such as poultry houses and chicken coops. By 1919 it was also building bodies for buses, charabancs and ambulances, becoming a limited company in 1923. It was probably at this time that it moved into new and larger premises at 80–108 Charles Street and diversified into more general building work; by 1926, the bodybuilding side of the business had been separated from the parent firm.

The bodybuilding business expanded rapidly and by 1930 Cowieson had become Scotland's leading bus builders. It was also using the rather awkward slogan, 'Bodies that made good, because they are made good'. Edinburgh Corporation and the Scottish General Omnibus Company had been important early customers and Cowieson-bodied single-deck Leylands were among Glasgow Corporation's first buses in 1924. There was subcontract work for local chassis manufacturer Albion from the mid-1920s, too. Double-deckers had followed by 1929, both lowbridge and highbridge types, and Cowieson patented its own lowbridge design with three nearside seats mounted slightly higher than the single offside seat and gangway; this was not as low as the Leyland lowbridge design and did not catch on.

Cowieson catered primarily for Scottish operators and both these 1930 examples fitted the pattern. The single-decker was for SMT and the double-decker for Glasgow.

Most Glasgow double-deckers in the 1930s had Cowieson bodies. Early examples had a piano-front style, but by the mid-1930s Cowieson bodies were characterized by a sloping front and rather fussy six-bay construction. Other Cowieson customers included Dundee Corporation and Belfast Corporation. However, by the mid-1930s there was less demand for Cowieson bodies: the work for Albion had reduced; Glasgow Corporation was turning elsewhere; and some sources suggest that quality had begun to slide as well. In 1938, a contract for more Glasgow double-deckers was reallocated to MCW when Cowieson's was unable to meet the delivery date. Meanwhile, it appears that some key staff left Cowieson to join Pickering (*q.v.*) in this period.

The last Cowieson bus bodies were built in 1939. The company did not return to bus bodywork after World War II, but remained active in the prefabricated buildings business until it was voluntarily wound up in 1953.

CRANLEIGH BODYBUILDERS

Cranleigh Bodybuilders seems also to have been known as Hutchings. It built single-deck bus bodywork in the mid-1920s.

CRAVENS

Cravens Railway Carriage & Wagon Co. Ltd was based in Sheffield and, as the name suggests, its primary business was railway rolling stock. However, the company also made tram bodies and was building bus and trolleybus bodies by 1927, offering both composite and all-metal types by June 1934.

During World War II, the company was engaged on work for the Air Ministry and it was no surprise that when it resumed bus bodying after the war it focused on such things as jig-drilling and interchangeable subassemblies. One notable contract was for 120 bodies on London Transport's RT-type AEC Regent double-deckers, but Cravens built these largely to its own design, with such features as five window bays instead of the four on the standardized RT bodies. As these non-standard features reduced the interchangeability of components that was such a feature of the RT class, they were soon sold out of service.

In 1964, Cravens sold out to East Lancs (*q.v.*), who at the same time tried to expand by opening Neepsend Coachworks (*q.v.*) in the Sheffield district of the same

There were coach bodies from the Sheffield firm as well, this 1930 example being a 'sun saloon parlour coach' on an AEC Regal chassis.

Double-deck buses and trolleybuses formed a large 1937 order for Portsmouth Corporation.

ABOVE: **A 1929 dual-entrance 32-seat single-decker by Cravens on AEC chassis for Stockport Corporation.**

RIGHT: **When favoured builders Park Royal and Weymann could not cope with the volume of new RT bodies for London Transport, Cravens was called in to help out. The company's design had five bays instead of four and these non-standard bodies were withdrawn early. This one was pictured in 1957 with Cream Bus Service of Stamford.**

name. The Neepsend business did not last, and Cravens were sold on to the Sheffield steel makers John Brown. Bus-body manufacture ceased, being concentrated in the hands of East Lancs.

CRAWFORD PRINCE-JOHNSON

Crawford Prince-Johnson Ltd was a Leicester company that also traded under the name of Quorn Coachworks (*q.v.*). The company's main work was with pantechnicon and mobile shop vehicles, but in the late 1940s and early 1950s it also built some single-deck bus and coach bodies. Among these were examples on Leyland Comet and normal-control Ford Thames chassis and a full-front coach on a Vulcan chassis. The Crawford Prince-Johnson bodies resemble Burlingham products and are often confused with them. With the surge in demand for PSV bodies over, the company returned to commercial bodywork. Its premises were at Melton Road in Syston.

CRELLIN DUPLEX

Crellin Duplex was not a coachbuilder, but a design that was manufactured between 1948 and 1952 under licence from its inventor, George Crellin. The first licence holder was the Lincolnshire Trailer Company (*q.v.*) and the second was Mann Egerton (*q.v.*). Only twenty are

thought to have been sold, as the design's advantage of fitting a large number of seats into the permitted PSV dimensions of the late 1940s were largely nullified when 30ft (9m) single-deck chassis became available.

The Crellin Duplex design is sometimes described as a half-deck coach, but that description is misleading. In practice, it had two layers of seats arranged in staggered 'compartments' of four, those on the lower deck facing in the opposite direction to those on the upper deck. The feet of those in the upper seats impinged on the lower-deck space, so that the overall height of the vehicle was only 12ft 6in (3.8m) – a foot shorter than a conventional lowbridge double-decker. The seating capacity was fifty, in the same footprint as that of a conventional coach that could carry fewer than forty passengers.

The Duplex was not George Crellin's first radical design on PSV chassis. In 1927 he had designed the Crellin Highway Motor Yacht – a sort of luxury caravan built as a prototype by Short Bros (*q.v.*) on a six-wheel Guy chassis.

CRERAR

Round about 1919, Peter Crerar set up a charabanc and bus-body business at Leadenflower Coachworks, Leadenflower Road, Crieff, in Perthshire. Crerar built a number of bodies for his own fleet and for many local operators in Perthshire and Fife, some on the Lancia chassis and Gilford chassis for which he became a local agent. He sold his coach-building business and works to two former employees in 1930, who re-established it as Forbes, Brebner & Co. (*q.v.*).

CRESBANK

Cresbank Coachworks at Garnet Road in Leeds was active in the PSV business between 1942 and 1949, mainly rebuilding worn-out bodywork.

CRESCENT

See Walton.

CROALL

John Croall & Sons Ltd was an Edinburgh firm that built horse trams in the 1870s. Before that, it had been a carriage-building works in Stirling, founded by William Croall. It resurfaced in the PSV field in 1927, claiming then to be 'Scotland's oldest body manufacturers'. It built bus bodies on a variety of chassis between then and 1929, operating from the Middlefield Motor Bodyworks, at Middlefield Street in Edinburgh's Leith Walk.

The Croall family was also Directors of the coach builder H.J. Mulliner & Co. Ltd, with a controlling interest in that company by 1936.

CROFT

The Croft Bodybuilding and Engineering Co. Ltd of Glasgow was established around 1940 as a motor body-builder and painter. It had premises at Croft Street, 1,009 Gallowgate, Glasgow E1. In 1943 it was designated to rebody earlier chassis with wartime utility-standard double-deck bodies and to carry out major body repairs as required.

After the war, Croft exploited the boom in demand by building more double-deck bodies, this time on Metal Sections frames, notably on Albion chassis for Glasgow and on Daimler chassis for Dundee. It built single-deck bodies using a design by Albion Motors originally drawn up for W. Alexander & Sons Ltd.

However, its PSV bodywork activities ceased in 1951; Croft remained in the commercial body field, later becoming a Ford dealer. After subsequent changes of ownership, it stopped trading in the early 1980s.

CROSBIE & COWLEY

This was an Isle of Man bodybuilder with premises in St George Street, Douglas. It built coach bodywork in the 1930s.

CROSS

J.A. Cross is recorded as the builder of some twenty-seat bodies on Dennis chassis for Lancaster Corporation in 1928 and 1929. Nothing more is known about the company.

CROSS & ELLIS

A 1930 26-seat coach from the Coventry builder, on a long-wheelbase Reo chassis.

Cross & Ellis Ltd of Coventry was established by two former Daimler employees in 1919. Better known now as a builder of car bodies, the company built some chara-banc bodies at an early stage in its existence and was still building small single-deck PSV bodies by 1930, when 18- to 19-seat types for Bean and 20- and 26-seat types for Reo chassis were on offer. The company went into liquidation in 1938.

CROSSLEY

The bodybuilding arm of Crossley Motors was active from 1926 to 1958, constructing single-deck buses and both single-deck and double-deck coaches. Many of its customers were in the north of England, around Crossley's Lancashire home, but Crossley bodies were being sold nationally by the 1940s.

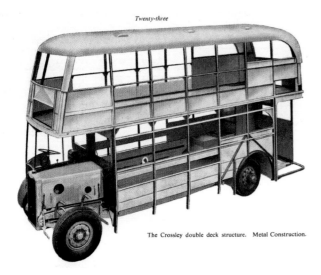

Twenty-three

The Crossley double deck structure. Metal Construction.

Characteristic of the late 1940s Crossley bodies was a stepped waistline at the rear, which disguised body reinforcement. Both the 'skeleton' body frame and the 1948 Barrow bus are on Crossley's own DD42 chassis.

Crossley Motors was founded in Manchester in 1906 as a division of the Crossley Brothers engine company. It moved to nearby Gorton in 1907, becoming a standalone company in 1910. In 1914 it bought another new site at Errwood Park in Stockport, soon after becoming a major supplier of lorry chassis to the army during the Great War. The company entered the bus market in 1928, offering chassis for others to body, but also providing its own bodywork to maximize profits. These bodies were built for both municipal and private operators.

The 1930s brought timber-framed double-deck bodies for Manchester on the Mancunian chassis, but the corporation was impressed by a metal-framed body built by Metro-Cammell in 1932. To keep the Manchester contract, Crossley agreed to finish Metro-Cammell metal-framed bodies at Gorton and to use the same frames for rebodying other makers' chassis. It announced its all-metal double-deck bodies in June 1933. A redesigned Mancunian with more modern, curvaceous bodywork and a much-improved interior arrived in 1935 and became known as the 'Streamliner'.

The link with Manchester was critical and the postwar double-deck body was designed to meet Manchester requirements. Available from 1945 for other makers'

The swept-down window lines and 'streamlined' flashes of this all-Crossley trolleybus from 1938 could only belong to a Manchester vehicle. The chassis was a TDD4 type and the body configuration was H28/26R.

This 1950 all-Crossley double-decker for Birmingham was to the customer's own design and even the identity of the chassis is concealed by the 'tin front' bonnet and radiator grille.

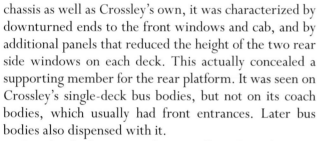

Later bodies had a straight waist, such as this 1951 all-Crossley example for Stockport with a forward entrance.

The stepped waist was evident on single-deckers, too, like this 1947 example for Lancaster on a Crossley SD42 chassis.

chassis as well as Crossley's own, it was characterized by downturned ends to the front windows and cab, and by additional panels that reduced the height of the two rear side windows on each deck. This actually concealed a supporting member for the rear platform. It was seen on Crossley's single-deck bus bodies, but not on its coach bodies, which usually had front entrances. Later bus bodies also dispensed with it.

Crossley bodies were always well made and consequently expensive. The body division played a major role in the company's business from 1945. However, the parent company sold out to AEC in 1948 to become part of the ACV sales organization. Crossley did the body design for the AEC Bridgemaster in the mid-1950s, but by this time its body division had become little more than a satellite of Park Royal, which also belonged to the ACV group. Risk of duplication with Park Royal led to the closure of the Crossley bodyworks in 1958. Crossley had built a total of 1,122 bodies for several different makes of chassis between 1945 and 1958.

CUMBERLAND COACHWORK

See Myers & Bowman Ltd.

CURTIS

The Curtis Automobile Co. Ltd had premises at Curtis Buildings, Abbey Road, London NW10 and offered bus bodywork in the 1920s and early 1930s. It may have merged with Duramin (*q.v.*) in 1929 to become Curtis Duramin Industries Ltd, which was voluntarily wound up in 1936.

CUTTEN

A company by this name built bus bodywork in the early 1920s, probably in Brighton.

DAGGART

The Daggart name comes up as the builder of bus bodywork on a Dodge PLB chassis for Knowles of Congleton in 1938, but nothing is known for certain about the company. It may well have been based in Cheshire.

DALES

F.D. & D.W. Dales Ltd (also shown as T.D. & W. Dales) were based at Ropery Street in Kingston-upon-Hull, where Barnaby (*q.v.*) also had premises. The company built some fourteen-seater bodywork in the 1920s or 1930s.

DARLAND-MASON

C.H. Darland-Mason was a Gilford dealer in Newcastle-upon-Tyne and in the late 1920s appears also to have constructed some bus bodywork for the chassis it sold.

DAVIDSON

Davidson (Trafford Park) Ltd was a Manchester PSV bodybuilder active between about 1920 and 1941, which described itself in the 1920s as 'the largest body-builders in the North'. The company built charabanc bodies in the beginning, including some for Midland Red, and later built both single-deck and double-deck bodies for several municipal operators, including Manchester, Salford and Portsmouth. It also built for independent operators, such as Fleming Bros of Redcar and Yelloway of Rochdale.

The company was later bought out by Eastwood & Kenning (*q.v.*).

DAVIES (1)

D.J. Davies Ltd was established in 1946 with premises on the Treforest Trading Estate at Pontypridd in Glamorgan. It built both coach and double-decker bodies, concentrating on local operators. Examples were Pioneer of Langharne, which took a Dennis Lance double-decker in 1949, while a Cardiff operator took a half-canopy body on a Dennis Lancet J3 chassis in 1950.

D.J. Davies also secured orders from St Helens Corporation for Leyland PD2s in 1954–6, but ceased activity in 1957.

DAVIES (2)

A second company called Davies was building bodywork for Welsh operators as early as 1932, when it constructed twenty-seat bus bodywork on a Bedford WLB chassis.

DAVIES (3)

The company of T. Davies was in business from around 1900 at La Charroterie in St Peter Port, Guernsey. It was building PSV bodywork as late as 1921.

The Largest Body-builders in the North

DAVIDSON (TRAFFORD PARK) LTD MANCHESTER
'Phones: 1098 - 1099 Trafford Park
'Grams: Autobodi, Manchester

A 1928 bus body on six-wheel Karrier chassis.

DBS

DBS Coachworks Ltd was at the Uxbridge Industrial Estate, on Wallingford Road in Uxbridge, Middlesex. The company was mainly known for minibus and commercial bodywork, but in 1954 also had some involvement with coach bodies.

DELL

Dell Coachbuilders Ltd was at Empress Road in Southampton when it started in 1966 and included some coach bodywork among its output of mainly commercial bodies. During the 1980s, the company became Dell Technical Vehicles Ltd and moved to Brokenford Lane in nearby Totton.

DE LUXE

It was inevitable that somebody would think of using this name as their own, but it is not clear who was behind the bus bodywork built in 1927 that bore it. The name certainly suggests that coach bodies may have been on the agenda as well.

DE MONTFORD

De Montford Commercial Bodies was more associated with commercial types than PSV bodies, as its name suggests. However, it did build some coach bodywork, probably around 1930.

The chassis maker built its own twenty-seat body for this Dennis Ace, new in 1935 to Blue Saloon of Guildford.

DENNIS

Even though Dennis Bros (1913) Ltd was primarily makers of chassis, the company also built bodywork for many of its own chassis in the 1920s and 1930s. By 1932, it had a standardized 32-seater ash-framed design for the Lancet single-deck type, which could also be fitted out as a 35-seater.

In 1938, Aldershot & District took a number of all-Dennis Lancets with 32-seater bodies. In the mid-1930s, there were also twenty-seater bodies available for the normal-control Ace chassis and bodies for the Arrow Minor and Falcon chassis as well.

DERBY

William Derby & Sons was a Belfast company with premises at 164 Antrim Road. It built some toastrack bodywork in 1930.

DEVON

Devon Coachbuilders Ltd built some coach bodywork in the early 1950s from premises at Potitor Garage, Potitor Lane, Torquay.

DEVONPORT

The Devonport name occurs as that of a coachbuilder that constructed bus bodies in the first half of the 1930s, but nothing more concrete is known.

DICK

G.W. Dick was at 5–9 High Street, Lochgelly, in Fife. The company was building motor vehicle bodies by about 1925 and is known to have made at least two bus bodies, on Karrier and Gilford chassis in 1925 and 1927. The original company closed in the late 1970s.

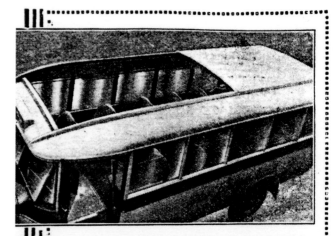

AT the moment we have a 26-Seater Body in stock ready for mounting, fitted with our patent sliding roof, which we venture to say at the moment is the only Roof *Rattle-proof and Rain-proof*. And can be *Opened and Closed in One Minute*. And Locks in any position.

Write for details of Price, etc.,

WILLIAM DICKENS,
COACH AND MOTOR BODY BUILDER,
PINFOLD GATE, LOUGHBOROUGH.
Telephone: Loughborough 135.

This 1930s advertisement shows the preoccupations of the time. Would the sliding roof rattle? Would it leak? And how quick was it to operate?

DICKENS

William Dickens described himself as a coach and motor bodybuilder, operating from Pinfold Gate in Loughborough, Leicestershire. Most of his PSV work seems to have been done during the 1920s, but by 1930 he was still advertising 26-seater bodywork for normal-control chassis.

DICK KERR

Dick, Kerr & Co. was mainly known for its railway and tramcar business in the late nineteeth century and the first decade of the twentieth century, when it had premises in Kilmarnock and Preston. The company was bought out by English Electric (*q.v.*) in 1919, but its name was used for some open-top double-deck bodywork on trolleybuses in the early 1920s.

DICKSON

Dickson Body Works Ltd started out as coach hirers, motor agents and engineers in Dundee during 1919. Initially at Clepington Road, the company was active from 1928 until 1940, by which date it had moved to 360 Strathmore Avenue. From 1928, it advertised as being a bus builder, car repairer and cellulose sprayer. It sold its bus bodies only to local operators; there were also four coach bodies in 1930. The bigger users were Alexander of Falkirk and Dundee Corporation.

Dickson's built mainly single-deck bodies, but there was a batch of double-deckers on Daimler COG6 chassis for Dundee in 1939–40. The Dickson Bodyworks was designated as a provider of essential bus-body repairs in 1943, but did not re-enter the PSV market after the war ended in 1945.

DISTURNAL

Richard Disturnal & Co. was established in the ironwork trade in 1830, with premises at Bridge Works, Wednesbury, Staffordshire. By January 1930, Disturnal was supplying the 'Twinslide' opening coach roof to body makers, although there is no evidence that the company was making complete bodies itself.

In the 1950s, John Brockhouse was an apprentice at Disturnal, before founding one of the largest engineering companies in the Black Country. He later returned the compliment by adding the Disturnal company to his empire.

DIXIE

W. Shepherd was the proprietor of the Dixie Garage at Market Bosworth in Leicestershire. In the early 1920s, he patented a bus body that could be converted for various

Bus Builders, Car Repairers and Cellulose Sprayers.

DICKSON BODY WORKS, LTD.,
166 Strathmartine Road and
360 Strathmore Avenue,
'Phone 85472.   DUNDEE.   'Phone 85472.

The Dundee bodybuilder constructed the centre-entrance body on this Daimler chassis for its local municipality in 1938.

other uses, including as a hearse and a livestock carrier. However, the Dixie name seems to have been applied more widely to describe multi-purpose bodies, irrespective of whether Dixie actually built them.

DIXON

Alfred Dixon Ltd was a West Bromwich bodybuilder active in the late 1920s and early 1930s. The company was based at Roebuck Lane and its work included single-deck buses and coaches on Dennis and the smaller Leyland chassis. Most were for Potteries area operators. It also built some van bodies on the Leyland Tiger chassis in the 1930s.

The company was sold to W.J. Smith & Son (*q.v.*) in the early 1930s.

DODSON

Dodson was an important builder of double-deck bus bodywork in the years around 1930 and was best known for catering to the requirements of the London independent operators.

Christopher Dodson founded his bodyworks at Willesden in London NW10. By 1907 he was building lorry bodies and by 1913 was building single-deck trolleybus bodies. Together with his brother, Frank, he founded Dodson Bros in 1921 as a bus operator on the Isle of Wight. Also known as Dodson & Campbell, this company later became the Vectis Bus Company and in

1929 Southern Vectis. Not surprisingly, its buses in this period all had Dodson bodies.

The Dodson concern developed the Charabus single-deck design in the early 1920s, with removable side windows to convert it from closed saloon to charabanc. By 1922, it was advertising double-deck bodies as well. It bodied a number of single-deck trolleybuses for Wolverhampton and built the bodywork on some prototype SMC (Sunbeam) motor bus chassis in 1928. Characteristic of Dodson double-deck designs was a three-window arrangement at the front upper deck, intended to allow the route boards to be changed from upstairs.

Dodson's location in north London made the company an obvious and popular choice to body double-deckers for the London independent or 'pirate' operators of the late 1920s and early 1930s. In 1930–1, the company also bodied a number of ST-class AEC Regents for Thomas Tilling in London to that operator's standard six-bay pattern with an outside staircase and balloon roof. A 1931 design extended the upper deck over the cab and added an enclosed staircase. However, when the London Passenger Transport Board was formed in 1933 and the London independents disappeared, so did Dodson's market and the company closed.

See also Metal Bodies.

DOMINION

The Dominion name is associated with some single-deck bus bodywork built in the second half of the 1920s. The company is thought to have been based in King's Lynn, Norfolk.

DORMOBILE

See Martin Walter.

DU CROS

W. & G. Du Cros had been a car sales operation and taxicab operator before 1914 and also manufactured its own chassis from premises at 177 The Vale, London W3. In 1920, the company sold out to STD Motors Ltd, which needed additional bodybuilding capacity next to its Talbot works. In the 1920s, Du Cros built lorry and charabanc chassis and in 1926 announced a new low-frame six-cylinder bus. Many of these bus chassis were

given bodywork by the Du Cros concern in the 1920s, including fifteen forward-entrance single-deckers for Bournemouth Corporation.

When STD Motors went into receivership in 1935, the Du Cros operation was closed down.

DUNCANSON'S

Duncanson's Ltd had started out as builders, but subsequently moved into motor body construction of all kinds. The company's address was Balmoral Works, at Scotstoun, in Glasgow. Only four PSV bodies are known, built between 1919 and 1924.

DUNNET

Alex (Sandy) Dunnet was a joiner in Wick, who also drove part-time for local operator James Begg. Dunnet constructed a single body on a Manchester chassis in 1928 for Begg.

DUPLE

In the seventy years of its existence, Duple became one of Britain's most prolific and most highly regarded builders of coach bodies. It tended to cater for customers in the southern parts of England before the 1960s, although its customer base spread wider in later years, especially following the acquisition of its major rival Burlingham in 1958.

Though best known as a builder of coaches, Duple also built service buses from the early days. This is a 1930 rear-entrance type on a Dennis Arrow chassis.

The company was founded by Herbert White in 1919 as Duple Bodies & Motors Ltd, with premises in the London borough of Hornsey. White had briefly built cars under the Bifort name at Fareham in Hampshire during 1914. The Bifort had been a car that could be transformed into a van and the Duple name was intended to suggest the same versatility. Duple's first activities were fitting bodies of this type to ex-military Ford Model Ts. As demand increased, the company moved to a new factory in Hendon, London NW9, during 1926. However, the critical year was 1928, when Duple decided to focus on the coach bodywork in which it had already dabbled and recruited Walter Ernest Brown, a former partner in Strachan & Brown (*q.v.*).

Now preserved, this 1933 Dennis Dart shows the styling flashes for which Duple would become famous.

There were double-deckers in the early days, too. This one was on a Dennis HV chassis for Shoeburyness Motor Services.

By 1930, Duple had already built coach bodies for major clients such as Royal Blue and the Great Western Railway. It was held in sufficient esteem to secure a large contract for the LGOC's new Green Line express coach fleet. The company also got in on the ground floor with Bedford and its selection as a recommended body supplier for the new WLB chassis in 1931 was the start of a close relationship with that chassis builder that would last for more than half a century. There was further expansion in 1932, with the acquisition of the London Lorries (*q.v.*) business and the Hendon site was further enlarged in 1934. The last car bodies (for Vauxhall) were built in 1935.

Duple coachwork was readily identifiable in the early 1930s and the company developed a good export business as well as selling to operators all over Britain. The typical Duple coach body had gently curving lines from front to rear, with stylish 'flashes' on the sides, often finished in contrasting colours. Sloping pillars were another feature, although Duple, like other builders of the time, would build almost any style to order, including direct copies of other coachbuilders' work.

The later 1930s saw some of Duple's standard coach designs being named. The Vista (with sloping pillars) was introduced in 1936 and the Hendonian (with vertical pillars) a year later. Both were designed for Bedford WTB chassis, with the Vista being updated to suit the new Bedford OB in 1939, so beginning Duple's long association with this chassis. There were substantial orders for single-deck bus bodies in this period, too.

During the war, the Hendon works was turned over to production of fuselages for the Halifax bomber, plus

Fairly typical of 1930s Duple designs is this 1935 coach on a six-cylinder Dennis Lancet chassis for Safeguard Coaches of Guildford.

This Duple coach was one of a fleet of twenty on Bristol JO6A chassis for Bristol Tramways in 1937.

other military work. But between 1942 and 1945 Duple became Britain's largest builder of 'utility' PSV bodies, constructing substantial numbers for the Bedford OWB single-deck chassis, along with both highbridge and lowbridge double-deckers.

From 1946, the company was renamed Duple Motor Bodies Ltd, restarting production with Vista bodies for the Bedford OB chassis. Coach bodies for heavyweight chassis entered production in May. The standard type deserved a more romantic name than it received – it was known simply as the A-type and was a most attractive style that drew heavily on pre-war designs. The B-type and C-type bodies had detail differences and there was a single-deck bus body called the D-type. For export customers, there was a metal-framed Almet body on the OB chassis, designed to be shipped in sections for local assembly. From 1948, the company also had a double-deck design, which found favour with Red & White and with SMT.

Although there were a few service bus bodies on the Bedford SB chassis, the 1950s saw Duple focus on

Red & White bought this Duple-bodied Albion double-decker in 1939.

coaches. The company made a determined start with its Vega coach body for the SB in 1950, a simple, lightweight front-engined chassis aimed at the independent coach operator. Initially built with Bedford's own front panel, then with an oval grille and finally with the much-liked 'butterfly grille', the Vega was a big success right through the decade. It gave way in 1959 to the Super Vega, an updated design with a wrap-around windscreen, half-spats for the rear wheels and another distinctive grille, which lasted in production until 1963. A version introduced for the new Ford Thames Trader lightweight chassis in 1959 and bearing a different grille was known as the Yeoman from 1961; on the Commer Avenger, meanwhile, the same design was called the Corinthian.

The side flashes of the 1930s remained on Duple bodies in the 1940s, even on this D-model, a service bus type on AEC Regal chassis.

There were even smaller designs from Duple, too – a scaled-down Vega was known as the Vista when fitted to Bedford C4 or C5 truck chassis. From 1959 this 29-seater was updated as a Super Vista and then from 1961 became a Bella Vista for the new small Bedford VAS chassis.

While success on the lightweight chassis ensured Duple's profitability in the 1950s, the company took some time to develop a successful design for underfloor-engined chassis. Its first attempts in 1950 hedged bets – the Ambassador embodied traditional Duple curves, while the disappointingly box-like Roadmaster had straight lines, small windows and bright metal side strips for decoration, all reflecting the influence of American designs. The Coronation Ambassador arrived in 1952, with a straighter waist rail than the original and straight side decoration.

The style began to settle down in 1953 as the Coronation Ambassador gave way to the curvaceous Elizabethan, distinguished by a reverse-rake pillar between cab and side windows. In 1955, the Elizabethan evolved into the

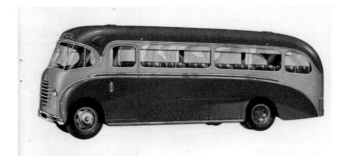

The Hendon coachbuilder was quick to design a body for the new lightweight Bedford SB and called it the Vega. This is a 1950 example, with the original Bedford-designed grille.

The Duple design for the Bedford OB chassis was a classic, combining the company's characteristic styling with well-proportioned lines on this small coach. This one dates from 1950.

The famous 'butterfly grille' is seen here on a 1956 Bedford SBG with a Duple Vega body for Henry Hulley & Sons of Baslow.

ABOVE: There was also a rather severe bus design for the SB chassis, though it was not common outside local authorities and the armed services.

RIGHT: The Britannia coach body of the 1950s for underfloor-engined chassis was another classic and is seen here on an AEC Reliance.

rather more gaudy Britannia. With regular facelifts, this lasted until 1963, although the last models retained few of the original 1950s curves. The Britannia was built with a centre or front entrance and, like the Vega, could be had with several different styles of side moulding.

Meanwhile, the company continued to expand. In 1952, it bought Nudd Brothers & Lockyer Ltd (*q.v.*), whose premises were used to develop and build metal-framed bodies at a time when Hendon was committed

The metal-framed Donington was often treated as a dual-purpose body, but always had more than enough of the Duple coach about it. This example was on a 1958 Tiger Cub chassis for Sunderland District.

The Super Vista body of 1959 was typically a 29-seater and had the famous butterfly grille.

Wrap-around screens and typical Duple side detailing characterize this Super Vega on a Bedford chassis.

BELLA VEGA/ TROOPER
41 passengers
Chassis: Bella Vega on Bedford; Trooper on Thames PSV

BELLA VISTA
29 passengers
Chassis: Bedford V.A.S.

CONTINENTAL
51 passengers
Chassis: A.E.C. or Leyland 11-metre underfloor engine

FIREFLY
41 passengers
Chassis: Bedford SB, Thames PSV or Albion Victor

MARINER 52 passengers
Chassis: Thames PSV 11-metre

VEGA MAJOR
52 passengers
Chassis: Bedford V.A.L.

The sheer variety of Duple bodies in the 1960s was confusing, but this 1964 catalogue page helps sort out what was what.

to composite types. Additional premises were bought in Loughborough in 1955 and a year later the Nudd Brothers and Loughborough factories were renamed Duple (Midland) Ltd. In 1958, the neighbouring Loughborough firm of Willowbrook (*q.v.*) was also acquired, although this company continued for some time to operate under its own name. Then 1960 saw the acquisition of Burlingham (*q.v.*), whose Blackpool premises became Duple Motor Bodies (Northern) Ltd in 1962. The Duple bodies built there are discussed under the heading for that company. From 1963, the former Yeates (*q.v.*) body shop at Loughborough was added to Duple's collection.

The curves largely disappeared from the Duple bodies of the 1960s, although they continued to favour the side decoration that made them unmistakably Hendon products. Straight waistlines, one-piece windscreens and deeper windows were the main characteristics. The Bella Vista on the new Bedford VAS chassis spearheaded the range for 1962; the Bella Vega a year later brought the same design to the SB chassis, while a version for the Ford Thames was called the Trooper. On the Bedford VAL three-axle chassis, the design became a Vega Major. All versions were characterized by an upright front and an angled pillar just ahead of the rear wheel arch. On 36ft (11m) underfloor-engined chassis for 1963, the style was known as a Commodore, although it lasted only a year before giving way to the Commander, which was always built at Blackpool.

From 1966, the Viceroy replaced most designs for lightweight chassis, but for the new 36ft Ford R226 there was the Mariner (originally introduced in 1964 as the Marauder). On 30ft (9m) chassis, the same design was an Empress on Ford R192, but a Bella Venture on Bedford VAM. The raked pillar over the rear wheel that had characterized many 1960s Duple designs disappeared in 1967 and for 1968 the Viceroy was restyled by Olsen Design as the Viceroy 36 for Bedford YRQ chassis; a variant of this then replaced the Commander on heavyweight chassis for 1970 as well.

However, even a major player like Duple was beginning to feel the pinch by the late 1960s. In 1968, the company closed its Hendon premises and relocated to Blackpool and the home of its Duple (Northern) subsidiary. The Willowbrook business was also sold off and in 1970 the White family, descendants of Duple's founder, sold the Duple company to Frank Ford. Ford had been a senior figure at Duple's arch-rival, Plaxton. The subsequent Duple story is explained under the entry for Duple (Northern).

New in the mid-1960s was the Viceroy, seen here on a Bedford chassis.

The Viscount of the mid-1960s also bought into the vogue for big windows. Again, the chassis is a Bedford.

The Vega design moved on again in the mid-1960s; this is a Super Vega from 1969 on a Bedford chassis.

The Viceroy 36 was for the 36ft Bedford VAL chassis, like this 1969 example.

DUPLE METSEC

See Metal Sections.

DUPLE (MIDLAND)

Duple Motor Bodies (Midland) Ltd was formed in 1952 when Duple took over Nudd Bros and Lockyer (*q.v.*) and its factory at Kegworth in Leicestershire. Among early commissions was a batch of former London Transport utility Guy double-deckers, built on reconditioned chassis for Edinburgh in 1953.

Duple (Midland) developed the Nudd Bros expertise with metal-framed bodies and from 1956 introduced the Donington coach body, named after the airfield where it was built. This was characterized by relatively small windows at a time when large windows were just becoming popular for coaches. Just over 100 were built before it was withdrawn in 1962; many were used as dual-purpose vehicles.

Duple (Midland) also built bus bodywork, including that for the Bedford SB chassis. This became a long-lived design, which, although slightly modified over the years, remained in production until 1976, latterly by Willowbrook (*q.v.*).

DUPLE (NORTHERN)

Duple Motor Bodies (Northern) Ltd was established in 1960 when Duple bought out the Burlingham (*q.v.*) company of Blackpool. It was active under that name until 1970, building a number of the Duple designs.

The Commander body featured the big windows typical of 1960s designs. This 1965 example was on AEC Reliance chassis for the Highland operator David Macbraynes Ltd.

The first all-new Duple (Northern) coach body was the metal-framed Continental, drawn up by the old Burlingham team as a high-floor 51-seater for fitting to 36ft (11m) chassis. This arrived in 1962 with conventional opening windows; a modified Alpine Continental with larger, fixed windows and forced-air ventilation was introduced a year later. However, some bodies with forced-air ventilation as well were later badged as simple Continental types.

The design introduced as a Burlingham Seagull 60 in 1959 for front-engined lightweight chassis gained a new grille and became a Seagull 61 before being replaced by a redesigned body called the Gannet. This dispensed with the raised centre roof section of the original, which had tended to leak. However, the Gannet lasted only until 1963, when it gave way to the Firefly, which, in turn, lasted until 1965. There was a 36ft version of the Firefly for underfloor-engined chassis, too, called the Dragonfly; its anachronistic centre entrance may explain why the design only found six buyers.

Blackpool took on construction of the Commander from 1964 and both this and the Viscount (intended for Bedford VAM and Ford R192 30ft/9m chassis) had more steel in their construction than the Hendon-built designs. Then, from 1968, Duple moved entirely into the Blackpool plant and the old Duple (Northern) name was subsequently dropped.

The all-metal, jig-built Dominant coach body replaced the Viceroy in 1972 and was broadly similar to the Plaxton Panorama Elite for which it was a deliberate competitor. There were versions for both lightweight and heavyweight chassis, and the Dominant became one of the most popular coach bodies of the 1970s, but the next decade saw Duple running into problems. First, the collapse of the lightweight coach market in 1981 halved its mid-1970s output, then increasing competition from continental European coachbuilders gradually ate into its heavyweight market.

Sales continued to slide, but Duple was saved from collapse in June 1983 when it was bought by the Hestair Group and renamed Hestair Duple. This ownership lasted until 1988, when Hestair sold Duple and the Dennis chassis business in a management buyout to a group calling itself Trinity Holdings. The new ownership and new name of Duple International lasted only a few months, before the business was closed in July 1989. Some Duple body designs were sold to the Carlyle Group and the jigs for others went to arch-rival Plaxton (*q.v.*), who also bought the spares and repair business that operated as Duple Services Ltd.

DURAMIN

The Duramin Engineering Co. Ltd was based at Hythe Road in London NW10 and built bus bodywork. It is thought to have become Curtis Duramin in 1929 after merging with Curtis (*q.v.*), another local firm.

DUTFIELD

Dutfield Motors Ltd was established in September 1947 at Portsmouth Road, Godalming; by July 1948 it was building one of its standard coach bodies a week and had also attracted export orders. These bodies were clearly inspired by Duple designs. Many Dutfield bodies in the late 1940s were on Tilling-Stevens chassis and the two companies had a joint sales organization.

The home market Dutfield body seems to have been known as the Hogger and was of composite construction with aluminium and steel panels on oak and ash frames. However, Hogger was also the name of a company with which Dutfield had links – from about 1949, Associated Deliveries, Dutfield, Hogger, Longford and Theale (*q.q.v.*) all seem to have worked together as a loose consortium of smaller coachbuilders.

Dutfield lasted only until 1950 in its original form, merging with Longford Coachworks of Neath and becoming Dutfield Longford Coachworks Ltd. Its registered premises were then in Reading, although the Godalming and Neath works both seem to have remained open. The company built a 32-seater coach for House of Watlington on Commer Avenger chassis in 1950, but probably closed down shortly afterwards.

EASTBOURNE AVIATION

The Eastbourne Aviation Company was founded in 1909 and had an airfield near the Crumbles, between Eastbourne and Pevensey Bay. It constructed Avro fighter aircraft during the 1914–18 war, but Eastbourne airfield closed in 1924. It is likely that the 32-seat Eastbourne Aviation bus bodies on AEC 401 chassis for Merthyr Tydfil Corporation constructed in 1924 were a final fling for the company.

EASTERN COACH WORKS

See ECW.

EASTERN COUNTIES

See ECW.

EAST LANCASHIRE COACH BUILDERS

Confusingly, there were two East Lancashire companies, this one being based at Bridlington (actually in east Yorkshire) and splitting the 'coachbuilders' part of its name into two – East Lancashire Coach Builders. This lesser of the two companies was based at Bessingby Way in Bridlington and was active only from around 1949 to 1952. It was formed out of the Yorkshire Equipment Company (also known as the West Yorkshire Equipment Co (*q.q.v.*)) and seems to have built double-deck and single-deck bodies for both trolleybuses and motor buses.

EAST LANCS

East Lancashire Coachbuilders Ltd was established in 1934 at Brookhouse Mills, Whalley New Road in Blackburn, Lancashire. The company's first bus bodies were on Leyland TD5 chassis for Bolton Corporation in 1938. During the war, East Lancs was designated as a supplier of new bus bodywork, but in practice had ample stocks of parts and kept going on these throughout the hostilites, never actually having to build a utility-pattern body. The company also rebodied a number of war-damaged buses in this period.

After the war, East Lancs forged links with Air Despatch (later Bruce (*q.q.v.*)) to gain wider distribution of its products and these companies built bodies to East Lancs designs. Meanwhile, East Lancs itself refurbished a number of bodies for St Helens Corporation in 1947–50.

LEFT: **Quite late for a front-engined single-decker, this 1953 Leyland Tiger PS2/14 had East Lancs B39F bodywork for the Burnley Colne and Nelson Joint Transport company.**

This 1965 Leyland PD2A/30 for St Helens Corporation carried an East Lancs H36/28R body.

Eastbourne was an East Lancs stronghold and in 1963 the corporation took delivery of this imposing AEC Regent V.

In 1964, the company purchased Cravens of Sheffield (*q.v.*), and established Neepsend (*q.v.*) as a subsidiary in Sheffield. Neepsend bodies carried East Lancs body numbers. In the 1960s, East Lancs became firmly established in the market, its key attraction being a willingness to build bespoke bodies for municipal operators rather than rely on a standardized design. Even so, the double-deck bodies built on Bristol VRT, Daimler Fleetline, Dennis Dominator and Leyland Atlantean chassis during the 1970s and early 1980s did share the same general proportions, window spacing and lipped GRP roof domes.

East Lancs continued with its policy of building to customers' individual requirements and from 1994 it expanded into new premises and developed a new range of single- and double-deck buses. Its modern designs depend on the Alusuisse system of construction, with bolted aluminium frames and composite floors and roofs. The company went into administration in 2007, but was immediately bought out by the Darwen Group, being rebranded as Darwen East Lancs. A year later, a subsidiary of the Darwen Group bought out bus maker Optare and East Lancs became part of that company.

EASTWOOD & KENNING

Eastwood & Kenning Ltd were builders of single- and double-deck bus bodywork in 1930–1, when the company was based at the Trafford Park Estate in Manchester. It took over Davidson (*q.v.*) and was associated with Reeve & Kenning (*q.v.*).

EATON (1)

Eaton Coachworks was the trading name of Herbert E. Taylor Co. Ltd, a Norfolk coachbuilder established in 1890. Eaton was active in the PSV market by the mid-1920s and in first half of the 1930s; it had works at Cringleford, but its head office was at 7 Queen Street in Norwich.

Eaton Coachworks, Cringleford, Norwich.

20-seater Allweather Coach on 6-cylinder "Chevrolet" Chassis.

This extended-chassis Chevrolet LQ was new in 1929 with Eaton twenty-seat bodywork. The owner was Guyton & Co. of Great Yarmouth.

Crossley 6-cylinder all-weather Coach as illustrated ready for immediate delivery, also W. & G. all-weather Coach and Reo, B.A.T. and Sunbeam Omnibuses in stock waiting colour instructions. Further particulars apply to—

HERBERT E. TAYLOR & CO., LTD.,
EATON COACHWORKS,
CRINGLEFORD, NORWICH.
'PHONE: EATON 52 (2 lines).
'GRAMS - "COACHWORK, EATON, NORFOLK."

Dating from 1930, this Eaton all-weather body was on a Crossley chassis for Norfolk Motor Services.

This front-entrance body from 1933 was another 32-seater, this time on a Bristol chassis.

The company seems to have built bodies mainly for local operators; some were on small chassis such as Reo and Thornycroft Cygnet types, but there were also many on Gilfords and a 1930 ADC 416D for Eastern Motorways of Norwich is also known.

This 'all-weather sunsaloon coach' was built on a Gilford chassis.

Also on a Crossley chassis, but dating from 1933, this was a B32R body from Eaton.

EATON (2)

Both bus and charabanc bodies were available from William Eaton of Manchester in the mid-1920s. The company had premises at Bank Street in the Clayton district.

ECOC

See ECW.

ECONOMY

See EMCOL.

ECW

Eastern Coach Works Ltd grew out of the bodyshops of United Automobile Services in Lowestoft, which had been set up in 1920. When the Tilling group bought United in 1931, it separated the East Anglian operations

In the early 1930s, Eastern Counties coachwork was finding customers all over the country. The buses here were delivered to Eastern Counties themselves, East Yorkshire, Hants & Dorset, North Western, United and West Yorkshire.

A six-bay layout was used for the H56R bodies on Leyland Titan chassis for Middlesborough Corporation in 1937.

A quite different five-bay design was used to rebody this Eastern Counties Leyland TD1 in 1938. The chassis dated from 1930 and was also re-engined, with a Gardner diesel.

from the rest of the company and created the Eastern Counties Omnibus Company to run them. With them went the bodyshops; increasing demand for what were simply known as ECOC bodies led to the establishment of a separate bodybuilding company in July 1936. This was Eastern Coach Works, or ECW as it was almost universally known. The company became very successful and was at one time the largest full-time employer in Lowestoft, with around 1,200 staff at its peak.

Lowestoft was considered in danger of enemy action during the 1939–45 war, so ECW moved its bodyworks to Irthlingborough. Here, it continued to build bodies to meet Government orders, but never had to build utility designs because it had sufficient stocks of parts in store. The company was also designated to rebody earlier chassis with utility-standard bodies.

ECW returned to Lowestoft when the war ended,

and by 1947 production was back at its pre-war levels. However, this was the year when the Tilling group was nationalized as the BTC, and with it went ECW. From then until 1965, ECW built bodies only for BTC operators (although there were also some for the Sheffield Corporation fleet run jointly with British Railways) and almost always with chassis or running gear from the nationalized Bristol concern. For each new Bristol chassis, ECW produced a standardized body design, which always managed to be elegant as well as functional; ECW bodies were devoid of the gratuitous styling touches that came to characterize many designs of the 1950s and 1960s, but they were invariably distinctive.

The designs for the underfloor-engined LS and MW were unspectacular, but pleasantly solid looking, and the big-windowed derivative of the MW 30ft (9m) express coach style built as a motorway coach for 36ft (11m)

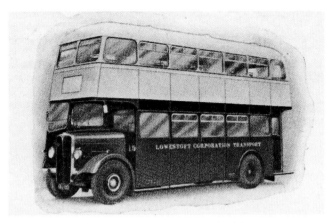

Ten years on, a five-bay layout was normal. This was an AEC Regent for Lowestoft Corporation, with aluminium panelling on wood frames.

Front engines and full-fronts were in vogue for a time. The ECW C31F body on this Eastern National Bristol L6B dates from 1950.

Although the chassis of this Eastern Counties Bristol JO5G dates from 1937, it is carrying a new body built by ECW in 1952.

Despite the later conversion to open-top for sea-front services, the body on this Eastern National 1953 Bristol KSW5G is typical of the four-bay types coming from ECW.

The Bristol Lodekka was a hugely important low-height design and of course always carried ECW bodywork. This is a 1966 FL type that was new to United Counties.

Even ECW had succumbed to the fashion for large side windows by 1969, when this Bristol RELH6G was built for Eastern Counties.

rear-engined RE chassis from 1962 was a masterpiece of understatement. The 1972 coach style that replaced it, still on RE chassis, boasted deeper windows and a double curvature windscreen. Standardization did not preclude innovation, either – in the 1950s, ECW worked with Bristol on such vehicles as the SC integral-construction single-decker and the Lodekka low-height double-decker.

From 1965, Leyland Motors owned a 25 per cent share of ECW, so the company once again began to build for the private sector, although as before its products were mostly on Bristol chassis, themselves also newly available outside the state-owned companies. Four years later, the Bristol and ECW association was further cemented when British Leyland (as Leyland had become) took that part of its business forward alongside the new venture that united it with the National Bus Company (successor to the BTC via the Transport Holding Company) and resulted in the Leyland National (*q.v.*). However, this all changed in 1982, when British Leyland assumed full control and ECW closed down in January 1987. Its factory was demolished and the site is now occupied by the North Quay Retail Park.

Edmonds of Thetford is a bodybuilder about whom almost nothing is known. This advertisement dates from 1924.

with which Jack Crabtree was involved. It was linked to Elite Coaches of Rochdale in this period. Jack Crabtree was later associated with Lewis & Crabtree, Shearing & Crabtree, Shearings of Oldham, Oldham Construction and Challenger (*q.q.v.*).

EDMONDS (1)

Active between 1923 and 1938, W.G. Edmonds & Co. Ltd built both single-deck and double-deck bus bodywork. The company was established in 1919 and had premises at Oliver Street, Linthorpe, in Middlesborough.

EDMONDS (2)

This Edmonds was a body maker at Thetford in Norfolk in the mid-1920s, but no further details have come to light.

ELDER

The name of Elder is associated with single-deck bus bodywork in the late 1920s, but no further details are known.

ELITE

Elite Bodies operated from Heywood between 1921 and 1924, and seems to have been the first of the companies

ELKINGTON

The Elkington Carriage Co. Ltd was first registered in 1922 and operated from the Great West Coach & Motor Works in London W4. The company also built horse boxes, but constructed single-deck bus bodies between 1929 and 1931.

ELLISON & SMITH LTD

This Manchester company was active in the 1920s as a builder of bus, coach and charabanc bodies. Its premises were at Magnet Works, Church Road, Gatley.

EMCOL

EMCOL was the trading name of the Economy Manufacturing Company, which was located in Ipswich from about 1924, but by 1929 had moved to London Road South in Lowestoft. The company built mainly for local operators, but appears also to have built a twenty-seat forward-entrance bus on a Reo Gold Crown chassis for a Scottish operator in 1931. Its bodies were all for small

This advertisement for a bus body on full-size single-deck chassis dates from 1929.

Mounted on the long Leyland Lion chassis, this English Electric 32-seater was delivered to Blackpool Corporation in 1929.

normal-control chassis. EMCOL seems to have closed down by 1933.

EMERALD

Emerald appears to have been an Isle of Man company that built single-deck bus bodywork towards the end of the 1920s. Isle of Man Road Services had several Emerald-bodied Thornycrofts.

ENGLISH

F. English Ltd was involved with bus and coach bodywork in 1946, from premises at 48 Poole Road, Branksome, Poole, in Dorset.

ENGLISH ELECTRIC

English Electric was active as a bus bodybuilder in the period 1932–40, although before that it had been the largest builder of tramcar bodies in Britain.

English Electric had been founded to build electric motors and in 1919 acquired the Preston tram builder Dick Kerr and Co. Two years earlier, this company had bought the United Electric Car Company. Tramcar bodybuilding continued in Preston and the later bus and trolleybus bodies were also built there.

The key English Electric double-deck body in the early days had a standardized six-bay design with wooden

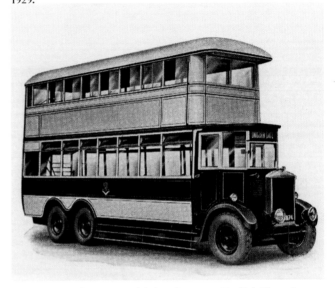

Again dating from 1929, this is a sixty-seat English Electric body on Karrier WL/62 chassis for Portsmouth Corporation.

This 1939 AEC Regent represents the final English Electric double-deck design.

frames and a vee-shaped 'piano front'. This was built on several makes of chassis and supplied widely across the UK. From 1934, an alternative five-bay all-metal body was available. On trolleybuses this had a modern bow-front style, but for motor buses there was a flat piano-front until 1936, when these bodies also took on bow-fronts.

Some of the early English Electric all-metal bodies gave trouble and most of the first batch on Leyland TD3 chassis (for Burnley, Colne and Nelson) needed reframing of their lower decks by 1937–8. As a result, the body was redesigned in 1937, but the damage had been done and there were not many customers. Nevertheless, English Electric found business building bodies for Manchester to that corporation's standardized design and supplied large batches in 1939–40.

English Electric also built single-deck bus bodies in

These were English Electric double-deckers in 1937. Only the Bradford AEC Regent in the centre has the latest five-bay design and the overhanging roof is still a feature.

On all these 1934 bodies, the roof overhangs the top deck windows and the top deck overhangs the cab. All are six-bay designs.

the mid-1930s and had some success in the coach market with operators such as Ribble, its Standerwick subsidiary, and Samuel Ledgard of Leeds. The side windows on these coach bodies were typically paired, while the cab front had a pronounced snout. Many were half-canopy types.

In 1939, the company built a single chassis-less trolleybus for London, but this was not a success. English Electric did not resume bus-body production after the war.

EVANS

A company called Evans built twenty-seat bus bodywork on Renault JX1 chassis for Altrincham & District in 1924. It may have operated from the town of Macclesfield.

FAHY

Fahy was a bodybuilder in the Republic of Ireland that was active in the 1920s, building bodies on chassis such as Dodge.

FARNSWORTH

Farnsworth & Co. Ltd of Columbia Street, Huthwaite, Sutton-in-Ashfield, Nottinghamshire built single-deck bodywork for quite a number of local operators in the early 1930s. Farnsworth took over the operations of R. Johnson (Blue Bird) of Huthwaite, running the company briefly until it was sold on to the Trent Motor Traction Co. of Derbyshire.

FARR

In the early 1920s, an F. Farr of Brown Street in Salisbury, Wiltshire, constructed single-deck bus bodies.

FEDERATED INDUSTRIES

Federated Industries Ltd was based at Stell Road in Aberdeen and was active as a PSV bodybuilder and rebuilder between 1949 and 1951. However, its core business was as a commercial bodybuilder. The company built a small number of single-deck bus and coach bodies for Scottish operators and even a pair of lowbridge double-deckers on AEC Regent III chassis in 1950.

The company still survives, in the sheet metalwork business.

FIELDING & BOTTOMLEY

Fielding & Bottomley Ltd was a joiner and builder at South Parade in Halifax. During the 1920s and the first half of the 1930s, the company added PSV bodywork to its repertoire, constructing both buses and coaches, the majority probably for local operators. An example of its work was a 26-seat, dual-entrance coach on a Gilford chassis in 1930 for an operator in Heckmond-wyke, Yorkshire.

FLEMING

There were bus bodies from this company in the first half of the 1920s, built at premises in the Yorkshire town of Redcar. The company may have been Fleming Bros (Redcar) Ltd, or possibly Gerald Fleming Ltd of Trunk Road Garage in the town.

FLEMING & SIEVEWRIGHT

The company with this name that built single-deck bus bodywork in 1921 has not been identified. It may be associated with the Fleming & Son that bought out Forder (q.v.) in 1926.

FORBES, BREBNER

Forbes, Brebner & Co. (initially Forbes & Brebner) was a bodybuilder with premises at Leadenflower Coach-works, Leadenflower Road, in Crieff. It was active in the early 1930s. James Forbes and George Brebner were former employees of Peter Crerar (q.v.), taking over his bodybuilding business and premises in 1930.

The last known bodies were built in 1933; some 1932 bodies on reconditioned Albion chassis for W. Alexander & Sons of Falkirk may have been subcontracted from that company's own bodyworks.

FORDER

Forder & Co. built charabanc bodies between 1911 and 1926 from premises at Cleveland Road in Wolverhampton. The company was bought out by Fleming & Son in 1926 and there is some suggestion that this may have been the same company as Fleming & Sievewright (q.v.).

FOWLER

W. & H. Fowler was a commercial bodybuilder in Leyland that had built a few PSV bodies in the 1930s, including a coach for a local operator on the six-wheel Leyland Tiger TS7T in 1936. In 1962, the company was bought out by local operator J.W. Fishwick & Sons and from then on was run as the company's in-house body manufacturer. Fishwick's transferred the business to the Golden Hill Lane Garage on Tuer Street.

Notable Fowler bodies for Fishwick's included its only double-decker, a 1972 Atlantean, and three single-deck Fleetlines in 1973.

FOX

G. Fox was probably a small Lancaster-based business. In 1928 it constructed a B26F body on an ADC 424 chassis for Lancaster Corporation, probably on subcontract from Barton Townley (*q.v.*).

FRANCIS

The Francis company that built bus and coach body-work between 1920 and 1935 may have been J. Fran-cis & Sons Ltd of The News, Conway Road, in Colwyn Bay.

FRY

Fry Bros was a London coachbuilder in the early 1920s, building single-deck bus and both open-top and closed double-deck bodywork. It was at Lion Wharf, Norman Road, London SE10. It may have been associated with Fry's Motor Works Ltd, which was established in 1910 by Sydney Fry at Lee High Road in Lewisham, London SE13.

Fry bodywork included five 1920 single-deckers for West Hartlepool and double-deckers for Birming-ham and Manchester in 1922. All these were on AEC chassis.

GARNER

Garner Motors Ltd was founded by Henry Garner in Birmingham, but later operated from premises at North Acton Road in London NW10. The company was active between 1922 and 1926 building single-deck bodies and was probably acquired by Hawson's of Sunbury-on-Thames (*q.v.*) to become Hawson-Garner Ltd.

GARRETT

Richard Garrett & Sons Ltd was an old-established engineering business at Leiston in Suffolk that could trace its origins back to 1778. The company built trolleybuses for which it constructed its own body-work; among the best known were those for the Mexborough & Swinton concern. There were also some single-deck bus bodies. The company was active from 1925–31.

GASH

R.E. Gash was based at Stourton in Surrey and constructed one or more bus bodies in 1929.

GENERAL AIRCRAFT

The General Aircraft company built one or more open-top double-deck bodies in the 1920s.

GENERAL LIGHTING

The General Lighting Co. of Huddersfield in Yorkshire built some single-deck bus bodywork in the 1920s.

GENERAL SEATING

The General Seating Co. Ltd was involved with open-top double-deck bodywork in 1920. Some bodies seem to have been built to a design by Hickman (*q.v.*). The General Seating company's registered office was at 13 City Road, London EC1, but by 1921 it had moved to 162 Grosvenor Road in London SW1.

GEORGE & JOBLING

George & Jobling had headquarters in Newcastle upon Tyne and had started out as a bicycle manufacturer, later expanding into motor vehicles and bodywork as well. The company had multiple outlets in the north of England and became a major retailer of cars.

It was building charabancs by 1912 and bodied a number of vehicles for operators in the north-east. There was even some double-deck bodywork in 1931, but the company seems to have disappeared soon after that.

GLENDOWER

The Glendower name appeared on single-deck bus bodies between 1919 and 1923, an example being on Daimler Y chassis for the British Automobile Traction Co. of Macclesfield. However, further details of the company itself are lacking.

GLOBE

The Globe company, which may have hailed from West Yorkshire, built some single-deck bus bodywork in 1922.

GLOSTER

See Gloucester Railway Carriage & Wagon Co. Ltd.

GLOUCESTER RAILWAY CARRIAGE & WAGON CO. LTD

The Gloucester Railway Carriage & Wagon Co. Ltd (GRCW) was founded in 1860 as the Gloucester Wagon

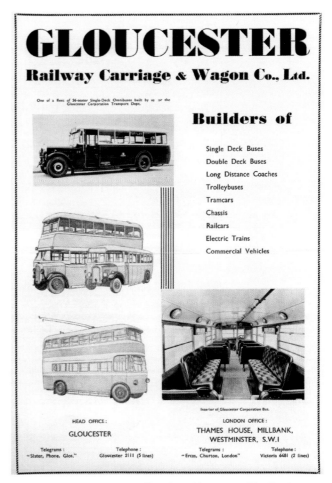

The Gloucester company offered a wide range of bodies in 1933, the top picture being a Thornycroft BC for Gloucester Corporation.

Co. Ltd. As its name suggests, its primary area of operation was the railway industry, but by the end of the 1920s

A pair of Gloucester double-deckers on Dennis Lance chassis for Walsall Corporation in 1934.

This was the sole Gloucester-built trolleybus, built in 1934, later operating as Southend Corporation no. 122.

it had also become involved in building trams and trolleybuses. The short-lived Gloucester Corporation was a major customer.

The company built and bodied its own trolleybus chassis in 1933, but there was only the one, which entered service with Southend Corporation in 1934. There were both single-deck and double-deck motor-bus bodies as well and Walsall Corporation took some of the latter with 'modern composite construction' in 1935. Later products carried the Gloster name.

GOODMAN

Goodman & Sons operated from the Sussex Coach & Motor Works at 70–74 Eastern Road, Brighton, in Sussex and was responsible for some single-deck bus bodywork in 1921.

GORDON

A Birmingham company with the name of Gordon Coachcraft Ltd built some coach bodies for Smith's Imperial Coaches Ltd in Birmingham between 1948 and 1950 at premises in Golden Hillock Road, opposite the old BSA factory. Gordon Coachcraft was in fact owned by the operator and the coaches were designed by his son, whose middle name was Gordon.

GRANT, CAMERON & CURLE

Between 1926 and 1931, this commercial bodybuilder constructed some bus bodies from premises at 83 Kennedy Street, in the Glasgow district of St Rollox. Most were on Thornycroft chassis. The company ceased trading in 1940 and its premises were turned over to the Scottish Commercial Motor Company (*q.v.*).

GRAY

A company with this name built five single-deck bus bodies for Aberdeen Corporation in 1930 on Thornycroft BC Forward Control chassis. The firm was probably William Gray & Company, of 139 Constitutional Street, whose main business was as timber merchants.

GRCW

See Gloucester Railway Carriage & Wagon Co. Ltd.

GREAT YARMOUTH COACHWORKS

Great Yarmouth Coachworks Ltd had premises at New River Road in Great Yarmouth and is thought to have built at least one coach body in 1949.

GREEN

A company by this name built some bus and coach bodies in 1949–50 at premises in Merthyr Tydfil, Wales.

GREENHOUS

The Greenhous company whose name appeared on some single-deck bus bodies in 1937–8 was probably Vincent Greenhous (Shrewsbury) Ltd, then of Greyfriars Motor Works, Shrewsbury, Shropshire. The company had begun as a bus operator, working between Bishop's Castle and Shrewsbury, but became a car dealership early on. It is doubtful whether the bodies that carried the Greenhous name were actually built by them; it is more likely that their construction was subcontracted to another company.

Vincent Greenhous remains a major car dealer chain in the Shropshire and Herefordshire areas.

GRIEVES

A company with this name built single-deck bus bodies in 1925–8, but no further information is available.

GROSE

Grose was a Northampton company that had started in the cycle industry during the nineteenth century. In 1900 it moved into new premises at Pike Lane and became Grose Ltd. The business gradually expanded into coachbuilding (among other things) and in 1914 established a subsidiary, the Northampton Motor Omnibus Co. Ltd, for which it built many bus bodies. This company was sold to United Counties in 1928.

In 1924 the company bought Crofts Carriage Works in Kingsthorpe Hollow, Northamptonshire, and began building high-class bodies for Rolls-Royce, Daimler and other top-of-the-range car chassis, as well as ambulance and both single-deck and double-deck PSV bodies.

During the 1930s Grose continued to build both bus and coach bodies for operators locally and as far away as Wales, while expanding to become a major car dealer in the area. Car dealerships gradually became its primary focus and there were no more bus bodies after World War II. Grose remains a major car dealer in the Northampton area today.

GURNEY NUTTING

J. Gurney Nutting & Co. Ltd was a long-established and highly regarded builder of luxury car bodywork that turned to coach bodies after World War II as an additional source of income. The company had been bought out by motor dealers Jack Barclay Ltd in 1945 and from 1947 was based at Ranalah Works, Lombard Road, Merton, London SW19.

The Merton works was turned over exclusively to PSV coach bodies in 1948, bodying Crossley, Daimler and Dennis chassis, many with full-front styles. Gurney Nutting also constructed some very distinctive bodywork on Sentinel platforms, some with rear spats, and during 1952 also bodied Foden underfloor-engined chassis. However, by the end of 1952 the major builders were dominating the market and Gurney Nutting was no longer competitive. About 125 coach bodies had been constructed when coachbuilding ceased at the end of 1953.

GUY

Guy Motors Ltd of Wolverhampton was, of course, a major manufacturer of bus, coach and trolleybus chassis for many years and between 1927 and 1955 it also built bodywork for some of its own chassis. So, for example, between 1923 and 1926 it constructed B20F bodies on BA and NN chassis for St Helens Corporation and from about 1930 was building both single-deck and double-deck bodies for its own trolleybus chassis.

Post-war work included many single-deck and double-deck bodies for municipalities from about 1948 and the company was versatile enough to build the bodies for a batch of underfloor-engined Arabs ordered by Huddersfield Corporation in 1951–3. In the early 1950s it also completed bodies on frames built by others, such as some on Park Royal frames for Lancaster City Transport.

New in 1950, this AEC Regal III has a Gurney Nutting C33F body. It was owned by Rochester & Marshall of Great Whttington. The body has generic Duple/ Harrington influences; the paired windows are interesting.

This open-staircase double-decker on a Leyland Titan chassis was built for Greenock Motor Services in the late 1920s.

Hall Lewis used its central London office address on this 1927 advertisement for single-deck bodywork.

Salford Corporation took a batch of these special Hall Lewis low-height fifty-seater bodies on Dennis H chassis in 1929. There were sunken gangways on either side of the top deck and angled seats facing forwards and outwards in two rows down the centre.

HALL LEWIS

Hall Lewis was the forerunner of Park Royal (*q.v.*) and was active in the bus-body business between 1924 and 1929.

The company was founded in Cardiff in 1889 as Hall, Lewis & Co. Ltd to manufacture, repair and lease railway vehicles. It subsequently opened several subsidiary operations around the country and during 1920 diversified into building bodies for prestige cars as well. In 1924, the company moved its headquarters to Abbey Road in Park Royal, London NW10, where it had been using the former munitions factory for railway wagon repair work. By the end of that year, it had begun building charabanc and small bus bodies, activities that went on to become a major element in its business over the next few years. Hall Lewis built bodies on ADC, AEC, Daimler, Guy, Karrier, Leyland and Maudslay motor-bus chassis, and possibly others.

There were also bodies for trolleybuses and in 1927 the company's first double-deck body was for a Karrier DDC trolleybus. At this stage, railway carriages were still being built at Park Royal and there was also some quality car bodybuilding. However, by the end of the decade the company was forced into liquidation, as a result of a decline in its railway business and increasing competition from other coachbuilders.

One of the principal creditors was Harry (Hymie) Yager, who formed Park Royal Coachworks out of the liquidated assets of Hall Lewis in April 1930.

HALLOWELL

George Hallowell operated from Wellway Coach Works in Morpeth, Northumberland, and constructed containers and horseboxes as well as bus bodies. The bus-bodying activity dated from around 1967.

HANBURY

A company called Hanbury & Co. was active building single-deck bus bodies in 1922. It was based at London Road, Thetford, in Norfolk.

HARDY

This Lancaster company may be included here under false

pretences, as its only known bodies date from 1918. J.A. Hardy was based at Halton Road in the city and in that year constructed the bodies on a pair of Edison battery-electric buses for the local corporation.

HARKNESS

Harkness Coachworks Ltd was the leading Belfast coach-builder and was active as a builder of bus bodies from 1925 until 1991. It was founded around 1886 in McTier Street, but by 1965 was at Northumberland Street. The company was also known variously as Harkness Coachworks (Belfast) Ltd, Harkness Coachworks Ltd and James Harkness & Son (Coachbuilders) Ltd.

The Belfast municipal fleet was largely bodied by Harkness, beginning in the 1920s and continuing for nearly half a century. The bodies were built to a very high standard. Harkness also assembled and panelled the bodies for the first batch of post-war GNR Gard-ners, using body frames supplied by Metal Sections in Birmingham. These were built between 1947 and 1949, the bodies being completed at the GNR's own works in Dundalk, and the same arrangement was used for a number of double-deckers for Belfast.

Large numbers of Belfast buses were bodied by local coachbuilder Harkness, including this 1948 Guy BTX trolleybus.

HARRINGTON

Thomas Harrington & Sons Ltd is one of the best-loved and best-documented of British coach bodybuilders and now has its own Harrington Society of enthusiasts. The company began life in 1897 in Brighton, constructing

The famous dorsal fin of the 1930s Harrington coach body is seen here on a preserved 1939 Leyland Cheetah.

horse-drawn carriages; it later began bodying motor cars and before the Great War had begun to specialize in commercial vehicles, buses and coaches. After 1919, the focus was on luxury coaches, with a few single-deck bus bodies and other general coachbuilding work.

Harrington always had a reputation for high build qual-ity and accordingly tended to sell at the more expensive end of the market. Despite strong sales of coach bodies in the early 1960s, largely to the BET fleets, the company by this stage needed more investment. When Harrington closed down in 1965, the design rights for its products passed to Plaxton; the final Harrington bodies were built in April 1966.

In 1930, Harrington moved into the purpose-built Sackville Works, at Old Shoreham Road in Hove. Despite its policy of focusing on luxury coach body-work, in 1933–4 it built a few double-deckers on Leyland TD3 chassis for Maidstone & District. It forged strong relationships with its major customers and developed a distinctive style. By the mid-1930s this included a stepped window line, no canopy over the engine and elegant, curvaceous contours. Towards the end of the decade, a further Harrington feature was a 'dorsal fin' on the rear dome, which doubled as an air extractor.

The 1939–45 war saw Harrington building West-land Lysander aircraft, which gave the workforce new skills in jig-building using lightweight alloy sections and extrusions. Many later Harrington bodies would be jig-built from aluminium, although in the late 1940s most bodies for the home market had steel-reinforced

The fin was also present on the famous miniature coaches made by a Harrington employee for seaside use.

hardwood frames. The company's first post-war products were some bus bodies on AEC Regal chassis, but it soon began to build coach bodies again. These were broadly similar to their pre-war counterparts and the characteristic dorsal fin remained available as an option, while deep chromed rear bumpers were always a distinguishing feature. There were some full-front bodies to suit the taste of the times, but these were essentially modified half-cab styles with no other special features. The final full-front bodies took on some elements of the new Wayfarer underfloor-engined coach style at the start of the 1950s, but Harrington built its last body on traditional front-engined chassis in 1951.

Meanwhile, the company built up a good export business, especially with South America and the British colonies in Africa. New models from 1948 were for Leyland Comet and Commer Avenger chassis; Harrington had always had a good relationship with the Rootes Group who owned Commer, having been Rootes agents in the 1930s. Nevertheless, the often-repeated story that Rootes actually bought Harrington at the start of the 1960s is inaccurate.

The company's output in the 1950s and 1960s is most easily understood by dividing it into body styles for heavyweight chassis and those for lightweight chassis. The heavyweights predominated, not least because they belonged to the more expensive end of the market, where Harrington preferred to work.

The Wayfarer (1951–61) was the first Harrington design for heavyweight underfloor-engined chassis, and also the first of the company's styles to be given a name. It was a sturdy, aluminium-framed body that went through four different Marks to become the company's longest-lived single design, but it lacked the lightness of touch associated with the earlier half-cab bodies. It became Harrington's first body for 30ft (9m) × 8ft (2.4m) chassis and the final Mk4 variant introduced the stepped-roof style that provided force-fed air inlets for the ventilation system.

Recognizing the threat posed by the integral Olympic from MCW and Leyland and the Monocoach from Park Royal and AEC, Harrington introduced its own integral-construction offering. As the company was also a sales

Harrington modified the front dome of its Wayfarer coach design to incorporate the star motif for Silver Star of Porton Down. This coach was built in 1955 on a Leyland Tiger Cub chassis.

The Cavalier coach body arrived at the end of the 1950s and was an instant classic. This example is on a 1964 AEC Reliance.

outlet for the Rootes Group, this used Commer Avenger running units. The Contender (1952–7) was usually marketed as a Harrington Contender and could be had as a coach, or with the squarer standard bus shape of the period. Some of the coach variants shared design elements with the contemporary Wayfarer, but the Contender was only moderately successful. During the 1950s, however, both this design and the Wayfarer allowed Harrington to develop expertise in the manufacture of increasingly large GRP mouldings, while at the same time pioneering durable laminates for interior panelling.

Harrington's next heavyweight design became its best-loved masterpiece. The Cavalier (1959–65) combined deep, wrap-around front and rear screens with big windows and a fresh yet modern approach. The stepped roof was still present for forced ventilation, the front and rear panels were GRP mouldings and the underfloor lockers had ingenious cantilever doors that made them easier to use in confined parking spaces. The design was so appealing that Harrington secured significant advance orders on the strength of drawings alone and there were large fleet orders from several BET operators. The all-aluminium Cavalier was introduced as a 41-seat design for 30ft (9m) chassis, but to meet the new size regulations in 1962 it was made available as a 43-seater of 31ft 5in (9.6m) for 30ft chassis (called Cavalier 315) and a 51-seater for 36ft (11m) chassis (Cavalier 36). Orders remained strong right up until Cavalier production ended

in 1965 and 359 of all types were built, of which 200 were on 30ft chassis, sixty-five the 315 design and ninety-four the Cavalier 36.

The Cavalier was joined by the Legionnaire (1963–5), designed specifically for the new small-wheeled Bedford VAL three-axle coach chassis, but beaten into the market by designs from Duple and Plaxton. The 52-seat Legionnaire was a square-rigged, straight-waisted design with a clear resemblance to the Cavalier's Grenadier successor. It was modified in 1964 and also adapted to suit the two-axle Ford Thames 36; a pair was also built on Guy Victory trambus chassis. However, the larger wheel arches needed for these two-axle chassis compromised the design. Just fifty-eight examples of all kinds were built.

The Grenadier (1962–6) was an updated Cavalier, designed from the outset for the latest 36ft × 8ft 2½in (2.5m) chassis dimensions. Fewer and larger side windows removed the compromises of the longer Cavalier bodies and there was less of a dip towards the rear. The peaks were still present and the front screens were even deeper, while improved ventilation allowed for fixed glazing in all side windows. Horizontal rather than vertical tail-lights provided a recognition point, even when South-down ordered its 1964 deliveries with Cavalier front-end panelling to prevent its fleet of those coaches looking out of date. The Grenadier was the only full-size coach still in production when the Harrington works closed in 1966.

The curved screens pioneered by the Cavalier body adapted quite well to the Crusader body for front-engined chasses, too. This is a 1961 Bedford SB3.

As far as lightweight chassis were concerned, Harrington had resumed post-war production with bodies on Commer Commando chassis during 1946. The Rootes connection ensured that the first Commer Avenger in 1948 had a Harrington body, although plenty of other coachbuilders soon got in on that act. Bedford's close ties with Duple and the success of that builder's Vista coach body made Harrington-bodied SBs less common after 1952. So Harrington tried the Avenger market again with a variant of the Wayfarer Mk2 style from 1954, but again without great success.

From 1958, the company made a determined assault on the lightweight market with the Crusader (1958–64), designed specifically for the Avenger, Bedford SB and new Ford Thames chassis. Although this was a standalone design (and borrowed a name briefly used by Plaxton (*q.v.*)), it can be seen as aiding the transition from the Wayfarer to the Cavalier bodies for underfloor-engined chassis. Always using large GRP mouldings for its front and rear panels, the Crusader moved closer to the Cavalier, with similar curved screens on its 1961 Mk2 incarnation, and closer still on the 1963 Mk3, then tending towards the Legionnaire for its final Mk4 version, which reverted from all-aluminium to composite construction in order to reduce cost. Deliberately designed for the cheaper end of the coach market, the Crusader was always intended as a cheaper, lightweight design, and some argue that it never felt as solid as earlier Harrington bodies.

Bus-body manufacture continued into the 1960s, although the Harrington service bus designs were by no means as distinguished as the coaches. The company also built many Black Marias for the Metropolitan Police. The connection with Rootes had already led to minibus conversions on Commer and Karrier van chassis during the 1950s and, from 1957 until the end, Harrington also had the contract for the 'in-house' Commer 1500 minibus bodies, which featured a clerestory roof made of GRP.

Between the 1930s and the mid-1950s, the company also put its name to a series of sixty-three quarter-scale road-legal model coaches for use at leisure resorts; these were mainly the work of an employee, Ernie Johnstone, but a dozen were constructed in the Hove works. All featured scale versions of Harrington body designs and many were powered by Villiers 125cc engines.

HARRIS (1)

Harris was a Yorkshire builder of single-deck bus bodies, active around 1927. Nothing further is known about the company.

HARRIS (2)

A.E. Harris Ltd was probably based at Penarth Road in Cardiff and was involved in PSV bodybuilding around 1938.

HARRIS & HASSEL

Harris & Hassel Ltd were agents for Reo chassis with premises at 24–32 St George's Road in Bristol. The company may have built some single-deck bodies in the second half of the 1920s, although this is in doubt. Harris & Hassel was re-established in 1929 and then again in 1931 after entering voluntary liquidation in November 1930.

HARRISON

Harrison of Dewsbury was established as a coachbuilding firm in the nineteenth century; in the first half of the 1920s it prospered as a builder of high-class car bodywork, mainly on prestige chassis. From around 1923 it also built some single-deck bus bodies and after the death of the Harrison brothers in 1927 switched entirely to commercial and PSV bodywork. Its last PSV bodies were probably built around 1938.

The company was initially called A. Harrison & Sons (Dewsbury) Ltd, with premises at Lower Peel Road in Dewsbury. It later became Harrison's of Dewsbury Ltd and was at Kings Mill in the Savile Town area of Dewsbury. It subsequently changed its name to the Universal Vehicle Group and enjoyed success in the UK ambulance market, but has since closed down.

HARTSHORN

J. & A. Hartshorn were based at 64 Ray Street, in the Derbyshire town of Heanor, and built single-deck bus bodies during the 1920s.

HARVEY (1)

The firm of Harvey Bros had started as blacksmiths in 1796; during the nineteenth century it built bodies for horse-drawn vehicles and by the early 1900s was constructing commercial bodies for motor vehicles. Based at 74 Waterside Street, Strathaven, in Lanarkshire, it built bus bodies between 1913 and 1954, always on Albion chassis and mostly as a subcontractor to Albion Motors. The company closed in 1956.

HARVEY (2)

This second Harvey company was also Scottish, actually operating from John Street, Stromness, in Orkney. W.S. Harvey was originally a builder of horse-drawn vehicles, but did his first motor-bus body in 1921. The company continued to trade (as W.S. Harvey & Son) after his death, becoming the leading commercial and bus builder on Orkney in the 1930s. All the bus bodies were small-capacity types for local operators and the last one was built in 1939.

HARWOOD

Harwood Bodybuilders Ltd built coach bodies between 1948 and 1953 from premises at Chorley New Road, Horwich, in Lancashire.

HASSALL

A company of this name built a single PSV body some time around 1950. It operated from Stoke-on-Trent in Staffordshire.

HAWLEY MILLS

Hawley Mills & Co. Ltd built both coach and pantechnicon bodies during the 1950s from premises at Charles Street, Walsall, in Staffordshire. The PSV activity appears to have ceased in or by 1962.

HAWSON

Hawson Ltd built both service bus and welfare bus bodies in the 1980s from premises at Windmill Lane, Sunbury-on-Thames, Middlesex. Its products were particularly associated with Bedford chassis. The company merged with Garner Motors (q.v.) to become Hawson-Garner Ltd and moved to West Portway, Andover, Hampshire.

HAYWARD

C.W. Hayward of Wolverhampton was perhaps best

This 26-seater all-weather body on an AJS Pilot chassis dates from 1929.

known for its motorcycle sidecars, but in the 1920s it diversified into car bodies as well. In 1925–6 the company was bought out by the AJS motorcycle firm, which subsequently branched out into the PSV market with the Pilot chassis in 1927. It was only natural that Hayward's should build bodywork for this and among those it did build was a 26-seater all-weather coach on the forward-control version of the chassis.

Still trading as C.W. Hayward, the company advertised in 1929 that it could build any type of bodywork on any chassis. AJS went into liquidation in 1931 and Hayward's probably went with it.

HAYWOOD

There were probably three separate PSV bodybuilders with the name of Haywood. One seems to have been based in Edinburgh and to have been active around 1930; the second, a builder of single-deck bus bodies in 1930–1, may have been James H. Haywood & Co. Ltd of Wilderspool Causeway, Warrington in Cheshire. The third, active from 1931–40, was probably based at Formby in Lancashre.

HEALEY

The Healey company that was building fourteen-seat bus bodies for Ford Model T chassis by 1922 was probably the same one that was later registered as C. Healey & Son (1927) Ltd, with premises at 27 Westgate Street in Gloucester.

HEAP

R. Heap & Sons was a firm of wheelwrights with premises at Clegg Street Garage in the Lancashire town of Haslingden. It constructed one or more single-deck bus bodies in 1919.

HEARN

The identity of the Hearn company active in the PSV field between 1926 and 1936 is in doubt. It may have been Martin Hearn of Hooton, Cheshire, or perhaps C. Hearn & Sons of Catherine Street, Darlaston, in Staffordshire.

HEAVER

John Thomas Heaver was a coachbuilder from Fulham in London who was drafted into the Army in 1915 at Bulford Camp in Wiltshire. Demobbed from military service, Heaver had set himself up in business by 1920 at Bulford Road in nearby Durrington.

Heaver Ltd was always a small coachbuilder. It was building on small Bedford chassis during the 1930s, supplying both bus and coach bodies for many local operators and some further afield as well. The company moved into full-front bodywork on front-engined chassis in the early 1950s. It also built a large number of bodies for Guernsey in the mid-1950s, many on Albion Victor chassis, but the business was closed and sold in 1958.

HENLEY

The Henley name may be a misreading for Healey (q.v.).

HENSON-SHAW

This company built bus and charabanc bodies in the 1920s, but no more detailed information is available.

HEYWOOD

Heywood was probably a Lancashire coachbuilder, active by the end of the 1914–18 war and into the early 1920s. Among its products were some single-deck bodies on Tilling-Stevens chassis for Widnes Corporation.

HICKMAN

The Hickman Body Building Co. Ltd had an address at 8 Grove Road in Balham, London SW12. By 1923 it had constructed both single-deck and double-deck bodywork, including on Dennis and Lancia chassis; by 1926 the company claimed that it always kept '20- to 26-seat bodies in stock ready for mounting'. In 1928, it constructed an O42RO body on a Daimler Y type chassis operated by Birch Bros; and in 1929 it was advertising 20-, 24-, 26- and 28-seater all-weather coaches on Dennis and Gilford chassis.

The company also built some bodywork on Karrier chassis under contract to the chassis maker.

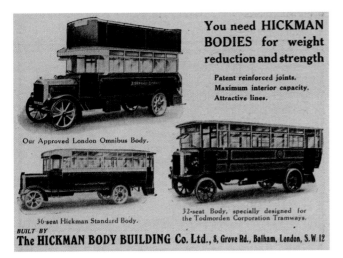

This 1924 advertisement shows an open-top double-decker for Aldershot & District (an 'approved London omnibus body'), a Hickman 'standard body' for Nottingham Corporation and a 32-seater for Todmorden Corporation.

HICKMOTT

Hickmott put its name to open-top double-decker bodywork in 1922, but nothing further is known about the company.

HILTON

James Hilton & Sons of Leigh in Lancashire rebuilt some worn-out bodies for St Helens Corporation between 1947 and 1950. The company appears to be the one with premises at Brookside Mill in Charles Street, which was better known for its domestic appliances.

HINDLE

A company of this name built bus and coach bodies in the period from 1931 to 1943. It may have been Hindle of Manchester Ltd, which had premises at 11–15 Barton Street in that city.

HOGGER

The name of J. Hogger is associated with a number of coach bodies built in the late 1940s and early 1950s. The company had premises at Portsmouth Road, Godalming, Surrey, and seems to have been part of a co-operative venture with Associated Deliveries, Dutfield, Longford and Theale (q.q.v.).

HOLBROOK

Samuel Holbrook Ltd came into being around 1937, having started life as Holbrook & Taylors Ltd (q.v.). The main focus of its work was on rebodying, examples including some 1939 coach bodies on 1935 Leyland Lioness chassis for Allenways of Birmingham. However, it also built on new chassis, the earliest being in 1938 on an AEC Regal chassis for Don Everall of Wolverhampton.

The company operated from premises in Park Lane, Fallings Park, Wolverhampton.

HOLBROOK & TAYLORS

Holbrook & Taylors Ltd was at Park Lane in Wolverhampton and also known as H.T. Bodies. However, in the 1920s the company was more commonly known as Taylors of Wolverhampton, mainly to distinguish it from Taylor of Norwich, which also traded as Eaton (q.v.). It was allegedly quite upset when its local municipality, Wolverhampton Corporation, bought a body from Taylor of Norwich.

By 1930, the company was offering fourteen- to twenty-seater bus bodies for Chevrolet and Ford commercial chassis, and that year it also constructed an early observation coach body that was named the Bella

This 'typical' coach body has an interesting roof design, distinguishing the driver's compartment very markedly from the saloon.

Vista – a name revived some thirty years later by Duple (*q.v.*). This had room for thirty passengers and had a toilet compartment underneath the raised rear seating area.

The company became Samuel Holbrook Ltd (*q.v.*) in the later 1930s.

HOLLINGSWORTH

J. Hollingsworth was constructing single-deck bus bodies in 1922 from premises in Hastings, Sussex. The company had addresses at Braybrooke Road and also at 3–15 Havelock Road.

HOLMES

Some records show Holmes as a coachbuilder in the East Midlands area at the start of the 1920s. The company appears to be identical with Sanderson & Holmes (*q.v.*).

HOMALLOY

Homalloy was the trading name of Holmes (Preston) Ltd, which built some single-deck bus bodies in 1922. The company later became Cravens Homalloy Ltd.

HOODS

Hoods was a coachbuilder responsible for single-deck bus bodywork in the Hastings area in 1919.

HOPKINS

The Hopkins name was associated with single-deck bus bodies in the period 1925–30, but the company has not been identified.

HORA

The company of E. & H. Hora Ltd was incorporated in December 1896 and combined the talents of wheel-wrights Ernest and Harold Hora with those of coach-builders Robert J. and John G. White. The company was based at 36A Peckham Road, in London's Camber-well district. Hora built a number of bodies for London

independent operators in the 1920s, but also found customers further afield.

In 1921 the company built a B28F body on Daimler chassis for the St Helens municipality in Lancashire and in 1922 bodied an AEC trolleybus.

HORSFIELD

This is a common but incorrect spelling for Hosfield (*q.v.*).

HOSFIELD

Active between 1922 and 1929, Hosfield Ltd built bus and coach bodies from premises at 131 Withington Road, Whalley Range, Manchester. Its products were mainly on locally manufactured Crossley chassis; Widnes Corporation also had some Hosfield-bodied Tilling-Stevens and North Western had some 26-seat Renaults.

HOUGHTON

The Houghton name was associated with single-deck bus bodies built between 1930 and 1936, but nothing further is known about the company.

HOYAL

The Hoyal Body Corporation built mainly luxury coaches, but also some single-deck and double-deck bus bodies from premises at Weybridge in the period from 1922 to 1931, when it went into voluntary liquidation.

This Hoyal service bus body was built for Aldershot & District in 1928.

Another 1928 body, this time on a larger chassis and built for SMT.

The company was better known for bodywork on small British sports cars and, as Chalmer & Hoyer, the name under which it was formed in 1921, it was the first company in England to use the Weymann patents for coachbuilding. An example of its PSV work was a B29D body on Daimler CH6 chassis that was bought by Dundee Corporation after serving as a demonstrator.

H.T. BODIES

See Holbrook & Taylor.

HUDSON

The Hudson Motor Engineering Co. Ltd was based at 15 Hudson Road in Sunderland. It built fourteen- and twenty-seat bus bodies for small chassis such as Reo and in 1927 also constructed a bus body of thirty-two seats on a Karrier six-wheel chassis.

The twenty-seater Hudson body shown here on Reo chassis and dating from 1927 appears to be typical of the company's work.

HUGHES

The identity of the Hughes company that built coach bodywork in 1949 has not been established for certain, but it may have been based at Leek in Staffordshire.

HUME

Hume appears to have been an Edinburgh company responsible for single-deck bus bodywork around 1930.

HUNTER & GARDINER

Hunter & Gardiner owned the Crown Garage at Lockerbie, Dumfriesshire, in the 1920s and early 1930s. They were motor dealers and also ran a local bus service; between 1921 and 1927 they may have built as many as three bus bodies for local operators.

HURST NELSON

Hurst, Nelson and Company Ltd was a railway rolling stock manufacturer at Motherwell in Scotland, established in 1893. After 1899, the company also became one of the largest builders of trams in the UK, but occasionally built motor-bus bodies as well. Most of its bus body-

A six-bay, piano-front H28/24R body by Hurst Nelson on a Crossley Condor chassis for Manchester Corporation in 1932.

LEFT: **The original Cowieson body on this 1930 Glasgow Corporation Leyland TD1 was burned out in 1931 and the chassis was rebodied by Hurst Nelson with an interesting design of a front upper-deck emergency exit.**

work was done before 1917, but in 1932–3 it constructed a batch of double-deck bodies for the Manchester municipality on Crossley Condor chassis.

HUTCHINGS

See Cranleigh.

IMMISCH

Immisch was actually a boat builder, with premises at Hampton on Thames in Middlesex and Maidenhead in Berkshire. As the Immisch Launch & Boat Co. Ltd, it specialized in building electric launches. However, it also created some open-top double-deckers in the period from 1913 to 1920 and was involved in rebodying some Dennis Subsidy chassis for Aldershot & District, using both single-deck and double-deck bodies taken from 1912–13 Leyland chassis.

IRELAND

Thomas Ireland and Sons Ltd of Lancaster was established in 1870 as an operator of horse-drawn coaches and cabs. A limited company was formed in 1916 (as Thomas Ireland and Son) at Royal Garages in Chapel Street. The company then ran a livery stable, hired cars, carriages and coaches, and ran a motor garage.

It went on to become a small coach operator in Lancaster and during the late 1940s constructed some coach bodies for its own use and for others.

IRVINE

Peter Irvine & Sons traded from Muirhall Garage, 197 Main Street, Salburgh, Lanarkshire. The company ran its own bus services, but by 1948 was also acting as a used PSV dealer. Between 1947 and 1950, Peter Irvine & Sons built or rebuilt a number of bodies on chassis for Scottish operators.

JACKETT

Jackett's Garages was a Swansea firm that constructed charabanc bodies in 1928. Its premises were at 17–21 Wassail Square.

JACKSON (1)

Jackson was an otherwise unidentified coachbuilder that was probably based in the area of Crewe, in Cheshire. It was building single-deck bus bodies for local operators on Leyland chassis by 1924 and was still active in 1936, when it built at least one body on a Dennis chassis. Some of its products ended up in the North Western fleet as the result of takeovers.

JACKSON (2)

This company was John Jackson & Sons of Mill Street in Dunfermline, Fife. It constructed bus bodies for Scottish operators between 1921 and 1930, but then moved into commercial vehicle bodywork.

In 1947, by which time it had moved to Pittencrieff Street, it was also responsible for a pair of van bodies on Daimler CVD6 bus chassis.

JACKSON (3)

Harry Jackson & Co. (Manchester) Ltd was building PSV bodies by 1966 from premises at Fairfield Street, Ardwick, Manchester 4. By the mid-1970s, the company had moved to 84 Oldfield Road in Salford, where it was continuing in business as a builder of van and trailer bodies.

JACQUES

Jacques Coachworks Ltd was at Church Street, Bentley, Doncaster, in Yorkshire. The company built the bodies on a pair of Bedfords and a TSM for the operator S.M. Wilson & Sons of Balby, Doncaster, between 1948 and 1951.

JEFFREY'S

Jeffrey's Commercial Motors (Swansea) Ltd had premises at Neath Road in Swansea's Morriston district. It was an established firm of commercial bodybuilders that turned its hand briefly to PSV bodies in the late 1940s. Among others, it built bodies for Austin K4SL, Bedford OWB, Crossley and Dennis chassis.

JENKINS

J.P. Jenkins & Co. of Harvington in Worcestershire was well established as a builder of bodies for local operators, constructing a number of small PSVs in the 1920s and 1930s. An interesting example was a Bedford 'coach bus' with sliding-head bodywork dating from 1931.

JENNINGS

Jennings Coachworks Ltd was based at Crewe Road in Sandbach, Cheshire. Originally known as J.H. Jennings & Sons, it was an old-established company that built some

car as well as commercial bodies in the 1930s. By 1931 it was building 32-seat post buses for A. Macintyre & Sons of Fort William, Scotland, and by 1932 was advertising coach bodies as well.

In later years, the company was better known for its welfare bus bodywork, for horseboxes and pantechnicons. However, it did build some more single-deck bus bodies in the second quarter of the 1960s. It later became a subsidiary of the lorry builder, ERF.

JENSEN

The Jensen brothers started in the coachbuilding business in 1928 with a special body on an Austin Seven car chassis. They were primarily car bodybuilders until the mid-1930s, when they produced their first complete vehicles and began work on integral-construction lorries at about the same time.

From 1948 they offered a PSV derivative of the design, for which they also built bodywork. However, sales of the Jensen lorry (always known as a JNSN, as were the PSVs) collapsed after a change in regulations in 1951 and Jensen stopped building buses and the bodywork for them in 1952. The company was based at Carter's Green in the Staffordshire town of West Bromwich.

JERSEY MOTOR PANELS

Jersey Motor Panels of St Helier took advantage of the need for refurbished bodywork after World War II, working on both bus and coach bodies. Among the vehicles it rebuilt were some 1932 AEC Regals for Mascot Coaches of St Helier that had belonged to City of Oxford Motor Services.

JOHNSON

Tom Johnson of Bradford in Yorkshire is recorded as a builder of single-deck bus bodywork in 1920.

JONES

T. Jones was an independent operator in the mid-Wales town of Llanidloes that built some single-deck bodies for its own use and some for other operators. It was active around 1974.

JONES BROS

The Jones Bros who put their name to a seventeen-seater PSV body in 1951 were probably Jones Bros (Coachbuilders) Ltd of 44 Kemp Road, London NW6, and who later moved to Albion Works, Old Oak, Common Lane, London NW10. The company also constructed commercial bodies, for the Post Office among other customers.

JUNCTION

The Junction Motor Bodybuilding Co. Ltd had premises at 161 Oldham Road, Miles Platting, in Manchester. It was briefly involved with coach bodybuilding in the second half of the 1940s, constructing a number of bodies on the Crossley chassis manufactured nearby.

KARRIER

Karrier Motors Ltd was established in Huddersfield in 1920 as a manufacturer of chassis. The company later moved to Luton (1934) and subsequently Dunstable (1970), then in 1970 became part of Chrysler (UK) Ltd.

Between 1923 and 1927, Karrier supposedly built bodywork for its own PSV chassis, including charabancs, single-deck service buses and double-deckers with both open and closed tops. However, some of the Karrier bodies were certainly subcontracted elsewhere; the double-deckers for Enterprise and Silver Dawn, for example, were actually built by Hickman (*q.v.*).

K.B. COACHBUILDERS

K.B. Coachbuilders (Darwen) Ltd was at Ellesmere Road in Darwen, Lancashire. The company was established in 1960 and briefly built coach bodywork. It ceased trading in 1983.

KELLY

J.H. Kelly built bus and coach bodywork at premises in Van Street, Parkhead, Glasgow E1, in the 1920s. The company had started out as a builder of commercial bodies in the early years of the century and from 1912 was also building passenger-carrying bodies.

In 1923, Mr Kelly retired and sold the business to William Beardmore & Co. (*q.v.*). Some distinctive bodies were built for local operators, still under the name of Kelly, but after 1929 Beardmore had its own commercial vehicle department and the Kelly name disappeared.

KEMP & NICHOLSON

This company had built horse-drawn vehicles in the nineteenth century and was specializing in agricultural engineering by 1930. It traded from the Scottish Central Works in Stirling. Kemp & Nicholson built a single bus body on an Albion chassis for a local operator in 1928.

KENEX

See Kent & Sussex Woodcraft.

KENT

A Kent Motor Co. involved with bus bodywork in the early 1930s may be identical with the Kent Motor Coachworks Ltd that was registered in January 1930 with premises at 89 Broad Street in Canterbury.

KENT & SUSSEX WOODCRAFT

Kent & Sussex Woodcraft Ltd had premises at Eastmead Works in Ashford, Kent, during the late 1940s. It entered the PSV bodywork market in 1949, focusing on coach bodies for the smaller chassis such as Austin CXD and also the Bedford SB. However, the company soon found a niche building minibuses and minibus conversions, so for much of the 1950s was known for that and as Kenex Coachworks Ltd. Other products included works bus types.

The company moved to new premises in Dover and in 1962 briefly re-entered the PSV market with a 25-/29-seater coach body for the new Ford Thames FC. However, this had hardly been registered before the company was

This fourteen-seater coach was available from Kenex on the Austin LD2 30cwt van chassis in the late 1950s.

taken over by Martin Walter Ltd (*q.v.*) in September 1962. The new owners continued the design, marketing it as the Romney, but it was soon discontinued.

KIDDLE

Kiddle Motor Bodies was a Bournemouth firm active in the PSV field during the first half of the 1920s. Its premises were at The Old Water Works in Tuckton. The company may be the same as the H.W. Kiddle & Sons who built, or more probably refurbished, single-deck bus bodies in the period 1942–6. This company still existed as a car body repairer in 2012.

KING & TAYLOR

King & Taylor Ltd was a Godalming company that became

involved with PSV bodywork in the post-war period of the late 1940s. The company built both bus and coach bodies, notably on Austin chassis. It subsequently became King & Taylor (Commercial) Ltd and is still active in the manufacture and sales of commercial vehicles.

KNAPE

J. Knape & Sons of Burnley, Lancashire, was building bus bodywork by 1906, when it constructed a double-decker for a local operator on a Critchley & Norris chassis. The same company built at least one ambulance body during the 1914–18 war and in 1923 constructed a single-decker for Colne Corporation. Between 1924 and 1927, several single-deckers on Leyland chassis for Burnley Corporation followed, but the company's involvement with PSV bodies seems to have ceased by the end of the decade.

KNIBBS

W.H. Knibbs & Sons Ltd had been established in the 1850s and became known during the 1920s as a builder of car bodies. It appears to have constructed some PSV bodywork in this period as well. The company was then based at Tipping Street, Ardwick, Manchester. It was subsequently renamed Knibbs & Parkyn, before going on to become a car dealership with the name of Knibbs of Salford.

K.W. BODIES LTD

See Lansdowne.

LAMBERT

W.G. Lambert Ltd was established in the late nineteenth century at Castle Street, Thetford, in Norfolk. Later, at Coach Works in Minstergate Street, the company built single-deck bus bodies in the 1920s for chassis such as the Chevrolet LQ.

LANCASHIRE AIRCRAFT LTD

See Samlesbury Engineering.

LANSDOWNE

Lansdowne K.W. Bodies Ltd, also known simply as K.W., built coach bodies from premises at Collins Avenue, Bispham, in Blackpool from about 1937. Active again in the late 1940s, the company built bodies for the Commer Avenger and some full-front types for Seddon Mk4 chassis.

By 1960, the company had moved to Wakefield Road in Blackpool, but PSV activity had ceased.

LATYMER

The rather pretentiously named Carrosserie Latymer (1915) Ltd built charabanc bodies in the first few years of the 1920s. It operated from the former London Road Car Co. depot at Pamber Street, London W10.

LAW

William Law set up in business in 1886 to build horse-drawn van and lorry bodies in the Glasgow district of Scotstoun. In 1907 it built its first charabanc body; in 1920 it briefly became Law & Hope Brothers, then in 1923 it became William Law & Son. Most of its small bus-body output was built between then and the end of 1927, for local operators. Glasgow Corporation took two Law bodies on Halley chassis in 1924.

LAWRIE

Robert Lawrie was a Paisley coachbuilder in the nineteenth century, becoming a coach and motor bodybuilder in the new century. The company is thought to have built around four PSV bodies, of which two dated from 1939. All were for local operators.

LAWTON

The Lawton Motor Bodybuilding Co. Ltd was based at Church Lawton, near Stoke-on-Trent in Staffordshire. It built its first PSV body in 1921 on a Ford chassis (although there is a counter-claim for a 1920 Karrier WDS being the first) and its last in 1954. Approximately 200 PSV bodies carried the Lawton name in that period, although the company also seems to have been a builder of hearses.

Most Lawton bodies went to local operators in the Burslem, Newcastle and Stoke area of South Cheshire and North Staffordshire. Late examples included a 35-seat half-canopy coach with forward entrance on Foden PVSC chassis in 1949.

LAYNE

G.H. Layne & Co. Ltd of Brigg in Lincolnshire was active in the 1920s and into the 1930s. The company is known to have constructed fourteen- to sixteen-seat

Lincolnshire bodybuilder G.H. Layne was offering fourteen- and sixteen-seater bodies on Chevrolet chassis in 1924.

bodies on Chevrolet 20/25cwt chassis and to have offered twenty-seaters on extended Chevrolet chassis as late as 1929. The company used the Glanford name for some of its bodies.

LEAVER

G.H. Leaver Ltd was probably a dealer, based at 16 Eanam, Blackburn, Lancashire. It may also have built single-deck bus bodywork in the second quarter of the 1920s.

LEE MOTORS

The Lee Motor Bodyworks (Bournemouth) Ltd was active in the PSV market building coach bodies between 1934 and 1950. The company was often known as Lee Motors. By 1952 it was focusing on school buses, such as twenty-seaters for the Dorset County Council Education Department.

LE HURAY

Le Huray was a Guernsey company established probably around 1900, but active in the PSV field between 1921 and 1948, building charabancs and single-deck bus bodies. The company was initially known as T. Le Huray, but later as Le Huray & Sons. It continued in business as VMW (Commercial) Ltd.

LEWIS

William Lewis & Sons (Cardiff) Ltd were at Tudor Lane in that city and built single-deck bus bodies in the middle 1920s.

LEWIS & CRABTREE

Lewis & Crabtree Motors Ltd was based at Starkey Works, Heywood, Lancashire, but also had premises in Manchester. It built charabanc, single-deck bus and coach bodies between 1928 and 1930 on chassis such as Gilford and Reo Major.

Mr Crabtree was Jack Crabtree, who had come from Elite Bodies Ltd and was later associated with Shearing & Crabtree, Shearings of Oldham, Oldham Construction and Challenger (q.q.v.).

LEX

In the early 1970s, the Lex sales and hire group diversified into vehicle bodywork from its premises at Ringwood Road, Totton, in Hampshire. There were coaches, single-deck buses and lorry-buses, as well as welfare buses.

The company was also known as Lex Commercial Ltd, Lex Commercial (SMB) Ltd, Lex Tillotson (Totton) Ltd and Lex Vehicle Engineering Ltd.

LEY

Frederick Ley of Turvey in Bedfordshire appears to have become involved with bus bodywork in the 1920s, but nothing else is known about him.

LEYLAND

The bodyshop attached to chassis manufacturer Leyland Motors Ltd consistently produced innovative and standard-setting designs until it was closed in 1954 to allow the company to focus on its core activities. Leyland had built bodywork for its own bus chassis since the first decade of the twentieth century and during the Great War the relevant skills had been kept intact as the company had built vehicles – mainly lorries – for the war effort.

From 1919, Leyland's policy was to buy back the vehicles it had built for the War Office (primarily the RAF) and to refurbish them before reselling them on the civilian market. Many of these chassis were rebodied as charabancs for the 1919 summer season; a basic Popular body was available on reconditioned chassis, while a better-equipped De Luxe type was usually fitted to new chassis. By the end of 1919, enclosed bodies were also being made. These were mainly built to order, although some of the more popular types were built for stock.

During the early 1920s, Leyland offered different bodies to suit each of its different chassis types, often naming the bodies after the operator who bought them. One was the Farington, on the A13 chassis (1924–7); this

Built in the early 1920s on an ex-RAF Leyland lorry chassis, this Leyland body was constructed entirely from wood.

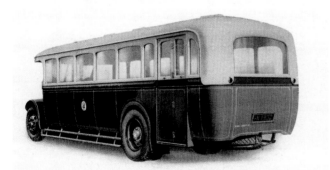

There was variety in the Leyland single-decker designs, too, which could be had with either front or rear entrance.

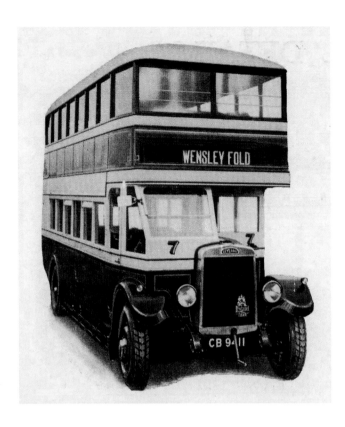

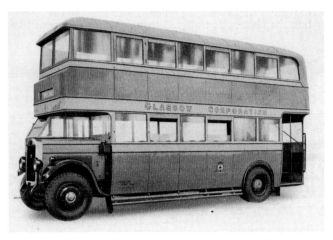

The difference in height between the lowbridge body on a Blackburn Titan and the Hybridge type on a similar chassis for Glasgow is mainly noticeable in the panel above the lower deck. Both date from the late 1920s.

name would be used again nearly thirty years later, by which time Leyland would also have a factory at Farington, near its main works in Leyland, Lancashire.

From 1927, the new body designed for the Titan TD1 chassis gathered together a number of practical features. It had a low overall height of just 13ft (4m), some 2–3ft (0.6–0.9m) lower than older designs. This was achieved partly by using a 'lowbridge' upper-deck layout, with a sunken gangway on one side – a design that set a trend for the next thirty years or more. The Lowbridge name was initially used as a trade name, although Leyland allowed the exclusivity to lapse. Although the body still had an open staircase, the upper deck extended over the cab; Leyland was not the first to use this style, but certainly popularized it. Above the cab was a distinctive 'piano-front' shape incorporating the destination indicator, and aluminium panelling kept overall weight down. By 1929, most of these bodies had an enclosed staircase and that year Leyland also introduced a highbridge alternative (marketed as Hybridge) with a 14ft (4.3m) overall height and central upper-deck gangway. From 1931, Leyland double-deck bodies incorporated an opening rear window in the upper deck that doubled as an emergency door. This went on to become a standard requirement on British double-deckers.

Leyland also built single-deck bus bodies for its own

chassis, but left coach-body manufacture to others. With the charabanc age now over, the Lion chassis was graced with a rather rectangular wooden-framed body that was a classic of its time, but gave way to a more modern and less upright style in 1930. Leyland bodies of both single- and double-deck types were in demand all over Britain and in the 1929–30 period the company had to find additional manufacturing capacity. Up to about 1932, some bodies were therefore built at Leyland's Trojan car works in Kingston-upon-Thames, Surrey, while others

The original steel-framed 'vee-front' double-deck bodies from Leyland gave a lot of trouble. Many were returned to the makers for remedial work; the owners of this one, Ledgard of Leeds, successfully demanded a new-style replacement body.

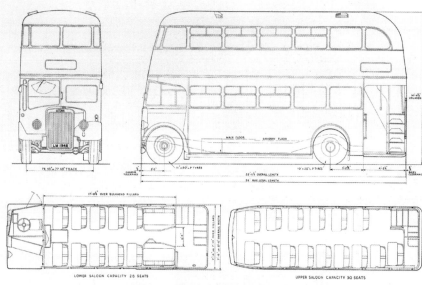

ARRANGEMENT OF 56-SEATER HYBRIDGE BODY ON PD. 2 CHASSIS

The post-war Leyland double-deck body could be had in lowbridge or Hybridge forms. These drawings show the difference in upper-deck layout and in appearance. As it had done twenty years earlier, the height of the panel below the top deck windows provides the external clue to the body type.

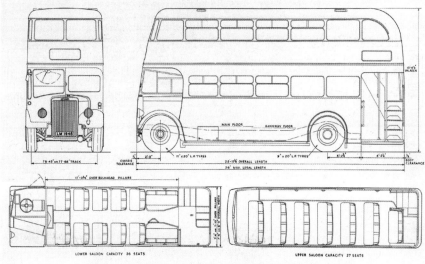

GENERAL ARRANGEMENT OF 53 SEATER LOWBRIDGE BODY ON PD.2 CHASSIS

were subcontracted to outside bodybuilders. Massey, Northern Counties, Roberts, Short Bros and Vickers (q.q.v.) all became involved, sometimes, but by no means always, building bodies to Leyland designs.

From 1933, all-metal construction was introduced for a new generation of single-deck bodies, yet more rounded and resolved in appearance than before. A coach version of this body was also made available and in 1936 the shape was revised.

Double-deck body design continued to evolve. In 1932, Leyland prototyped a metal-framed design (bodies were usually of composite construction, with wooden frames), which became available in 1934. It was a six-bay design, distinguished by a vee-shaped front above the cab – 'Every part rustproofed and jig-built' read a 1935 advertisement. These early all-metal bodies gave a lot of trouble in service, so were replaced from 1936 by a revised design with a flat front and five window bays. Designed by Colin Bailey, who had learned about metal framing at Metro-Cammell, these 'Bailey bodies' were sturdy and their clean and well-balanced lines set a standard that endured into the 1950s. Unique batches were built with full-fronts especially for Lytham St Annes and in the late 1930s 100 went to London Transport as the STD class, quite extensively modified to harmonize with the existing STL class AEC

One of Leyland's most attractive coach bodies was rarely seen outside the major BET fleets, but this one went to Gibsons of Leicester when new in 1951. It was on a Leyland Royal Tiger chassis.

STEEL FRAMED BODY

Exhibited for the first time at the Scottish Show, the latest steel-framed body contains many new constructional features. The Single-decker "Service-type" body seats up to 39 passengers and is described in Catalogue 525, which will be forwarded on request

list **£370** price

by Leyland

HEAD OFFICE AND WORKS: LEYLAND · LANCS

Steel-framed bodies were introduced in 1934 and here is one in 39-seat single-deck service bus form on, of course, a Leyland chassis.

The vee-front body was replaced in 1936 by the Bailey type, normally built to a standard design, but on this Leicester example fitted with an odd side indicator box.

Regents. By 1938, Leyland was also looking at integral construction, but development of its double-deck trolleybus design was curtailed by the war and the sole prototype served out its days with London Transport.

There was no bus-body production at Leyland during the 1939–45 war, as the works was entirely turned over to production of military trucks and tanks. Body construction resumed in 1946 with a mildly modified Bailey design of double-decker that had a deeper cab front side window and other less visible changes. The demand for double-deckers was such that there were no new Leyland single-deck bodies in the 1940s. As 8ft (2.4m) wide bodies became permissible from 1950, so Leyland economized on jigs by retaining the front end panelling of the 7ft 6in (2.3m) bodies, which then tapered outwards to meet the 8ft wide front bulkhead. But another new design arrived in 1950. This was the Farington type, with five-bay design, neatly radiused window corners and nearly flush glazing. It again proved a durable classic and remained in production until the Leyland body shop was closed.

Meanwhile, the switch to underfloor-engined single-deck chassis had prompted Leyland to design its own bodies for the type. The service bus body for the Royal Tiger was well-proportioned, if quite square in outline, while the coach design with lantern-style windscreen was designed in conjunction with major customer Ribble and became another highly regarded classic.

LEYLAND NATIONAL

The Leyland National deserves an entry of its own because it was built quite separately from the Leyland bodyworks that had closed down in the 1950s. It was an integral-construction single-decker with modular construction, employing interchangeable sections that allowed easy repairs and the flexibility to produce alternative lengths on the assembly lines. All examples were built and bodied at a dedicated plant established at Lillyhall, near Workington in Cumbria. Body elements of the National were also used in railcars for British Rail.

The National was introduced in 1972 and had been designed as a joint project between Leyland and the National Bus Company, whose members were obliged to buy it. The design replaced the variety of single-deckers made at different plants within the Leyland group. All the early Nationals were bus types, but from 1974 coach seating became available as an alternative; sadly, there

Though somewhat derided at the time as a 'standardized' design, the Leyland National grew old gracefully. This example from the Fishwick fleet was actually new in 1977, but is visually similar to the 1975 and earlier models.

was no accompanying variation in the rather severe lines of the body to bear witness to the difference.

Characteristic of the early National was a large pod on the roof, which contained the heating equipment; this was reduced in size in 1974, before disappearing altogether in 1978 when a simplified National appeared. From 1979 the model became the National 2 and in this guise remained in production until 1985. Over 7,000 were built in all.

Few of the odd Crellin-Duplex bodies came from Lincs Trailer. This was a 1949 example on a Leyland Tiger PS2/3 chassis for Norfolk Motor Services of Great Yarmouth.

LINCS TRAILER CO. LTD

The Lincs Trailer Company tried to find a foothold in the PSV body market during the boom period of the late 1940s with the intriguing coach design patented by George Crellin in 1948. This was known as the Crellin-Duplex (*q.v.*) and Lincs Trailer had built the 46-seat prototype and demonstrator on a Guy chassis by October 1949.

During June 1950, the company announced a 51-seater derivative of the design for underfloor-engined chassis, but had no further involvement with PSV bodies. The Crellin-Duplex patents passed to Mann Egerton (*q.v.*) late in 1951. Lincs Trailer operated from premises at Ashby Ville Road in Scunthorpe.

LINDSAY

W.L. Lindsay was a Dundee firm that built some charabanc and single-deck bus bodies for the local corporation during 1921. There may have been others. The company's main business was motor engineering and it remained in that trade until 1944, with premises at North End Vehicle Works, 136 Strathmartine Road.

LITTLEBOROUGH

The Littleborough Motor & Engineering Co. Ltd took its name from Littleborough, near Manchester, where it was based. Its creations included an all-weather body on a Leyland Lioness chassis in November 1929.

Built for a Haslingden operator in 1929, this all-weather body was on a Leyland Lioness chassis.

This 1931 body on Tilling-Stevens chassis for Westcliff Motor Services was pictured outside the London Lorries premises when new.

Quite why this 26-seat all-weather design by London Lorries in 1928 was called the QP type is unclear.

LONDON LORRIES

As its name suggested, London Lorries Ltd was initially a builder of commercial motor bodies. From 1918 it was at Spring Place in the Kentish Town district of London and its first PSV bodies probably appeared in 1922. These were all-weather coaches, promoted as having a low-line design. The company specialized in all-weather bodies during the 1920s, but its range included single-deck buses and coaches as well as charabancs.

In 1931, one of the company's coach bodies won a silver medal at the Commercial Motor Show and in 1932 London Lorries built its first double-deckers – on Leyland Titan chassis for Swan Saloon Services of Swansea. However, later that year its business was acquired by Duple (*q.v.*).

LONGFORD

The owners of Neath & Cardiff Luxury Coaches at Neath Abbey decided to spread its coachbuilding skills beyond vehicles in its own fleet during 1947, so it established the Longford Manufacturing and Coachbuilding Co. Ltd at Neath. Among other work, the company rebodied some pre-war chassis for the West Riding Automobile Co. Ltd. Longford became part of the co-operative that included Associated Deliveries, Dutfield, Hogger and Theale (*q.q.v.*).

By the time Neath & Cardiff passed into BET ownership in 1953, coachbuilding activity had ceased.

The Bedford chassis of this coach may have been a rebuilt lorry chassis. The Longford coach body dates from about 1949.

LONGWELL GREEN

Longwell Green Coachworks Ltd was established around 1944 by the Bence family of Bristol, who also owned bus services and car dealerships. It had formerly been Bence Motor Bodies Ltd (*q.v.*) and took its name from the Bristol district where it was based, in Kingsfield Lane. Bus, coach and commercial bodies were all on offer by 1946 and 1949 PSV bodies included coaches on Daimler and Maudslay chassis, plus 29- and 33-seaters on the Leyland Comet. There were double-deckers on Leyland Titan PD1 chassis for the Bristol Omnibus Company, too.

During the 1950s, bus bodies on underfloor-engined chassis proved popular with operators in South Wales. Longwell Green ceased to make PSV bodywork in the 1960s, but the company continued to build commercial bodies and during the 1980s was even involved with custom-building Range Rovers for the Middle East.

LOUTH

As its name suggests, Louth Motor Bodies Ltd was based at Louth in Lincolnshire. The company is known to have built single-deck bus bodywork in 1921.

LOVE & MAXWELL

This company was a joiners and bodybuilders at Glenboig in Lanarkshire. It built a single bus body for a Glenboig operator in 1948, using mostly wooden construction.

LOVELLS

A Lovells Motor Co. built charabanc bodies, probably in the early 1920s.

LUCAS

The London firm of F.W. Lucas claimed to be 'motor coach specialists', although it also advertised its history as dating back to 1844. The company built fourteen-seat saloon bodies and all-weather types, and was based at 240 Brixton Hill, London SW2.

LYDNEY

The huge demand for new bus and coach bodies in the late 1940s led the Plymouth firm of Mumford (*q.v.*) to look for new premises. Major operator Red & White offered the company premises at Harbour Road on the Lydney Industrial Estate in Gloucestershire in 1947. It was a good deal for all concerned – Red & White gained an in-house bodyworks, while Mumford, now renamed Lydney, gained good business.

The Lydney works built buses, coaches and double-deckers for several local operators, including United Welsh. However, the company closed down in 1952 and all work in hand (which included several bodies for underfloor-engined Leyland Royal Tigers) was transferred to the Bristol Tramways bodyworks at Brislington (*see* BBW).

LYON & PYE

Lyon & Pye was a St Helens engineering company that participated in the local Corporation's scheme for refurbishing its worn-out bus bodies between 1947 and 1950.

MACDONALD

Duncan MacDonald was a bodybuilder on the Isle of Lewis, catering for the local market in the 1920s and 1930s. Just one 1923 body on Ford chassis has been provisionally identified as his.

MACKEOWN & CLUGHAN

A company of this name is credited with building bus bodywork in 1930. It may have been based in Belfast, but nothing more is known for certain.

MACLEOD

John MacLeod of Port of Ness in Lewis constructed some bus bodies in the 1920s for local operators. The company's name is sometimes given as McLeod and in some records appears as McCleon of Ness.

MACPHERSON

John MacPherson Ltd built bus bodywork between 1924 and 1931 from premises at Orchard Street, Newcastle upon Tyne.

MACRAE & DICK

This company was established in the nineteenth century in Inverness as a hirer of horse-drawn vehicles. It progressed to motor vehicles in the early twentieth century and began to body some PSVs. Only one has been firmly identified, and that was built in 1920, but there were more.

Macrae & Dick remains active today as a car dealer.

MAINS

Mains & Co. Ltd was a motor bodybuilder in Ayr in Scotland, with premises in Burns' Statue Square. Its first bus body probably dated from 1921, but most of its products were bus bodies in 1929–31 for Ayr & District Motor Services. These had visual similarities to contemporary Porteous (*q.v.*) designs, although no direct link has been proven.

The company continued to trade until about 1975, but there are no known PSV bodies after 1931.

MALLETT

The Mallett company of St Sampson, Guernsey probably began as a carpentry and wheelwright's business, but also advertised itself in the early 1930s as a builder of motor bodies. The company seems to have been founded around 1920 as F. Mallett at Mont Martin; by 1933 it was at Les Banques, La Rue des Bas Courtils; and it later became F. Mallett & Son. It also traded as St Sampsons Coach and Motor Works (the name of the Les Banques premises), but it is not clear whether any PSV bodies were built under this name.

MANHIRE CHANDLER

Manhire Chandler & Co. Ltd was a commercial bodybuilder with premises at Barry Road, London NW10. It was incorporated in 1900.

During the 1950s it constructed some coach bodies from premises at Ealing Road, Alperton, in Middlesex. The company was taken over by Wilsdon of Solihull (*q.v.*) in the mid-1960s.

MANN EGERTON

Mann Egerton & Co. Ltd claimed to have been established in 1898; indeed, that may have been the date when electrical engineer Gerald Mann and pioneer motorist Hubert Egerton first worked together. However, the company itself was founded in Prince of Wales

The practical interpretation of your ideas

While there are obvious advantages, particularly on the score of price, to be gained from purchasing a standard design we recognise that operators may wish to introduce certain individual effects or may want the general styling to conform to that of the existing fleet.

The luxury coach illustrated is a good example of the practical interpretation of personal ideas. Built for Mountain Transport Services Ltd., it embodies the salient features of the Mann Egerton standard 31-seater Norfolk Coach but the basic design has been modified to allow for the special styling that is a distinctive feature of the coaches operated by the Mountain Transport Services Company.

Facilities are also available for building special bodies, and designs, specifications and quotations for coachwork, to suit any make of chassis, will be submitted on request.

Modern Coachbuilding by Mann Egerton

MANN EGERTON & CO. LTD., NORWICH.   Telephone 23291

This 1949 advertisement explained that the coach body pictured on Austin chassis had been specially modified from the company's standard Norfolk design to suit the requirements of Mountain Transport Services Ltd.

Road, Norwich, in 1905 to sell cars and carry out electrical installation work. It added car bodywork manufacture to its portfolio in 1909 and during the 1939–45 war made military ambulance bodies, among other items.

After the war, Mann Egerton abandoned car bodywork (with a single exception in 1951), turning to PSV bodies. Now at Cromer Road in Norwich, it was best known for its coach bodies on Austin CXB chassis and for its timber-framed single-deck service bus body as exemplified by London Transport T (AEC Regal) and TD (Leyland Tiger) vehicles of 1948–9. However, the company also built double-deckers, including some on Daimler chassis for Newcastle in 1950 and Glasgow Corporation in 1951 and that year it also became the licensee for the Crellin Duplex coach design (*q.v.* and *see* Lincs Trailer Co).

The company's last bodies for the home market were probably built in 1952, but as late as 1956 there was a 45-seat single-deck bus body called the Equator for export. The company subsequently remained in business with a chain of car dealerships.

MANNERS (1)

A company responsible for some single-deck bus bodies in the 1920s may have been J.D. Manners of Wokingham Road, Bracknell, in Berkshire.

MANNERS (2)

A company thought to have been W. Manners of Pocklington in Yorkshire is credited with a single forty-seater bus body.

MANNING

The Southport firm of W. Manning & Sons was an agent for Reo chassis in the mid-1920s, constructing all-weather and saloon bodywork for some of them. The company was based at 64 Compton Road in Birkdale and also ran a fleet of coaches with bodies of its own design.

MANSONS

Mansons is believed to have been a Belfast PSV coachbuilder at the start of the 1930s.

MARGHAM

Harry Margham & Sons Ltd was based at Newport on the Isle of Wight and became involved with the PSV business in the 1920s when it reconditioned some bus bodies for local operator Dodson Bros. The company continued its occasional association with the bus and coach body business from premises at Towngate, Lower St James Street until 1948 and also became active as a builder of hearses.

Today, Towngate has been rebuilt as a retail park, but Margham Stores still has premises in Newport and operates as a supplier of automotive refinishing products.

MARKHAM

A company called Markham was involved with single-deck bus bodywork from premises in Slough, Berkshire, at the end of the 1920s.

MARKS

F.W. Marks & Sons Ltd had premises at Shaftesbury Road, Wilton, in Wiltshire, where it built bus and charabanc bodies in the late 1920s.

MARNELL

Almost nothing is known about the Marnell company that put its name to some bus bodywork in the mid-1930s.

MARSDEN

Marsden (Coachbuilders) Ltd of Warrington, Lancashire, carried out some refurbishment of older bodywork for St Helens Corporation in the 1947–50 period. Marsden's was a commercial bodybuilder, which remained in that field after this brief brush with PSVs.

MARSHALL

David Marshall set up a garage business in Cambridge in 1909 and from that grew a vast business empire. Marshall Motor Bodies Ltd was an arm of this, estab-

One of our standard 20-seater Saloon buses on a Reo Major chassis.

28-SEATER REO PULLMAN
All-weather Safety Coach.

One of a fleet of Coaches built and run by W. Manning & Sons, designers of body. Acknowledged to be safest coach on road; being built only 12 in. from the ground, it cannot turn ove. It has a door to each compartment, also windscreens across each. Four-wheel brakes, free from draughts and dust; when fitted with the "All-weather" screens can be used for winter work—not being made of glass these give the coach a lighter weight on the tyres and are not dangerous in case of accidents. Open photograph is of a 28-seater which has been run by ourselves 30,000 miles with repair cost of 25/- and front tyres still on.

W. MANNING & SONS,
(Established 1895.)   Automobile Agents, Motor Body Builders,
(Telephone:— 408.)   and Agents for the REO CHASSIS.
64, COMPTON ROAD, BIRKDALE, SOUTHPORT.

Reo agents, coach operators and bodybuilders, W. Manning & Sons had the PSV scene sewn up in the Southport area by 1927.

Typically well-proportioned, this is a 1963 Marshall Camagna service bus body on an AEC Reliance chassis for Leicester City Transport.

The dual-entrance 44-seat bodywork on this 1971 AEC Swift was by Marshall for St Helens Corporation.

lished in Cambridge in the late 1940s, but the company's major involvement with PSV bodies began after it had taken over Mulliners (*q.v.*) in 1959. The company was renamed Marshall of Cambridge (Engineering) Ltd, with some early bodies being marketed as Marshall-Mulliner types. It was based at Airport Works, Newmarket Road, Cambridge.

During the 1960s, Marshall was a major builder of single-deck buses and coaches, often to standardized designs for the BET group of operators. There were double-deck bodies, too, although the company built only a single prototype coach (in 1962) before deciding to leave that market alone. The service bus bodies were notably smart and well-proportioned, generally also attracting a good reputation for durability.

Many Marshall designs had names beginning with Cam- to indicate their Cambridge origins (examples are Camagna, Camair, Cambrette, Cambridgian, Cambus and Campaigner). The Camuter was an integral design with a Perkins engine mounted at the rear; it was adopted by Bedford as the JJL, but no production followed.

Marshall pulled out of the PSV market in 1982, but re-entered it ten years later after buying designs from Carlyle Conversions, which had been established in 1984 at Edgbaston in Birmingham. Marshall Bus then lasted until 2002, when its assets were sold to MCV Bus and Coach.

MARSTON

John Marston & Co., later John Marston's Carriage Works Ltd, operated from 21–28 Bradford Street in Birmingham. Although founded as early as 1900, the company was active in the PSV field from 1919 to 1928 as a builder of single-deck bus bodies.

MARTIN (1)

Beginning probably in 1929, J. Martin (Bournemouth) Ltd constructed coach bodies from premises at 16–18 Cutlands Road. The same company later traded as J. Martin (Bournemouth) (1931) Ltd and may have been responsible for the single-deck bodywork on Thorny-croft BC chassis for Bournemouth Corporation in the early 1930s. Martin seems to have been active until the mid-1930s.

MARTIN (2)

James Martin (Kirkintilloch) Ltd was active as a body-builder between 1924 and 1938. The company was a dealership for both Ford and Leyland, although it also bodied other chassis, always for local operators. Its address was Kelvin Valley Works, Kilsyth Road, Kirkin-tilloch, Dunbartonshire.

MARTIN WALTER

Martin Walter is best known as the company that converted Bedford vans into estate cars in the 1950s, progressing from that to camper and caravan conver-sions on a variety of chassis. Yet the company had a far more extensive history that went right back to 1773: it was involved in the harness and saddlery business in the beginning, then moving into carriage-building and, in the early 20th century, car bodybuilding.

By the start of the twentieth century it was still a saddlery business, later moving into cycles and sports goods. The 1920s and 1930s saw it making a name for itself as a car body manufacturer, eventually specializing in drophead coupé types. The car body business was sold to Abbey Coachworks in 1937, but Martin Walter Ltd remained active from its Folkestone premises.

The company's involvement with PSVs centred on minibuses, but it also built some coach bodies in the 1960s and continued some designs by Kenex (q.v.) after it bought that company in 1962. The company later changed its name to Dormobile Ltd, using the trade name of its best-known caravan conversion, but went into receivership in 1994.

MASHFORD

Mashford was a boat builder at Cremyll in Cornwall, but between 1948 and 1955 turned its hand to coach bodywork to meet the strong demand of the period. It built just six bodies in all – two in 1948, two in 1949 and two more in 1955. Among the recipient chassis were Austin CXB types.

MASON

G.H. Mason & Co. Ltd was a builder of bus and coach bodies in the late 1920s. The company's address was 94–96 Percy St, Newcastle upon Tyne, but the bodyworks may have been at 69 West Street in Gateshead.

MASSEY

Massey Brothers (Pemberton) Ltd was established by three brothers in 1904 as a timber merchant and building contractor at Pemberton, near Wigan in Lancashire. From 1919, the company began building bodywork for cars, vans and charabancs. The PSV bodywork side of the business grew rapidly during the 1920s, with both bus and tram orders for Wigan Corporation and buses for other local operators. The first double-deckers came in 1927, on six-wheel Guy FCX and AEC Renown chassis, and soon also for the new Leyland TD1. The Massey bodyshops also built a number of bodies under contract to Leyland in the 1929–30 period, when that company's own body shops were under pressure.

Not best known for its coach bodywork, Massey nevertheless responded to demand in the late 1940s.

This front-entrance Leyland Titan PD2/37 was bodied by Massey for Lancaster in 1960.

Now preserved, this 1966 Leyland PD2 of Wigan Corporation shows the majestic lines of Massey's later front-entrance highbridge body.

The 1930s saw Massey concentrating on double-deck bodies, both highbridge and lowbridge types, and for trolleybuses as well as motor buses. Local municipalities were key customers, as were Cumberland Motor Services, but there were occasional orders from independent operators as well. Massey bodies were sturdily constructed and this earned them a good reputation. They were also quite distinctive, the typical body having D-shaped end windows on the lower deck and curved tops to the front upper-deck widows.

During the 1939–45 war, Massey built utility double-deck bodies for Guy and Daimler chassis, its style being distinguished by a combination of severe angularity and a deep roof. Immediately after the war, the company found itself very busy with reconstructing bomb-damaged buildings as well as new bus bodies; there was bus-body refurbishment work as well. New double-deck designs mostly retained the characteristic curved top deck windows, although the company built several variations on its basic design to suit customer preferences. As before, municipalities were its primary customers.

From 1962, Massey stopped its building and construction work, but continued to build bus bodies until 1967, when it sold out to Northern Counties (*q.v.*) of nearby Wigan.

MAUDSLAYS

Maudslays (Leeds) Ltd was a commercial vehicle builder with premises at White Lyon Road, off Tong Road, and at Grove Coach Works on the Dewsbury Road. It is best known for building mobile library bodies, but also constructed some bus bodywork in the 1960s.

MAULE

The Maule company responsible for some bus bodywork in 1919 may have been E. Maule & Son of Skinner Street, Stockton-on-Tees.

MAYHEW

Mayhew Industrial Systems Ltd, of 39 Victoria St, London SW1, was building all-metal bus bodies in the very early 1920s.

MAYROW

An otherwise unidentified company called Mayrow built single-deck bus bodywork in 1920.

MAYTHORN

Maythorn & Son was founded at Biggleswade in Bedfordshire as a carriage builder in 1842. The company became a car bodybuilder in the early twentieth century and was noted for its work on prestigious chassis, especially Daimlers, with whom it had a special relationship. From 1920 Maythorn & Son became a subsidiary of the London coachbuilder, Hooper.

The company appears to have built some PSV bodywork in 1930, perhaps to offset falling demand for car bodies, but went bankrupt in 1931.

McCLEON

See MacLeod.

MCCW

These initials stand for the Metropolitan-Cammell Carriage and Wagon Co. Ltd. *See* Metro-Cammell, MCW.

McFARLANE

Daniel McFarlane owned the Argyll Motor Garage in Dunoon and offered motor bodies between about 1920 and 1935. Just one 1921 charabanc body has been confirmed as his.

McHARDY & ELLIOTT

No details of the bodies built by this Edinburgh company have come to light. It lasted from 1920 to 1924 and moved premises from Chapel Street to West Nicholson Street and finally to Abbeyhill.

McINTYRE

McIntyre Ltd, of 13 Duncan Street in Greenock,

Renfrewshire, was a commercial bodybuilder. The company may have bodied at least one bus under contract to Albion in 1930, but is better known for a brief flurry of PSV bodybuilding activity in 1949–50, when it constructed three coach bodies for a local operator.

McLAY

William McLay set up as a blacksmith at Kirkintilloch, Dunbartonshire, in 1878. Moving into bicycles, he then entered the motor trade and became active in a number of areas. His first charabanc bodies were probably built in the early 1920s, but the company built mainly commercial bodies until 1969, when it designed a crew bus body for the former Austin-Morris mid-sized bus chassis. This was quickly developed into a PSV design and the company continued to build this and similar designs on other chassis until 1985. In this period, its main activities were building minibus, mobile library and welfare bus bodies.

McLay's Garage Ltd was at 60 High St, Kirkintilloch.

Making the stubby proportions of the Leyland EA440 chassis work as a coach was difficult, but McLay had a good try in the early 1970s. The design was called the Wayfarer.

McLENNAN

Bus operator A. & C. McLennan of Spitalfields, London E1, built coach and some bus bodies mainly for its own fleet between 1947 and 1963, but also constructed a small number for other local operators.

McLEOD

See MacLeod.

MCV

The initials stand for Marshall (Cambridge) Vehicles. *See* Marshall.

MCW

MCW was one of the leading players in the bus body-building business for a period of nearly sixty years, from the early 1930s until 1989. The initials MCW stand for Metropolitan-Cammell-Weymann Ltd, which was a joint sales organization set up in 1932 by the Metropolitan-Cammell Carriage & Wagon Co. Ltd of Birmingham (*q.v.*) and Weymann Motor Bodies of Addlestone (*q.v.*). It was established at a time when the bus industry was still feeling the effects of the Great Depression. Metro-Cammell

MCW combined Metro-Cammell's experience in steel bodies with Weymann's experience in flexible types. The picture in this 1933 advertisement is of an AEC Regal for South Wales Transport, with BEF-standard body.

Again metal-framed, this AEC Regent was one of several for Rhondda in 1934.

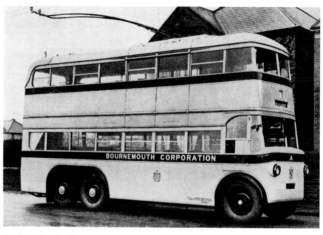

A double-deck trolleybus body on Sunbeam six-wheel chassis for Bournemouth, dating from 1934.

A neat five-bay design for the 1939 Brighton, Hove & District trolleybus intake.

This metal-bodied rear-entrance single-decker on Albion chassis was new in 1933 to Central SMT.

BELOW: The Hermes single-deck bus body was announced in 1952 as a lightweight design for underfloor-engined chassis. It is seen here on an AEC Reliance.

London Transport demanded its own design of single-deck bodywork for the RF class on AEC Regal IV chassis in the early 1950s.

The Leyland Oympian was an integral single-decker using Tiger Cub running units and constructed by Weymann. First deliveries were made in 1954.

This neat service bus body on a 1961 Leyland Tiger Cub chassis was for Edinburgh. The body was actually by Weymann.

The MCW Aurora style of the late 1950s is seen here with a forward entrance on Leyland PD3 chassis.

and Weymann were a good fit for each other, as Metro-Cammell had a promising metal-framed body but was a railway company with little experience of selling to bus operators, while Weymann had the sales organization but was still focused on bodies of composite construction.

MCW was not itself a maker of bodywork, although in later years bodies were built to common designs by both factories and carried MCW identification plates. By 1948, the combined output of the Metro-Cammell and Weymann plants was over 2,000 bodies a year. The Weymann factory was closed in 1966 and separate Metro-Cammell and Weymann brand names were dropped at the same time.

Light weight was an MCW preoccupation from quite early and in 1939–40 the company built a batch of special lightweight double-deck bodies for Coventry Corporation. Although these needed a mid-life rebuild while more conventional bodies did not, they were important pioneers. In 1948, MCW entered into a joint agreement with Leyland to build the underfloor-engined Olympic integral single-decker; though never numerous on the home market, the Olympic sold well for export, although the lightweight Olympian that followed did less well.

Built on a Leyland PD3 chassis for Ribble in 1962, this was one of a batch closely similar to earlier bodies for the same operator by Burlingham. They were nicknamed 'tanks'.

The lightweight double-deck Orion body, introduced in 1952, was a major success on Leyland PD2 and other chassis. It had a slimmed-down version of MCW's steel-framed structure, minimal panel bracing and fixed side windows, plus lacked many interior refinements in order to save around a ton in weight and also to reduce manufacturing costs. Its character was rather cruelly defined by an Edinburgh Baillie, who described the local Orion-bodied fleet as 'ungainly, inelegant, shivering masses of tin'. Later versions added opening windows and, inevitably, some weight. Nevertheless, the Orion's use of direct rubber glazing with fibreglass front and rear domes was widely copied.

MCW benefited from the closure of Leyland's body-works in 1954 and worked closely with Leyland on the development of bodies for the rear-engined Atlantean chassis, securing a sizeable proportion of early orders as a result. During the 1960s, the MCW name was most commonly associated with double-deck types, although the Weymann works at Addlestone built a number of single-deck bodies for BET fleets.

In the 1970s, MCW was still riding high as a builder of double-deckers, notably with a revised design for the rear-engined Leyland Atlantean and Daimler Fleet-line chassis that attracted fleet orders from the likes of Liverpool Corporation and Tyne & Wear PTE. Another volume contract in this period was for London Regional Transport's DMS double-deckers on Daimler Fleetline chassis, which was shared with Park Royal (q.v.).

By contrast, coach bodies were never an MCW strength. The company did make a determined assault on the lightweight coach market during the 1960s, announcing related designs called the Amethyst (for Bedford SB chassis) and Topaz (for the Bedford VAL) in 1962. Both were built by Weymann, but they were unhappy shapes. The Amethyst remained a one-off, while the Topaz was completely redesigned as the Topaz II for 1965. Even then, only six were built; small coach operators preferred the established names of Duple, Harrington and Plaxton. Undeterred, MCW tried again with the 1966 Athena, intended for Bedford VAM and Ford R192 chassis; no buyers were found and the body was restyled

Taking the boxiness away from the rear-engined double-decker became a challenge in the 1960s. These are three different MCW styles: Leyland Atlanteans for Liverpool and Nottingham; and a Daimler Fleetline for Manchester.

The Metro-Scania integral single-decker was not a success; the body design hinted at US transit buses.

and relaunched the following year as the Metropolitan. There were few takers and from 1969 the design was subcontracted to Strachans (*q.v.*), who built just ten on Ford chassis, despite high hopes of more.

MCW could see that the arrival of the Leyland National, built entirely at Workington, would reduce the numbers of chassis for them to body. So in 1969 the company got together with Swedish commercial vehicle builder Scania to develop the new Metro-Scania single-decker. Only a handful of these were built, but the design was further developed to deliver the Scania Metropolitan double-decker, based on a Scania chassis and distinguished by the asymmetric windscreen (deeper on the nearside) of its MCW body. Though a total of 662 were sold before production ended in 1978, many had a short service life because the body structure suffered badly from corrosion. MCW replaced the Metropolitan on its assembly lines with the Metrobus from 1977.

MELLIN

Mellin was an Aberdeen company that built single-deck bus bodywork in 1948, but nothing more is known about it.

MELTZ

See Metal Bodies.

METAL BODIES

Wooden body framing was the norm for PSVs until the mid-1930s, but as early as 1911 a Mr Max Meltz of London established some principles for using metal framing. He went into business with the idea in 1931 (as Meltz & Son, Longfield Avenue, Ealing) and built several 28-seater bodies for the Majestic Express fleet of Manchester and other operators. Some of these bodies had the driver's cab wholly separate from the saloon.

From March 1932, the company traded as Metal Bodies Ltd from the Dodson (*q.v.*) premises at Cobbold Road in Willesden, London NW10, but Meltz was no longer a director, having been supplanted by members of the Dodson family. Meltz himself joined Short Bros (*q.v.*) in Rochester to work on the development of aluminium bodywork, then moved to Strachans (*q.v.*) in 1933 to work on that company's metal-framed designs.

METALCRAFT

Metalcraft (Staffordshire) Ltd was founded at Newcastle-under-Lyme early in 1946 to build coach bodies in the seller's market of the post-war years. It probably busied itself with repair and refurbishment work for a while, but had recruited a senior employee from Lawton (*q.v.*) in nearby Stoke-on-Trent as General Manager and delivered its first single-deck bus and coach bodies on Tilling-Stevens chassis in 1947.

Metalcraft's ability to deliver stylish and sturdy bodies quickly earned it a full order book and in 1949 it moved from Gindley Lane in Blythe Bridge to larger premises at Blythe Bridge aerodrome, Stoke-on-Trent. Crossley, Daimler, Foden, Leyland and Maudslay chassis all received Metalcraft bodies in this period and went to independent operators. In 1950, the company built some van and trailer bodies, to offset a drop in PSV body orders; it even made some bodies for car manufacturer Alvis. That year, it also bodied its first underfloor-engined chassis with a pair of Leyland Royal Tigers for Don Everall of Wolverhampton.

Two new designs for the 1951 season were previewed on Foden chassis, one fairly conventional and the other a multi-windowed Continental design. Many of the 1951 bodies featured a new ventilation system with a 'cockscomb' inlet above the windscreens and an oval outlet above the rear window. There were bodies for Guy Wolf, Commer Avenger and Bedford SB lightweight chassis, too. Orders declined again in 1952, as domestic sales of the rear-engined Foden chassis collapsed and Metalcraft's close association with it began to count against the company.

Some refurbishing work for PMT, lengthening second-hand double-deck bodies to fit newer chassis, kept the company going, but sales collapsed completely in 1953. General Manager Roy Snape returned to Lawton and Metalcraft went into voluntary liquidation in 1954. Its Blythe Bridge premises later became home to washing-machine maker Creda. The company had built around 110 complete PSV bodies in the eight years of its existence. Most went to independent operators, but Llandudno Corporation had also been a customer, notably buying a pair of Foden single-deckers for the service to the top of the Great Orme.

METAL SECTIONS

Metal Sections was a supplier of prefabricated metal sections for a variety of uses, but began to supply framing sections for bus bodybuilders before eventually deciding to enter the PSV body business on its own behalf. It became well known in the late 1940s and early 1950s for its CKD bus bodies, supplied mainly for export. There were double-deckers, as well as single-deck buses and coaches.

The company was based at Warley in the West Midlands, but also had premises in Oldbury (initially Broadwell Works in Broadwell Road, then at Birmingham Road and also at Tividale Works, Dudley Road, West Tividale, Worcestershire). The company's well-known slogan was 'We supply a bus in a box.' A notable order in the 1960s was 341 bodies for Córas Iompair Éireann Leyland Atlanteans, to a design by the operator; they were assembled in Ireland. The business was acquired by Duple (q.v.) in 1981 and continued thereafter as Duple Metsec.

METCALFES

Metcalfes (London) Ltd claimed premises in Regent Street, London W1, and at Lincoln Works in Romford, Essex, by 1924. By 1928, the company was also at Stuart Works in Hamilton, South Lanarkshire, where it built more than 150 bodies for the Glasgow General Omnibus & Motor Services Ltd of Hamilton. Metcalfes built single-deck bodywork, including a so-called 'sun and air saloon' and a 32-seat service bus called the Mastiff that was found on AEC Reliance chassis.

By 1935, it had become F. Metcalfe & Son, and was still building bodies as late as 1938.

Dating from 1928, this 32-seater bus was built on a Maudslay ML4 chassis.

On AEC Reliance chassis in 1929, this was Metcalfes' 'New Mastiff' 32-seat body.

METRO-CAMMELL

The Metropolitan Carriage, Wagon & Finance Co. Ltd was established in Birmingham in 1845 to build railway rolling stock. It changed its name in 1912 to the Metropolitan-Cammell Carriage & Wagon Co. Ltd (MCCW); from July 1932 its bus and coach products were marketed by the joint sales organization MCW (q.v.); and from 1966 when Weymann (the W of MCW) closed down, it became Metropolitan-Cammell Ltd.

The Metro-Cammell name remained primarily associated with the railway vehicles that the company continued to build, although it is sometimes used to describe bodies built during the MCW joint organization period, as a way of indicating that the body was built by Metro-Cammell in Birmingham rather than by Weymann at Addlestone.

The Metro-Cammell bus-body plant was initially at Washwood Heath in Birmingham. However, in 1947 it was transferred to Elmdon Works in Saltley, still in Birmingham, in order to make more room for railway vehicle manufacture at Washwood Heath. The Elmdon Works had been a wartime 'shadow' factory run by Austin on behalf of the Ministry of Aircraft Production and had constructed Short Stirling bombers.

Metro-Cammell built its first bus body in 1929 and was always known for double-deck types. These were metal-framed from the earliest times and the basic

This 1947 Leyland PD1 for Salford carried a Metro-Cammell H26/24R body.

Two views of the all-metal London ST design constructed by Metro-Cammell in 1930 on AEC Regent chassis.

By 1950, when this body was built on Guy Arab chassis for Birmingham, Metro-Cammell bodies were usually sold as MCW types. This was clearly built in the Midlands and not at Addlestone, however.

Again built in the Midlands, this 1953 body on the 'tin-front' version of the Leyland Titan PD2 was one of Edinburgh Corporation's vast tram replacement fleet.

Metro-Cammell design remained in production through the 1930s. Notable users were Manchester, which had large numbers on Crossley Mancunian chassis.

After the MCW period was over, Metro-Cammell's main bus product at its Elmdon works was the export-only single-decker Leyland Olympic. This continued until 1969, when a shrinking market persuaded the board of the Laird Group (which by then owned the company) to sell Elmdon and to relocate bus building back at the original 'A Shop' in Washwood Heath. Here (as related above under MCW), the company built the Scania Metropolitan and Metrobus double-deckers during the 1960s and into the 1980s.

However, competition from abroad and the later restructuring of British Rail into private franchises ate into the railway vehicle business, while deregulation of the bus industry in 1986 was followed by a fall in demand for bus bodies. The last Metrobus was built in 1989 and that year Metro-Cammell was sold to GEC Alsthom (later known as Alstom without the 'h'). Railway work continued until 2004, when the company was closed.

METSEC

This was a trade name for Metal Sections (*q.v.*).

M.H. CARS

M.H. Cars Ltd built double-deck bodies in the first half of the 1960s under that name, subsequently becoming M.H. Coachwork Ltd. It was based at Dunmore, Antrim Road, Belfast 15. The company subsequently became Potters of Belfast.

MIDGELEY

Working from premises at North Valley Works, Ingrow, near Keighley in Yorkshire, W. Midgeley & Sons built single-deck bus bodies in the 1920s.

MIDLAND

Midland was a trading name of J.C. Sword, of County Garage, Carlisle Road, Airdrie, in Lanarkshire. Sword ran Midland Bus Services from 1924 and from 1927 built a number of bus and coach bodies for his own use. However, from 1928 he also built for other operators, in both Scotland and Northern Ireland.

The Midland bodying business continued until 1931, when the company was absorbed by Western SMT.

Córas Iompair Éireann assembled this Metsec 'bus in a box' in Ireland on a Leyland Atlantean chassis in 1966; the body design was essentially its own.

MIDLAND COUNTIES

Midland Counties built bus bodywork in the mid-1930s, but no further information is available about the company.

MIDLAND LIGHT BODIES

Midland Light Bodies Ltd was at Holbrook Lane in Coventry from 1921 to 1936, but little is known about its work. Nick Walker, in his *A–Z British Coachbuilders 1919–1960*, suggests that the company acted as a subcontractor, supplying parts and assemblies to other coachbuilders. It was active in the car-body business, but was also a commercial bodybuilder, with an output that included pantechnicons. There were some bus bodies in the first half of the 1930s.

MIDLAND RAILWAY

The Midland Railway Carriage & Wagon Co. Ltd built bodies for trams and double-deck buses and was active in the PSV world between 1901 and 1923. It was later acquired by Metropolitan-Cammell.

MILLERS

Millers was a company from Hammersmith in London that built a fourteen-seater body that ended up on a chassis owned by Eastern Counties some time around 1920.

MITCHELL (1)

John Mitchell (Greenock) Ltd was primarily a commercial vehicle dealer, with premises initially at 5 Brougham Street, then 14 Robertson Street, and finally Globe Motor Works at 4 Grey Place in Greenock, Renfrewshire. He was active as a builder of bus and coach bodywork between 1911 and 1932, in all cases for local operators.

MITCHELL (2)

The business of Robert Mitchell & Son Ltd, of 18 Shaftesbury Street, Cranstonhill, in Glasgow, began building bodies for horse-drawn vehicles in the nineteenth century alongside the veterinary practice that was the company's origins.

During the 1920s, it developed the motor-bodybuilding side of the business, mainly focusing on commercial types, but also constructing bus bodies in the mid- and late 1920s; some bodies were built under contract to Albion Motors, which wanted to supply complete vehicles. The last bodies were built in 1930 for Edinburgh Corporation.

MORGAN

The Morgan company built a fabric-panelled coach on Leyland Lion PLSC3 chassis for a Blackpool operator in the late 1920s. Nothing further is known.

MORLEY

The name of J.O. Morley is associated with a rear-entrance 32-seat coach body built in 1931 on AEC Regal chassis for Provincial of Leicester.

MOTOR & ACCESSORIES

The Motor & Accessories Co. of 40 Waterford Road, Walham Green, London SW6, had probably started out supplying what its name implied. However, by January 1925 it was also building saloon-type bus bodies on chassis such as Lancia, using what it called 'light-steel construction'.

MOTOR BODIES

Motor Bodies (Luton) Ltd, was registered as a business in May 1920 and built some single-deck bus bodywork in the ensuing decade. It was initially at Lincoln Road and later at 326 Dunstable Road in Luton.

MOTTS

Motts may have been based at Colchester, Essex. The company was associated with coach bodywork in the mid-1930s.

MOULTON

Inventor Alex Moulton, better known for his folding bicycle and Hydrolastic fluid-based suspension used on BMC cars, designed an eight-wheel underfloor-engined coach of integral construction and had it built by his own company. The single prototype was completed in 1970 but never entered service and is now preserved at the Science Museum in Wroughton, Wiltshire.

MOUNT PLEASANT

An otherwise unknown company called Mount Pleasant built some bus and coach bodywork in 1933. The Mount Pleasant name was later revived for a company building replica bodywork.

MULLINERS

Although Mulliners Ltd of Bordesley Green in Birmingham had historic and family links with the two other Mulliner bodybuilding firms – Arthur Mulliner of Northampton (q.v.) and H.J. Mulliner in London – it was actually a completely separate company. It built car bodies for Daimler and Calthorpe before the 1914–18 war and after a 1924 management buyout specialized in contract bodywork for a number of major car manufacturers. Mulliners forged close links with the Rootes Group of companies, with the Daimler-Lanchester combine and with Alvis in the 1930s.

The 1939–45 war brought military vehicle and aircraft contracts and Mulliners also secured a contract to supply single-deck bus bodies for the Bedford OWB. So although car bodybuilding resumed when peace came, Mulliners also continued working in the PSV market. There were Bedford OBs from 1946 and even an observation coach body on Morris-Commercial chassis for the Morris Works Band.

The 1950s saw Mulliners building bus bodies for the armed forces and other Government agencies on Bedford SB chassis. Some municipalities were also customers, one being Douglas, which bought some Mulliner-bodied Guy Otters in 1957. In 1958, the company exhibited a rather self-consciously futuristic coach body on a Guy Warrior chassis at the Commercial Motor Show, but that same year was bought out by car manufacturer Standard-Triumph and ceased to build PSV bodies. The PSV body interests went to Marshall of Cambridge and from 1962

This single-deck Mulliners design on Austin chassis dates from the late 1940s.

Mulliners was fully absorbed into the Leyland combine, which by then owned Standard-Triumph.

MULLINER (ARTHUR)

Arthur Mulliner of Northampton was best known for its car bodies, but as business became harder in the 1930s the company also took on some PSV work. Arthur Mulliner had premises at 78–85 and 123–133 Bridge Street in Northampton. In 1939, the company sold out to Henlys, the car distributor, and its PSV coachbuilding activities ceased.

The small coach chassis with full-front bodies built in the later 1940s and sometimes attributed to Arthur Mulliner were actually built by Mulliners of Bordesley Green (q.v.).

MULLINS

The Mullins name is associated with coach bodywork in 1938, but nothing more is known about the company.

MUMFORD

Mumford's was a small coachbuilder that sold bodies mainly to operators in the south-west of England in the 1920s and 1930s. Its works were at Billacombe, but its trading address was at Salisbury Road, Plymouth, Devon.

Although this
advertisement
dates from 1929, the
photograph shows
what is probably a
1928 ADC chassis with
a single-decker body
for Cornish Buses.

A 'GOOD' BODY
IS A
"MUMFORD"

designed by men closely in touch with actual
bus operation and has all operators' needs
cared for.

Right through the making of our bodies "quality first"
is the watchword—we use the very best of paints and
varnishes, the finest upholstering cloths and hides,
fittings and equipment.

In the hands of our experienced and skilled craftsmen
a good body must result. Once more we say that you
cannot do better than have MUMFORD COACHWORK.
Write TO-DAY for specification, photo and prices.

KEEN PRICES   PROMPT DELIVERY.

W. MUMFORD LTD., SALISBURY RD., PLYMOUTH
BODYWORK FACTORY, BILLACOMBE.

W. Mumford Ltd was established in Plymouth in 1900 by William Mumford, whose family had been coachbuilders and wheelwrights in the area since the middle of the nineteenth century. Work focused initially on car and taxi bodies, but with a move to more spacious premises in 1915, Mumford's began building bus bodies.

It became a limited company in 1922. By 1925, Mumford's was claiming to have built many convertible touring bodies for Chevrolet, Durant, Morris, Overland and other chassis. From 1933, a new garage business was opened at Abbey Garage, Saint Andrew Street, in the town. In the 1930s, the company rebodied many older chassis for Western and Southern National. Plymouth Corporation favoured Mumford bodies in the 1930s, but much of the company's work was on smaller single-deck chassis, such as the Dennis Ace, for independent operators.

At the end of 1938, Mumford's was absorbed into Western Motor Holdings Ltd and the company was turned over to war work in 1939. Although the company was briefly involved with PSV bodywork again after the war, building, for example, a coach body on Tilling-Stevens chassis in 1946 for a Lancashire operator, its days as a bus builder were effectively over. The bodybuilding activities moved to Gloucestershire and were reorganized as Lydney (*q.v.*) in 1947.

Mumford's still exists as a car dealership chain in Devon.

MURPHY

James Murphy & Sons (Dundalk) Ltd was established in 1915 and was active in the PSV market between 1951 and 1972. It appears to have catered only for Irish operators. Its address was Dublin Road, Dundalk, in County Louth.

MYERS & BOWMAN LTD

Myers & Bowman Ltd was based at Prospect Garage, Distington, in Cumberland, trading as Cumberland Coachwork. The company was formed in 1921 and is today a Toyota car dealer with premises on the Lillyhall Industrial Estate at Distington.

During World War II, Myers & Bowman repaired military vehicles and in 1946 set up a new factory with a Development Agency grant to build single-deck bus and coach bodies. About forty bodies were built before the coach-building activity ceased in 1951, including several coaches on Commer Q4 lorry chassis that went to operators as far away as Cornwall.

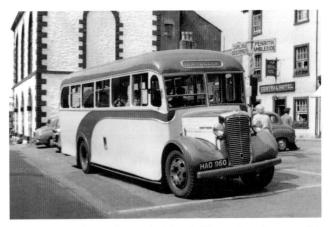

Weightman's of Keswick took this rebuilt wartime Commer Q4
lorry chassis in 1948, with a B32F body by local coachbuilder
Myers & Bowman.

NATIONAL STEAM CAR

The National Steam Car Co. was based at Chelmsford in Essex and was also known as Thomas Clarkson. It built open-top double-deck bodywork for other operators between 1912 and 1922.

NCB

See Northern Coachbuilders.

NCME

See Northern Counties.

NCV

See Nottingham Commercial Vehicles Ltd.

NEAL

The Neal name is associated with some coach bodywork in the 1930s, but nothing more is known about the company.

NEATH

Neath Coachbuilders Ltd was located at Cilfrew, Neath, in Glamorgan. The company built some coach bodies from 1947 for local operators and is still in business today as a builder of commercial vehicle bodies.

NEEPSEND

When East Lancs (*q.v.*) bought the Sheffield-based Cravens (*q.v.*) bodybuilding business in 1964, the company decided to increase its production capacity by setting up a subsidiary. This subsidiary was Neepsend Coachworks Ltd, with premises at 442 Penistone Road, Sheffield; the name was taken from the Sheffield suburb of Neepsend where the works was situated.

Neepsend built double-deck bodies to East Lancs designs between 1964 and 1968; the bodies actually carried East Lancs numbers. The Neepsend works was then closed and business was concentrated at the East Lancs premises in Blackburn.

NEW AVON

Avon Bodies Ltd was founded in 1919 as a coachbuilder and was based at Millers Road in Warwick. It was reconstructed as the New Avon Body Co. Ltd in 1922 and for most of the 1920s and 1930s focused on car bodywork, in particular on Standard chassis. However, it seems to have built some single-deck bus bodies as well in 1929–30.

By 1933, New Avon had moved to Wharfe Road, Emscote, near Warwick. Although the car bodywork business was doing well, New Avon kept one eye on commercial bodywork and entered the market for that in the late 1930s. After World War II, contracts for new bodies dried up and the company turned to repair work and hearse manufacture.

During 1973, New Avon was taken over by Ladbroke Bodies, continuing as a bespoke car converter, mainly of Jaguars, until 1985.

NEWMAN

Fred Newman was an independent operator from Walworth in south-east London who constructed open-top double-deckers for his own use from 1914. His company is a likely candidate for the Newman that rebodied a Tilling-Stevens TS3 chassis for Southdown in 1927, as a thirty-seat rear-entrance bus.

NEWNS

E.J. Newns Ltd was founded in Surrey, probably at Long Ditton, in 1924. By 1926, it had moved to nearby Thames Ditton, where it had premises at Portsmouth Road. It was best known for its car bodywork in the 1920s and 1930s, but was also building coach bodies by 1929.

Newns had the sole agency for the Newmelts sliding head by May 1931 and was focusing on all-metal construction. Among the bodies it built that year was a 26-seater on Lancia chassis. The company seems to have ceased all coachbuilding work after 1939, but later changed its name to Eagle Components (the brand name Eagle had often appeared on its car bodies) and survived into the 1970s.

NEWPORT

The Newport name associated with PSV bodywork probably indicates the Newport (Mon) Motor Co. Ltd, of Clarence Road in Newport, Monmouthshire.

NICHOLLS

The Nicholls company that built charabanc bodywork in 1928 is likely to be identical with Nicholls & Son Ltd, which traded from the Bedford Carriage & Motor Works in St Mary's Square, Bedford.

NICHOLSON

William Nicholson, of Bondgate in the Yorkshire town of Otley, built charabanc bodywork between 1912 and 1929.

NOBLE

The name of Noble is associated with the bodywork on a vehicle registered in Devon in 1930, but no other information about the company is known.

NORFOLK

The Norfolk company is known because of the thirty-seat dual-entrance bus bodywork it constructed in 1924 on Commer chassis for Glasgow. However, no further details of the company have come to light.

NORMAN

John Norman & Co. was a Cardiff bodybuilder that built some bus and coach bodies between 1923 and 1926. The company was based at 1 Market Road, Canton, Cardiff.

NORMAND & THOMSON

Normand & Thomson was a brass founder, coppersmith and engineering company based in Dunfermline, Fife, from 1905. However, for a period in the first half of the 1920s, it was also a garage proprietor at 99 Chalmers Street, and here it built a few bus and commercial bodies. The known buses were for local operators.

Normand & Thomson still existed in 2012, with premises in Dalgety Bay, where it was active in the steel business.

NORTHERN COACHBUILDERS

Northern Coachbuilders Ltd, often known by its acronym of NCB, can trace its origins back to 1920, when Samuel Smith established the Ringtons Tea Company in Newcastle upon Tyne. The company delivered by horse and cart in its early days, before moving into the construction of its own carts. From this, Northern Coachbuilders was formed in 1931, with premises at Claremont Road.

NCB began building bodywork for trams and trolleybuses and also diversified into the construction of electric delivery vehicles, especially milk floats. The Smith family established Smith's Delivery Vehicles to handle this side of the business. Later renamed Smith's Electric Vehicles and usually known as SEV, this company went on to become the world's largest manufacturer of electric vehicles. Its US subsidiary bought the parent company in 2011 and SEV is now based in Kansas City, Missouri.

In the 1930s, the NCB clientele was mainly local to the north-east of England, but it became established on a national basis after being designated to build utility double-deck bodies during the 1939–45 war. Its remit was to rebody existing chassis; among others, it rebodied twenty trolleybuses for London Transport and built a number of utility bodies to Park Royal designs on London Transport Guy Arab chassis. During this period, the company operated from a former airship hangar at Cramlington, which it shared with the Smith's electric vehicles business.

The wartime utility double-deck body evolved into a standard post-war design, which became available late in 1946 and was fitted to bus and trolleybus chassis by AEC, Daimler, Guy and Leyland. These early post-war bodies had some similarities to contemporary Weymann designs, but earned a bad reputation for sagging thanks to NCB's use of unseasoned timber – a necessity brought about by post-war supply shortages.

In 1949, NCB recruited Bill Bramham as Director and General Manager. Bramham had most recently held the same post at ECW (q.v.) and before that at Roe (q.v.); he brought with him elements of both companies' work. From 1950, NCB double-deck bodies took on a marked similarity to the ECW style of the late 1940s and were of all-metal construction with a new type of continuous-rail construction that echoed earlier Roe practice. The new design was built on both trolleybus and motor-bus chassis, but NCB came to an unexpected end in 1951 when a death-duty liability caused the company to be wound up. Its production machinery and other assets were bought by Roe (*q.v.*), but the company name did not survive.

NORTHERN COUNTIES

Northern Counties started life as Wigan Coachworks at Wigan Lane in Wigan and before the Great War had built some bus bodywork. In 1919, it was incorporated into a new company by Henry Lewis and became Northern Counties Motor & Engineering Co. Ltd. It is often known as NCME, as an easy way of distinguishing it from Northern Coachbuilders (NCB) (*q.v.*). The company started by building car bodies, but was building single-deck bus bodies for local customers by 1921 and by 1924 had abandoned car bodies. Both single-deck and double-deck bus bodies came from the company, but there were very few coaches. When the Leyland body shop came under pressure around 1930, Northern Counties was one of the companies that built bodies under contract to help out, sometimes using Leyland's own designs.

During the 1930s, Northern Counties' own double-deck bodies were characterized by narrow upper deck front windows with curved tops and thick corner pillars.

A 1959 Guy Arab IV with Northern Counties body, ordered new by Lancashire United Transport.

Potteries had this 1949 Leyland Titan rebodied by Northern Counties to lowbridge specification. The chassis is, unusually, an export-specification OPD2 type.

By the late 1930s, these had been joined by D-shaped side windows at each end of the lower deck. The company was then designated as a maker of utility bodywork during the 1939–45 war and most of the bodies it built had steel-framed construction. After the war, the company established a reputation for quality, creating a loyal client base that embraced not only Lancashire operators, but notably also included Potteries Motor Traction in the Midlands and reached as far south as Southdown. Its 1940s double-deck design had distinctive lower-deck windows in pairs with separate glass opening vents above them.

The 1950s brought both lowbridge and highbridge double-deckers from Northern Counties and a major customer was Lancashire United Transport (LUT). However, one of the best-known Northern Counties designs was for Southdown, for whom the company built a large fleet of full-front Queen Mary forward-entrance bodies on Leyland Titan PD3 chassis in the late 1950s and early 1960s. There were single-deck designs, too, one of them being adapted in 1960 with coach seats to make a dual-purpose bus for LUT.

Southdown took large quantities of these full-front bodies on Leyland PD3 chassis, now known as 'Queen Mary' types. This one was new in 1961.

In 1967, Northern Counties bought Massey Bros (*q.v.*) of nearby Pemberton, turning its factory into a paint shop and final assembly area. When a number of municipal operators in Lancashire and Cheshire amalgamated under the 1968 Transport Act to form the SELNEC (South East Lancashire, North East Cheshire) group, Northern Counties worked closely with the new authority to develop a standardized design for fleet replacements. When further reorganization turned SELNEC into the Greater Manchester PTE in 1974, Northern Counties continued to supply a large proportion of the new fleet's bodywork.

A 1975 collaboration with Foden to produce a semi-integral double-decker, the Foden-NC, was not successful and was abandoned in 1978. The 1980s were lean years, but Northern Counties survived and became a major supplier again as demand picked up in the 1990s. In 1995, the company was purchased by the Henlys group, which already owned Plaxton (*q.v.*), and from 1999 the Northern Counties name was dropped and all bodies wore Plaxton nameplates. From 2001, this changed again to TransBus International, the name of the new joint venture between Henlys and the Mayflower Corporation, which owned bodybuilder Alexander (*q.v.*) and chassis manufacturer Dennis.

When the Mayflower group failed in 2004, TransBus was sold to private investors and became Alexander Dennis. The old Northern Counties premises in Wigan were closed shortly afterwards, in January 2005.

NORTHERN MOTOR UTILITIES

Northern Motor Utilities Ltd was best known as a builder of commercial vehicle bodies and in the early days was especially associated with bodywork for the Rowntree chocolate company. Between 1928 and 1949 it also built some bus and coach bodies at its works in Walmsgate, York. The company's head office was at Foss Islands Road in the same city.

NORTHMOOR

The Northmoor name comes up in connection with some coach bodywork built in 1929, but there is no further information to identify the company.

NOTTINGHAM COMMERCIAL VEHICLES

Nottingham Commercial Vehicles Ltd built a single B29F body on a Bedford VAS chassis in 1962, calling it an NCV Alba body. The company was based at Bulwell Forest Works, Hucknall Road, Nottingham.

NUDD BROS

Nudd Bros and Lockyer Ltd was based at Ashby Road, Kegworth, in Leicestershire. It had earlier been known simply as Nudd Bros and had premises at Chilwell and on the Kegworth side of the old Castle Donington airfield. Co-founder Sydney Nudd was the son-in-law of T.H. Barton, owner of the Chilwell operator Barton.

The company became involved with bus bodywork in the late 1940s when it specialized in rebuilding worn-out bodywork that was overdue for repair after neglect during the 1939–45 war. In practice, these rebuilds sometimes amounted to an almost completely new body. Notable among them was a number of vehicles for BMMO (Midland Red) between 1949 and 1951; between 1951 and 1953, Nudd Bros also built a batch of single-deck bodies for Midland Red on that company's S13 chassis. There was also a number of coach bodies to Nudd Bros' own design.

The company sold out to Duple (*q.v.*) in 1952 and was renamed Duple (Midland). The former Nudd Bros work was absorbed by Willowbrook (*q.v.*), when Duple bought that company in 1958.

123

O'GORMAN

O'Gorman Bros were bodybuilders active at Clonmel, Co. Tipperary in the Irish Republic in the later 1920s. The late 1920s were a busy period for Irish coachbuilders and by 1928 the company was employing over 100 men. It built bus bodies on Mercedes-Benz and Graham chassis, among others, but also built commercial bodywork.

There were several changes of name after 1933 – O'Gormans, John O'Gorman & Sons, J.F. O'Gorman (1933) Ltd and J.F. O'Gorman Ltd – but the company was liquidated in 1943 after the death of founder J.F. O'Gorman.

OLDHAM CONSTRUCTION

This was one of the many companies with which Jack Crabtree was involved. It appears to have existed only briefly, during 1935, when he was also involved with Shearing & Crabtree Ltd and with Shearings of Oldham (q.q.v.).

OLDLAND

Oldland Motor Bodybuilders Ltd was best known for its commercial vehicle and ambulance bodies in the 1940s and 1950s, but also built some coach bodies from its premises at Victoria Works, High Street, Oldland Common, Bristol.

OLYMPIA

Olympia built tram, trolleybus and single-deck bus bodywork in the first half of the 1920s. The company is thought to have been Olympia Motors of 162 Melton Road in Leeds.

ORMAC

Ormac Coachworks Ltd opened for business in 1947, operating from Walmer Bridge, Longton, Preston, in Lancashire. The company built single-deck bus and coach bodies for about three years, some on Bedford chassis, but did not stay the course; a receiver was appointed in February 1950. An early example was a C20F type for a Scottish operator on a Guy Wolf chassis in 1947.

OSBORNE & HASSELL

Osborne & Hassell built coach bodywork in 1933 and is thought to have been located in Salisbury.

OSGOOD

An otherwise unknown Kent company called Osgood built a fourteen-seater body for W. Davis & Sons (Sevenoaks) on a Ford chassis in 1919.

OULTON BROAD

Oulton Broad Coachworks was based at Oulton Broad, near Lowestoft, Suffolk, and had some involvement with coach bodybuilding. Despite the geographical coincidence, it had no connection with Waveney (q.v.).

OWEN (1)

In the late 1920s, a company called Owen constructed some single-deck bus bodywork. It has been tentatively identified as W. Owen & Sons of Oxford Garage, Somerset Road, Llandudno.

OWEN (2)

A. Owen Ltd built single-deck buses and welfare-type bodies between 1954 and 1962 from premises in Clapham, London SW14.

OXLEY

Oxley Coachcraft was best known for its camper vans and minibuses, but also became involved with coach bodywork in 1974. It was based at Craven Street in Hull, Yorkshire.

PAGE & HUNT LTD
FARNHAM · · · SURREY
Telephone: Farnham 682-683

COACHMAKERS and DESIGNERS of ANY TYPE of BODY WHETHER PRIVATE or COMMERCIAL
Immediate delivery on acceptance of price and specification.

This coach body in a 1929 advertisement for the company features both forward and rear entrances.

PAGE

Page was a Colchester company involved with coach bodies in the first half of the 1930s. The company appears to have been based at 38 Church Street in Colchester, Essex, and its full name to have been P.G. Page.

PAGE & HUNT

Page & Hunt operated from premises at Wrecclesham, near Farnham in Surrey. Arthur Page was a coachpainter and former partner in another coachbuilding business, and Oliver Hunt put up the money for their joint venture in 1920. The company was active as a builder of car bodies during the 1920s; in 1929 it claimed to be a coachmaker and designer of any type of body, whether for commercial or private use. An advertisement of a picture of a single-deck coach body was used.

However, in September that year the company went into voluntary liquidation. Its London sales manager, E.D. Abbott, took over the Page & Hunt premises and equipment, and set up a new company in his own name. Abbott's (*q.v.*) continued with the construction of bus bodies.

PALMER (1)

Palmer's (Dover) Ltd was based at Cherry Tree Avenue and constructed some PSV bodies in the first half of the 1920s. The company appears to have been associated with Connaught (*q.v.*).

PALMER (2)

Another company called Palmer that constructed coach and single-deck bus bodies in the first half of the 1920s has been tentatively identified as Palmer Coachbuilders Ltd of Western Works, Twickenham Road, Hanworth, in Middlesex.

PAPLEY

James W. Papley was a wheelwright and motor body-builder at Burgh Road, Lerwick, on the Shetland Islands. He built a few small-capacity bus bodies for local operators between 1925 and 1937, but the business did not survive the 1939–45 war.

PARK

William Park was a Glasgow smith and cartwright who began building bodies for horse-drawn vehicles and then moved into the motor body business. He became a specialist in ambulances, but also built small numbers of PSV bodies in the early 1920s. After 1935, Park's known bus bodies were welfare types on Albion chassis for Glasgow Corporation. The company was at 40 Crawford Street in Partick and later at 40–44 Kilbirnie Street, off Eglington Street.

PARKES

Parkes of Rochester in Kent constructed single-deck bus bodywork in 1925. Nothing more is known about the company.

PARK ROYAL

Park Royal was one of Britain's top bus and coach body-builders from 1930 to 1980. It was formed in April 1930 out of the ashes of Hall Lewis (*q.v.*) and was initially called Park Royal Coachworks Ltd. Based at Abbey Road, Park Royal, in London NW10, the company was run by the Yager family until October 1946, when it was turned into a public company with the new name of Park Royal Vehicles. In July 1947, it absorbed the Roe (*q.v.*) body-building company of Leeds. From 1948 it belonged to the Associated Commercial Vehicles (ACV) group; in

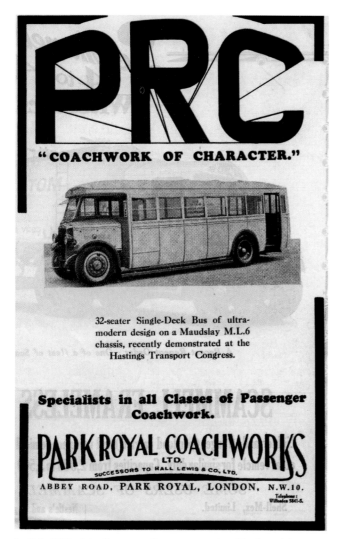

In this 1930 advertisement, the company is still advertising itself as 'Successors to Hall Lewis & Co. Ltd'. The bus had a B32R body on Maudslay ML6 chassis.

Confident enough by later in 1930 to omit any reference to Hall Lewis, the company pictured one of its B30R-bodied AEC Regals for Western Welsh.

This B32R body was on a 1931 AEC Regal for Rhondda

A Glasgow double-decker, with that operator's ungainly destination indicator, represents the early Park Royal offerings, with three front windows on the top deck.

Those three top windows are present again on this 1933 H52R body on a Daimler chassis for an unidentified operator.

The company's new metal-framed double-deck design had a steeply sloping front. It is seen here on a 1935 delivery for Huddersfield and a 1936 AEC Regent for Provincial of Gosport.

1962 it was absorbed into the Leyland Motor Corporation along with its ACV parent and in 1968 the group title was changed to British Leyland Motor Corporation when further mergers with car and commercial vehicle makers took place. The company finally closed in 1979 as a result of changes elsewhere in the Leyland group.

During the 1930s, Park Royal developed a strong relationship with London chassis builder AEC and the two companies' products were often associated. The standard Park Royal double-deck body of the period was based on designs from AEC for its 1931 Regent demonstrators. A small number of railcars with AEC engines was built alongside the primary work of bus production. Nevertheless, the early years under Hymie Yager were not always happy ones and in mid-1934 Park Royal's General Manager and many of his staff resigned and

went to Weymann (q.v.). Park Royal recruited Bill Black from Beadle (q.v.) to take over at the helm and by the end of the 1930s the company was building around 1,000 bodies a year, for operators all over Britain and also overseas.

Wartime saw the company building military vehicles and components for Halifax bombers as part of the London Aircraft Production Group, but Park Royal was also among the more prolific builders of wartime utility double-deck bodies between 1942 and 1945. It had built the prototype on a Guy Arab 5LW in March 1942. The Park Royal utilities nevertheless had their own

This is the rear view of a 1936 H28/28R body on an AEC Regent chassis for Morecambe & Heysham Corporation.

The Royalist coach body is seen here on an Albion Viking chassis.

London Transport's classic RT design was jig-built by a number of coachbuilders, including Park Royal. A small number was built for other operators, including St Helens Corporation, which took this example in 1950.

The body design for the AEC Bridgemaster needed a two-tone finish to relieve its rather square lines. This one, originally a demonstrator, was sold to Liverpool.

characteristics, notably a peaked dome at the front of the upper deck.

After the war, Park Royal became the lead body-builder for London's new RT class Regents, constructing a total of 3,280 bodies for them between 1946 and 1954. In the late 1940s, the company became part of the newly established Associated Commercial Vehicles (ACV) group, together with bodybuilder Roe (q.v.), and this brought even closer co-operation with AEC, who were also part of the group. Working together, the two companies established a formidable partnership that supplied major fleets all over the UK and, in particular, secured the contracts to build nearly 2,000 of London Transport's new semi-integral Routemasters from 1958.

Some of the Routemaster thinking was reflected in another AEC/PRV collaboration, the semi-integral Bridgemaster low-height double-decker of 1956. However, this was not a great success because operators preferred more choice of bodywork. From 1958, the standard Park Royal double-deck design, often seen on AEC Regent V chassis, then adopted a lightweight structure very like MCW's Orion body and more or less dictated by the demands of the BET group of operators. Not all those delivered had the same severity of line, but most had a distinctive ventilator above the top-deck windows, in some cases associated with forced-air ventilation.

In post-war years, single-deck bodies were in the minority at Park Royal, although the company did produce the frames for the 1950–2 GNR Gardner buses, which were completed in the GNR workshops. From 1953, it collaborated with AEC on the integral-construction Monocoach service bus, but this was never a strong seller and lasted only until 1958.

Coach bodies of the period included the 1954 Royalist design, which reflected ECW influences – not surprising because Park Royal's new Director and General Manager had come from ECW. However, coaches were not really Park Royal's forte; it was much more comfortable building dual-purpose designs, of which companies such as Aldershot & District and East Kent took good numbers in the early 1960s. These were built to a BET standard pattern that was also constructed by Alexander, Weymann and Willowbrook (q.q.v.). The Royalist name was revived in the late 1960s for a coach body on the new rear-engined Albion Victor, but only six were made.

As the era of front-engined double-deckers drew to a close, Park Royal and Roe, which was still using its own name, collaborated on a new standardized double-deck design for the rear-engined Leyland Atlantean and Daimler Fleetline chassis. This was introduced in 1968 and earned the company good sales from municipal operators. In its turn, it gave way to Park Royal's design for the new Leyland Titan B15 double-decker in 1977. However, when production of this vehicle was moved to the Leyland National (q.v.) plant at Workington in September 1979, the Park Royal company closed down. The old factory site was subsequently turned into a business park.

PARSONS

Active in the 1960s, a company called Parsons built some single-deck bus bodies. The company has been tentatively identified as Parsons & Parsons Garage Ltd, of Potter Street, Harlow, in Essex.

PASS

Thomas Pass Ltd built some bus and charabanc bodies in Coventry in 1920–1, but ran into financial difficulties that year. It sold its premises in Hill Street to another coachbuilding company that quickly took on the name of Carbodies. The Pass company had been established in the mid-nineteenth century and originally had premises at West Orchard and Little Park Street, in Coventry.

PEARCE & DOBSON

This company built single-deck bus and charabanc bodies in the first half of the 1920s, operating from premises at Grove Street, Stockton-on-Tees.

PEARSONS

Pearsons was an old-established Liverpool firm of coachbuilders that capitalized on the demand for new bodywork immediately after World War II. Originally at 3, 5 and 7 Shaw Street, Liverpool 6, it occupied new and larger premises in Overbury Street during the war years, where the workforce constructed large numbers of vehicles for the military and for some Government departments.

Once the war was over, Pearsons began by rebuilding ex-military vehicles, then moved into reconditioning worn-out PSV bodies and constructing new bodies for older chassis. From 1948, there were bodies on Austin, Bedford, Commer, Daimler and Leyland chassis, and some double-deckers followed in 1949. These were built in a new works at 168 Smithdown Lane, Liverpool 8. However, once the boom was over, Pearsons withdrew from the PSV market and its last bus bodies appear to have been built in 1951.

Pearsons also ran coaching companies, starting with Happy Days Motorways (James Pearson & Sons) that was sold to Ribble and Crosville in 1935. After the

Neat, if not particularly original, is this 1948 coach body on an AEC Regal chassis.

There is both Duple and Harrington influence in this 1948 body by Pearsons on a Daimler CVD6 chassis. It was new to Harman's Motor Service of Wolverhampton.

Pearsons four-bay double-deck body is seen here on an AEC Regent chassis.

requisite period of abstention from coaching activities, it then established Sunniways Coaches (Pearsons of Liverpool) Ltd in 1946.

PENMAN

A.C. Penman Ltd initially operated from the Queensbury Motor Works in Dumfries, having been established in the nineteenth century to build and repair horse-drawn carriages. From 1901, the company began supplying bodies for Albion cars and from 1906 there were small buses as well. In the 1920s, a separate coachbuilding works was opened at Rosefield in Dumfries. There was a variety of bus bodies through to 1936, but by then the company was better known as a builder of truck bodies and cabs. Some welfare-type bus bodies were constructed in the 1950s, but since 1945 Penman has been primarily a maker of specialist bodywork.

The company still exists as a commercial and military vehicle builder, now with the name of Penman Engineering Ltd and based at the Heathall Industrial Estate in Locharbriggs, Dumfries.

PENNINE COACHCRAFT

Pennine Coachcraft was set up in 1960 as a wholly owned subsidiary of the chassis maker Seddon, to build bodies for its own range of PSVs and trucks. It also built single-deck bodies on other manufacturers' chassis during the 1960s, including both underfloor-engined types (such as AEC Reliance) and rear-engined types (AEC Swift, Bristol RE, Daimler Fleetline and Leyland Atlantean).

Looking more like a toy than a real bus is this Pennine-bodied Seddon midibus for SELNEC, dating from 1972.

The company operated from Moss Lane Works, Royton, Oldham, in Lancashire until its closure in 1975 after Seddon (by then Seddon Atkinson) had been bought by International Harvester.

PERFECTA

Perfecta Bodies constructed double-deck bodywork in the 1930s, apparently from premises in the Greater London area.

PETERSON

Arthur Peterson was a commercial and passenger vehicle bodybuilder from Market Street, Lerwick, on the Shetland Islands. He built PSV bodies for local operators between 1924 and 1934.

PETTY

Petty was a firm of coachbuilders from Hitchin in Hertfordshire, active in the 1920s and early 1930s. Daniel Petty had been a wheelwright in Cheshunt, Herts, from around 1910 and joined forces with his younger brother Edward to create D. & E. Petty. By 1923, they were building charabanc bodies.

In 1928, the two brothers moved to High Wycombe, Bucks, where they became involved with Wycombe Motor Bodies (*q.v.*), which built bodies for Gilford chassis. In their absence, a third brother, Frank, kept the Cheshunt business going. In 1929 the brothers returned, to larger premises in Hitchin at the junction of Park Street, Queen Street and Bridge Street. They built only single-deck bodywork, much of it on AJS chassis. So when AJS went under in 1931, Petty went with it and the company's coachbuilding activities ended in 1932.

Nevertheless, the company carried on as a car dealership and in 1935 Petty Bros Ltd of Cheshunt was advertising a batch of 32-seater AEC Regal coaches from a cancelled order. The Hitchin factory became a London Transport bus garage in September 1933.

PHILLIPS

Henry Phillips & Sons Ltd was listed as an omnibus builder in trade directories for Bridgend, Wales, at the end of the 1920s. Its address was Central Garage, on Darwen Road.

PHOENIX (1)

The Phoenix Coachworks Ltd was established at Church Street in Ware, Hertfordshire, at the end of the 1914–18 war. It built both bus and coach bodies in the first half of the 1920s, but was taken over by the works foreman, W.L. Thurgood (*q.v.*), in April 1925. It subsequently took his name.

PHOENIX (2)

The Phoenix Cabinet and Joinery Co. of Todmorden, Yorkshire, constructed at least five open-top double-deck bodies on Leyland chassis for the local municipal operator between 1921 and 1925. A 1921 example has been preserved by well-known early Leyland aficionado Mike Sutcliffe and is usually on display at the Manchester Museum of Transport.

PHOENIX (3)

Phoenix Coachworks Ltd was a name also used by Arnold & Comben (*q.v.*). This company had a head office in London but its works were at East Street, Farnham, in Surrey. Its 1925 offerings included fourteen- and twenty-seat bodies on Berliet, Chevrolet and Reo chassis, and in 1928 it claimed to have built 'England's first sleeping coach' with two 'decks'.

In 1929, Phoenix was absorbed into the new company established by E.D. Abbott (*q.v.*) in Farnham and some early advertisements for that company used the Phoenix name.

PICKERING

R.Y. Pickering & Co. Ltd was established at Wishaw in Lanarkshire in 1864, initially as a builder and repairer of railway rolling stock. However, a series of business reversals in the early years of the twentieth century led to the Pickering family being ousted. Under new management, the company gradually returned to health and then turned to new markets in the early 1920s; among these, it began to construct bus bodies in 1922.

Although bodies were offered for a variety of chassis, the one pictured in this 1925 advertisement is a twenty-seater on Reo chassis.

Only a small number of bus bodies was built before Pickering became a subcontractor to chassis manufacturer Albion in 1927, constructing bodies so that Albion could offer complete vehicles for sale. There were tram bodies, too, initially for Glasgow Corporation in 1928. The Pickering order book was full in the early 1930s, most bus bodies being single-deck types, while the orders for tramcars continued, including a contract for repair work from the London Passenger Transport Board. By the time war broke out in 1939 the company had put its name on more than 300 bus bodies and around twenty tram bodies in all. Almost without exception, these had been for Scottish operators.

However, a series of deaths and illnesses within the senior management led to the company being taken over in 1938 by the ship builders Lithgow Ltd of Port Glasgow. The Pickering name was nevertheless retained and during the 1939–45 war the company was designated as a manufacturer of gun tractors and light military vehicles. From 1942 it also joined the select band of bodybuilders who constructed double-deck bodies to the wartime utility specification. Over seventy utility bodies came from the Pickering works, most of them highbridge types, but these quickly acquired a reputation for structural deterioration; there were single-deck 'utility' bodies on Albion chassis, too, from late 1945. During the war and the early post-war period, the Pickering works also overhauled or reconditioned large numbers of PSVs.

After the war, Pickering continued to build bus bodies for a few more years and also remained involved with

Like many other makers of the time, Pickering catered mainly for local operators, the 1926 example here being for Lanarkshire.

tramcars; among its last were ten double-deckers for Aberdeen Corporation Tramways in 1949. The last of more than 200 post-war bus bodies was constructed in 1950.

The company continued to operate in the heavy engineering business until the mid-1960s, when it merged with North British Welding Company to become Norbrit-Pickering Engineering Ltd in Wishaw. This company in turn was dissolved in 1987.

PICKTREE

The Picktree Coach & Engineering Co. Ltd was established in September 1947 at Picktree Lane, Chester-le-Street, in County Durham. The owners seem to have aimed to cash in on the post-war boom in demand for coach bodywork; siting their business almost next door to the local Northern General depot can hardly have been coincidental. Indeed, some sources claim that this operator had a financial interest in Picktree.

One way or another, most of Picktree's output did indeed go to Northern General. The company secured the design services of Doug Pargeter, who had been with Northern Coachbuilders, and produced half-cab single-deckers that included some intriguing AEC Regal rebuilds and by 1954 some underfloor-engined Guy Arab coaches.

The company's coachbuilding activities were over by the mid-1950s, but it continued in business as a motor dealer, eventually closing down in 1996.

PITT (1)

Pitt & Sons built some single-deck bus bodies from premises at Salisbury Street, Fordingbridge, Hampshire, in the early 1920s.

PITT (2)

A second company called Pitt, this time Norman H. Pitt, offered coach bodies from premises at Salisbury Street in Amesbury, Wiltshire, at the end of the 1920s.

PLAXTON

Plaxton is one of the oldest names on the current British PSV scene, having been founded as a joinery workshop in Scarborough, Yorkshire, in 1907 by Frederick William Plaxton. The company first expanded into building work, but from 1919 began to build charabanc bodies on Ford Model T chassis. More important at the time was car bodywork, with Plaxton building on several prestigious makes, although it became associated mainly with Crossley.

As demand for luxury cars declined in the early 1930s, the charabanc and coach-body business became more important. Demand was strong enough for Plaxton to expand in 1936 into new premises at Seamer Road, still in Scarborough. Although many buyers in the early days had been local to Scarborough, the company's use of independent dealers as agents allowed its products to reach a

This 1929 offering is neat, but hardly special in appearance; it was quality that gained Plaxton its name.

Dating from 1938 is this 26-seat Plaxton coach body on a Bedford WTB chassis. It was new to E.C. James of Pembroke Dock.

F. Oade & Sons Ltd of Heckmondwike, Yorkshire, bought this Plaxton C32F body on Leyland Tiger TS8 chassis in 1939. Plaxton called this its type D3 design.

wider market, thereby bringing great success with independent operators throughout the north of England.

By the middle of the decade, Plaxton had settled on a distinctive house style, featuring a very rounded front profile, a sloping tail and side windows that were grouped together. Side sweeps, often painted in a colour that contrasted with the main body, were also a characteristic. Plaxton bodies were common on AEC Regal and Leyland Tiger chassis among the heavyweights, while there were many for the lightweight coach market on Bedford and Dodge chassis.

The factory was given over to aircraft production during World War II, but returned to its former business at the end of 1945. In the late 1940s, it drew on its 1930s designs for front-engined chassis and also bodied smaller types like the Austin CXB and Bedford OB, but like many other companies found the transition to styles suitable for underfloor-engined types rather tricky. These early post-war bodies were known only by alphanumeric codes such as L3 and Q2.

Names for the Plaxton bodies arrived at the 1950 Commercial Motor Show, which also brought two new designs for the latest 30ft (9m) by 8ft (2.4m) dimensions. The Envoy was for front-engined chassis and the Crusader for underfloor-engined types; many early examples of both types had rear wheel spats. However, the Crusader name quickly disappeared in favour of Venturer and that name was then used for designs on lightweight front-engined chassis as well, such as the Bedford SB and Commer Avenger. So the slightly awkward-looking Venturer became Plaxton's standard design from 1952. Both centre-entrance and front-entrance variants were available and the Venturer II introduced wrap-around

glazing at the rear and the oval grille that embraced the headlamps, a Plaxton trademark feature for many years to come.

The Venturer gave way to the Consort at the Commercial Motor Show in 1956. A brief move to a differently shaped grille persuaded Plaxton to return to the style its customers loved and there were four variants of the Consort before it was replaced in 1961 by the Embassy. This was an evolutionary design, the major difference being in the window line; an optional raised-floor version moved the driver forwards to allow room for more seats

This striking thirty-seat body from 1947 was on a Bedford OB chassis modified to forward-control. The vehicle was new to Galley of Newcastle.

The oval grille was a trademark of Plaxton design by 1960, when this Consort body was built on Ford Thames chassis.

This was Plaxton's Venturer body, a 1954 example on Commer Avenger chassis for Ripponden & District.

and there were even a few 36ft (11m) versions of this multi-window design. There were also some single-deck bus bodies – never a Plaxton strength – in this period. These carried the Highway name and were introduced in 1957; adding a Consort front end made the dual-purpose Conway design in 1959.

However, it was the 1959-season Panorama that opened a new era for the company and presented the first credible threat to Duple's domination of the coach market for many years. It resulted from a request for a distinctive new style from Sheffield United Tours. Though it bowed to contemporary taste with a large chrome grille and was to some extent derived from the existing Consort, the Panorama also made pioneering use of forced ventilation (made by Smiths Instruments). This allowed fixed side windows, of which there were only three, but all were much larger than on other contemporary styles. The resulting clean side profile was immediately distinctive and very pleasing, as well as providing an excellent view out for the passengers. With periodic updates, but always retaining the classic lines of the original, the Panorama remained in production right through to 1975.

In 1961, Plaxton expanded into a new factory at East-field, while retaining its original premises as well. The Panorama was refreshed with paired headlamps and a version for the latest 36ft chassis became available, Britain's first 36ft coach probably being a Panorama-bodied AEC Reliance for Sheffield United Tours. There were still only three huge side windows and the design became a major success for the company. It found favour with both independent operators and the large fleets, Ribble becoming a major customer for the type. The Panorama

was further refreshed for 1963 with a clever roof design that made the body look even longer than it was and a two-piece wrap-around rear window; a version for the three-axle Bedford VAL was also introduced, bearing the simple name of Val.

For 1965, the Panorama was further revised by Ogle Design, taking on a new front end and being marketed as Panorama I and Panorama II types. The Panorama I was the big seller and Midland Red took a large quantity. The Panorama II was a cheaper option without the forced ventilation and with vent windows in the large side glasses. Both were available for underfloor-engined heavyweight and front-engined lightweight chassis alike and those on Bedford VAM chassis were sometimes badged as 'Vam' types. Plaxton also built a small number of coach bodies for the new rear-engined Leyland Panther in the 1960s, but sales never amounted to much.

Panorama I production ended in 1970, but a new Panorama Elite model had been announced during 1968. This was another Ogle design for Plaxton and featured gently curved side windows for the first time on a British-built

The full-size design was scaled down for the short Albion Nimbus chassis – arguably without complete success.

coach, while the interior made extensive but tasteful use of modern laminate materials. It was also available with a dual-purpose specification, in order to qualify for the Government's Bus Grant. A mildly modified Panorama Elite II followed in 1970 and the final iteration of the series was the Panorama Elite III with new vertical rear lights and (on most examples) the emergency exit at the rear rather than the front. Many of these later Panorama bodies went on to Bristol RE chassis for the operators of the National Bus Company. The Panorama Elite was again a huge success, with more than 6,000 of all types built in a seven-year production run.

While the Panorama catered for the buyers of under-floor-engined heavyweight chassis, those who wanted Plaxton coachwork on lightweight front-engined chassis such as the Bedford SB and Ford Thames were offered the Embassy. Though recognizably a Plaxton design, this was altogether more conservative, with multiple side windows. A version of the Embassy was also put forward for the three-axle Bedford VAL in 1962, but it did not prove popular and Plaxton replaced it with an Embassy II design incorporating the long side windows of the Panorama. After 1962, there was also a Plaxton bus body, called the Derwent; this was a significant development for Plaxton and was successful with several operators in the north-east, although it was never as popular as the coach types and went out of production in 1977.

The Panorama Elite gave way to the Supreme in 1975, now of (almost) all-metal construction after Duple had

The big-windowed Panorama was a hugely influential classic design. Here it is on a 36ft Leyland Leopard delivered in 1964 to Ribble subsidiary Standerwick.

The Panorama was adapted for the three-axle Bedford VAL chassis, too. This one, for Baddeley Bros of Holmfirth, Yorkshire, dates from 1969.

Though this 1951 body is typically assured behind the front axle line, the front end shows the difficulties even major coachbuilders had in building full-fronts on vertical-engined chassis. Underneath is a 30ft (9m) Maudslay Marathon; the real registration of this coach was DHL 245 and it went to Hudson of Leeds.

The Panorama design was long-lived – this is a 1974 Panorama Elite III version on Bedford YRQ chassis.

made good sales with its all-metal Dominant competitor for the Panorama. Once again, this was a major success, allowing Plaxton to retain its position at the top of the UK market. Six marks of Supreme were eventually built for different sizes of chassis and there was even a semi-integral version, while the Mini Supreme was exactly what its name suggested.

The Supreme's introduction was followed in 1976 by that of the Viewmaster, the first European-style high-floor coach body (with luggage room under the floor) to be made in Britain. This took time to attract UK buyers, but did prove popular in Europe. Plaxton became a subsidiary of Alexander Dennis in 2007 and remains Britain's leading coachbuilder today.

PLYMOUTH COMMERCIAL

Plymouth Commercial Bodies Ltd was based at Colebrook, Plympton, near Plymouth in Devon and built coach bodywork in 1968.

POCHIN

Cedric Pochin set up a joinery business in Manchester in 1935 and was later joined by his brother, Arthur. The company has since diversified into the construction industry and property development, and is today known as the Pochin Group.

In 1947–8, it briefly flirted with bus-body construction as well, building a total of just six bodies on Leyland Tiger PS1 chassis from premises at Middlewich in Cheshire.

POLLON

S.F. Pollon Ltd was a Manchester company that built single-deck bus bodies in the early 1920s.

PORTEOUS

James Porteous had opened a blacksmith's business in Linlithgow, West Lothian, during the late nineteenth century, but in about 1907 added a coachbuilding operation at a separate address, 283 High Street. In 1915, James Porteous & Sons moved to Bo'ness Road, Linlithgow. Here, they built bus bodies on a variety of chassis between 1919 and 1936, including many that were subcontracted from Albion Motors. All went to Scottish operators. The Porteous business had closed by 1938.

PORTSMOUTH AVIATION

Very little information has been discovered about Portsmouth Aviation, which built a number of coach bodies in the years following the 1939–45 war. These included a number of C32R types on Bristol L6B chassis for Wilts & Dorset.

As its name suggests, the company was associated with the aircraft industry. It had its headquarters at Portsmouth Airport and had started life as Portsmouth, Southsea and Isle of Wight Aviation in 1932; it had earlier been based on the Isle of Wight with the name Inland Flying Services and flew local air-ferry services.

The company had already begun to expand its business by carrying out aircraft maintenance and modification before the 1939–45 war. During that period, it was obliged to focus on aircraft repair work for the military and when peace came it seems to have reacted like so many other companies that had acquired a pool of skilled labour in the war. It changed its name to Portsmouth Aviation in 1946 and, in addition to designing its own aircraft, turned to the boom industry of PSV bodybuilding. This was not to last, however, and Portsmouth Aviation bodywork remained rare, petering out altogether at the start of the 1950s.

The company remains in business, still at Portsmouth Airport.

PORTSMOUTH COMMERCIAL

Portsmouth Commercial Motors was based in the town of the same name and was building bus bodywork at the end of the 1920s.

POTTER

Potter of Belfast was formerly M.H. Cars (*q.v.*). It was active as early as the 1920s, when it built single-deck bus bodies on Leyland Lion chassis for the Great Southern Railway in the Irish Republic. During the later 1960s it was taken over by Alexander's of Falkirk, becoming W. Alexander & Sons (Belfast) Ltd. *See* Alexander (Belfast).

PRAILLS

Praills Motors Ltd was based at Holmer Road in Hereford and was part of the larger Praill Group of garages. By 1949, the company was refurbishing the utility bodies on wartime Bedford OWB chassis, fitting them with interior panelling, luggage racks and even Dunlopillo seats. It also offered 'unregistered' Bedford chassis fitted with brand-new 28- or 29-seat coach bodies, although these were in fact bodied by Longford (*q.v.*).

PRESTON

The Preston Motor Bodybuilding Co. was active from 1919 and in the early 1920s. It probably catered only for local operators. Among its products were interchangeable lorry and charabanc bodies for Scout Motor Services of Preston, on ex-military Leyland lorry chassis, and some rebodies of similar chassis for Ribble.

PROGRESSIVE

The Progressive Motor Co. of Pembroke Works, Pembroke Street, London N1 built single-deck bus and charabanc bodies in the first half of the 1920s.

PUMPHREY

The Pumphrey that built some coach bodies in the mid-1930s may be P.W. Pumphrey of Premiere Garage in Flint, Wales. The company was an agent for Dodge chassis in the 1930s.

PYE

Pye appears to have been a Lancashire firm that built single-deck bus bodies in the 1920s.

QUORN

Crawford Prince-Johnson Ltd (*q.v.*) was a Leicester company that also traded under the name of Quorn Coachworks in the early 1950s.

RAINE

Herbert Raine & Sons was founded in 1893 and from quite early times undertook commercial bodybuilding work. PSV bodies were a natural outcome of this and there were bus and coach bodies in the 1930s. However, Raine is best known for its wartime work, when it extensively rebuilt worn-out bodies, mainly for operators in the north-east.

It continued this activity in the boom period of the late 1940s and also mounted a number of older bodies on to new chassis. Thereafter, the company reverted to commercial bodies and to repair work, before finally closing in 2001. Its address was Tower Coachworks, King Street, Spennymoor, County Durham.

RAINFORTH

Based at Monks Road in Lincoln, W. Rainforth & Sons Ltd was an old-established agricultural iron works that could trace its origins back to around 1880. The company was particularly associated with lightweight chassis in the 1930s, building on extended Chevrolet chassis. It was an approved bodybuilder for the Bedford WLB and WHB and also constructed a few bodies on the WLG chassis.

It built a batch of twenty Leyland Cubs for the Lincolnshire Road Car Co. and a pair of futuristic coach bodies on Leyland Tiger chassis, but subsequently became bankrupt. Resurrected, the company continued until around 1950, its 1940s products including a pair of Leyland Tigers for Wright of Louth. *See also* Applewhite.

RAMSAY

Ramsay (Peebles) Ltd was a motor trader at St Andrews Road in Peebles, Scotland. In 1949, it built a single thirty-seat coach on Commer Commando chassis for a local operator.

RAMSDEN

'Any type of body supplied for mounting on any type of chassis' was how Joseph Ramsden advertised his coach-building business in the 1920s. It was not a particularly original approach, but it typified the aspirations of any number of small bodybuilders. Joseph Ramsden Ltd had been formed in April 1920 and described itself as 'The Motor Bodybuilders' and was based at Valley Road, Liversedge, in Yorkshire. Among the company's products were saloon bodies for Hebble and South Yorkshire Motors.

Ramsden was still advertising its wares in 1930, but seems to have disappeared from the PSV scene in 1933.

R&K

See Reeve & Kenning.

RANDSOME

The name of Randsome Bodybuilders is associated with some charabancs built in the 1920s, but nothing more is known of the company responsible. The name may be nothing more than a corruption of Ransomes (*q.v.*).

RANSOMES, SIMS & JEFFERIES

Bus bodybuilding was only one of the multiple activities carried out by Ransomes, Sims and Jefferies Ltd. This

The Ramsden business managed to capture orders from some large operators, such as Hebble.

This 31-seat bus body on Karrier chassis was built in 1930 for Heather Bell Services at Tow Law in Weardale.

Built on a Dennis chassis in 1926, this Ransomes bus body for Yorkshire Woollen District was to standard British Electric Federation design.

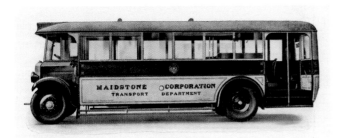

This 1929 31-seat Ransomes bus body on Leyland chassis was one of four for Maidstone Corporation.

At the other end of the country, this Ransomes service bus body was for the LNER in Aberdeen, again in 1929.

On a smaller Dennis chassis is this 1929 Ransomes saloon body for the Ortona Motor Co. of Cambridge.

Ipswich company had become a major producer of agricultural machinery after being established at Norwich in 1789 as an iron foundry. In the nineteenth century it had diversified into railway equipment (although this part of the business was separated in 1869) and in the early twentieth century it also became involved in trolleybus manufacture.

Bodywork was a natural extension of this side of the business and the company began building van bodies in September 1920 and bus bodies a month later. The company of course bodied its own single-deck and double-deck trolleybus chassis, as well as building charabanc and saloon bodies on other makers' chassis. 'There is a Ransomes' body for any type of chassis,' read one advertisement of the time. Ransomes Bus Bodies would build to BET specifications, too.

Examples of its work included a 1928 single-decker on Leyland PLSC3 chassis for St Helens Corporation; a batch of six-wheel Guys for Derby Corporation in 1930; single-deckers on Tilling-Stevens chassis, again for Derby, in 1931; and some double-deckers for Eastbourne Corporation on AEC Regent chassis the same year. During the 1930s, Ransomes also built bus bodies for export, one notable order being for the Egypt General Omnibus

Company. Commercial bodies included a number of box vans for the Post Office and some Austin 7s for the War Office.

The last Ransomes bodies seem to have been built in 1941, when the company was turned over to war work, although the last chassis (for Norway) was not built until 1948. The company's well-known address was always Orwell Works, in Ipswich.

READING

Alfred Reading set up his business at Southsea, Hampshire, in the 1880s to build the bodies for horse-drawn vehicles. He became an agent for Rover cars and constructed commercial bodywork, including some for ice-cream vans.

During the 1939–45 war, Reading & Co. Ltd built ambulance bodies. Its first brush with PSV bodywork seems to have been in 1943, when it rebodied a 1930s AEC Regal as a double-decker for local operator Provincial (Gosport & Fareham).

After the war, Reading continued to work closely with Provincial on some of its unique rebuilds of both double-deckers and single-deckers in the 1950s and 1960s. Reading built many single-deckers for other concerns, some double-deckers on AEC Regent III chassis for companies such as Wake's Services, and also bodied a number of double-deck motor buses and trolleybuses for Portsmouth Corporation.

In 1949, it was Reading who built the first body on a Jensen chassis, a full-front type of composite construction. It developed a fourteen-seat body called the Lilliput for smaller PSV chassis, such as Austin and Karrier types; there was also a 21-seater on Dennis Pax chassis for Jersey in 1950. Between 1960 and 1965, Reading built a number of bus bodies on the small Albion Nimbus underfloor-engined chassis for Guernsey and a few on the small Bedford VAS.

The business was later sold to Sparshatts (*q.v.*) and later to Wadham Stringer (*q.v.*), and eventually closed in 1974.

REAL / REALL

REAL was named after its founder, R.E. Allman, who established the REAL Carriage Works at Kew Bridge, London. He had done his apprenticeship with Brown, Hughes & Strachan (*see* Strachan & Brown) in 1912 and had been with Sopwith Aviation during the 1914–18 war.

REAL was founded in 1921 and initially focused on building charabanc and bus bodies. Chassis were the usual mix of the time and included Bean, Chevrolet, Dennis, GMC, Lancia, Morris and Reo. There was a move to Pope's Lane in Ealing, London W5, in 1929 and the company subsequently expanded into building car bodies as well.

These two saloon bodies on Chevrolet chassis, seen in a 1929 advertisement, were typical of their times.

The design seen here on a 1932 advertisement was also quite conventional.

This coach on Gilford chassis, with clerestory roof for the Westminster Omnibus Company, dates from 1928.

The company continued building single-deck bus bodies on smaller chassis such as Commers in the first half of the 1930s, but in 1936 went into voluntary liquidation and re-emerged as REALL (Coachbuilders) Ltd with premises at 468–74 Bath Road, Cippenham, Buckinghamshire; the double-L in the company name seems to have been introduced at this stage. This final incarnation of the company seems to have built only hearses, school buses and commercial bodies, and lasted until 1966, when it closed down and its existing commitments were taken on by the Eagle Engineering Co. Ltd and by Warwick & Allways Welding Ltd of Aldershot, Hampshire.

REDHEAD'S

Redhead's advertisements seem to have been calculated to make it look like a larger company than it really was. The company was established at 346 Lewisham High Street, London SE13, in 1927 and the following year invited would-be buyers to contact its Coaching Services Department. There were charabanc, bus and coach bodies on chassis such as Gilford, but Redhead's of Lewisham seems to have faded out by 1930.

REES & GRIFFITHS

Charabanc, bus and coach bodies all came from the Rees & Griffiths premises, variously reported as being in Stourbridge and Stourport (both in Worcestershire). The company seems to have started in 1926 and to have remained in business until the late 1930s. An example of its work was a single-decker built in May 1932 on a Tilling-Stevens chassis for an operator in Cheadle, Cheshire.

REEVE & KENNING

Harry Reeve founded his business in 1888 to build horse-drawn vehicles and, after his death in 1925, his son Jack went into partnership with George Kenning. Reeve & Kenning Ltd was established at Bridge Street, Pilsley, near Chesterfield, that year. Among the company's early products was a trolleybus body on Clough, Smith chassis. During the late 1920s, Reeve & Kenning picked up business from the local Chesterfield Corporation and by the early 1930s was building single-deck bus bodies on Leyland chassis. There were fourteen-seat bodies for smaller chassis, too. The company's products were sometimes known by the R&K Coachwork name.

On Bristol B-type 'Superbus' chassis is this thirty-seat centre-entrance body for Chesterfield.

The company became Reeve (Coachbuilders) Ltd in 1958, was sold to T.H. Burgess Holdings in 1974 and became Reeve Burgess, still at Pilsley. Reeve Burgess became a subsidiary of Plaxton in 1980 and closed down in 1991. In its later incarnations, the company was very much associated with minibus conversions and mobile libraries.

See also Eastwood & Kenning.

REGENT

The Regent Carriage Company built some single-deck bus bodies in 1920–1, but nothing more is known about the company.

REID

R. Reid & Son was a motor bodybuilder at 2 North Brown Street, Carnoustie, Scotland, by 1920. Most of its work was on cars and commercial vehicles, but it did build two double-deck bodies on AEC Regent chassis for Dundee Corporation in 1932 and also rebodied some Thornycroft J chassis for Dundee & District in 1920.

REYNOLDS

Reynolds Bros (Barnsley) Ltd was one of the many small coachbuilders active in the late 1920s. It built both single-deck and double-deck bodies from premises at Peel Street in Barnsley, examples of the former being twenty-seaters on Graham-Dodge chassis in 1925 for Ideal Service (R. Taylor & Son) and on Reo chassis in 1927 for another operator.

RHODES

J. Rhodes & Son (Bingley) Ltd seem to have had only a brief flirtation with the PSV world. In August 1952, this company, which had premises at Castlefields in Bingley, Yorkshire, built a sixteen-seater coach on a Bedford chassis.

RIDLEY

A company called Ridley built some charabanc bodies in the 1920s, but nothing more is known.

This Daimler CB with twenty-seater body was
'90% new' in 1924, with bodywork by Roberts in
Shepherd's Bush.

That was winter, this is summer; and for the 1925 summer
season J.M. Roberts promoted its 'saloon coaches', with
folding roof.

Another refurbished Daimler chassis is under this 32-seater
body from 1927.

RIMMER, HARRISON & SUTHERLAND

Rimmer, Harrison & Sutherland was a Southport company
that became briefly involved in the PSV business in
1946–7, when it built eleven open buses of twenty-three
seats each on ex-WD Bedford QL lorry chassis. These
were used on Southport Corporation's beach-bus service
and there were a dozen in all, the prototype having been
built in the Corporation's own workshops.

ROBERTS (1)

Based in West Bromwich, Staffordshire, this Roberts
company was responsible for some single-deck bus bodies
in 1920.

ROBERTS (2)

Josiah Morris Roberts clearly liked to show who was in
charge of J.M. Roberts & Son Ltd, as he invited buyers
to deal 'direct with me' at Cathnor Motor Works, Cathnor Road, Shepherd's Bush, London W12. He was active
by 1923, assembling both chassis (mainly Daimler) and
bodies from used and Government surplus parts.

However, the extent of his bodybuilding business is
in doubt, as he was primarily a dealer. He probably sold
mainly to London area operators, offering charabancs by
1924 and saloon coaches and buses as well by May 1927.
No later traces of the company have come to light.

ROBERTS (3)

Roberts (Wakefield) was established as early as 1856 as a
builder of railway rolling stock, but the company's entry
to the PSV market was not made until the end of the
1920s. By then, it was known as Charles Roberts & Co.
Ltd and had premises at Horbury Junction, near Wakefield, Yorkshire.

By March 1929, the company was advertising van
bodies and by September the PSV types had been added
in a list that included 'omnibuses, saloon coaches, vans,
lorries, trailers [and] road tankers for all classes of
liquids'. When the Leyland bodyshops were under pressure around 1930, it seems to have been this Roberts (and
not one of the many others) that helped out by building
bodies under contract, sometimes using Leyland designs.

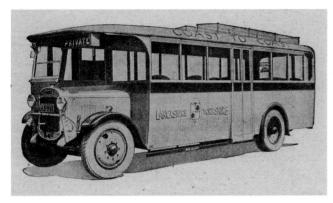

Intended for long-distance express services from the Lancashire coast to the Yorkshire coast, this coach, bodied by Roberts of Wakefield dates from 1929.

This time, the body is a twenty-seater 'sun saloon de luxe coach' on Dennis chassis for a Yorkshire operator. It dates from 1930.

This 1930 26-seater on Albion chassis is an all-weather design incorporating a fixed rear roof to support a luggage rack.

The piano-front double-deck body by Roberts of Wakefield on the 1931 Leyland Titan for Bolton Corporation was very much in the contemporary idiom.

By 1931 there were also double-deck Roberts bodies, including some 48-seaters on Leyland Titan chassis for Bolton and later on AEC Regent chassis for Halifax. From 1933 there were bodies for Guy trolleybuses, too.

The company made a return to PSV work after the 1939–45 war, building a number of metal-framed double-deck types between 1947 and 1950 for municipal operators such as Leigh (Lancashire), Nottingham and Sheffield. Roberts also built some of the final Sheffield tramcars in 1952 and the single-deck 'Coronation' trams for Blackpool in 1953.

ROBERTS (4)

J. Roberts was a Llandudno company active in the PSV world in the late 1920s and possibly also the early 1930s. It seems to have served only local operators, most notably Llandudno Corporation, which took some five toastrack

bodies on Dennis and Guy chassis between 1928 and 1930. It is not clear what happened to Roberts after that.

ROBERTS (5)

A. Roberts from Hastings in Sussex built some coach bodywork in 1936, but no further information has yet come to light.

ROBERTS (6)

Griffith J. Roberts was established as a coachbuilder at 3A Lower Grangegorman in Dublin in 1933. The company built both bus and coach bodies until about 1953, some notable examples being the special airport coaches on Bedford OB chassis for CIE's airport services in 1949.

ROBIN HOOD

Robin Hood was both a body repair and bodybuilding company, trading under the names of Robin Hood Repairs Ltd and Robin Hood Vehicle Builders Ltd from 1973. It was initially at Fareham in Hampshire and from here it built a number of single-deck coach bodies, as well as minibus conversions and welfare-type vehicles.

The company opened a second factory at Rotherham in 1988, which in 1989 became Phoenix International. The Fareham company nevertheless remained in business and today trades as Robin Hood Coachbuilders Ltd.

ROBINS & DAY

Robins & Day was offering charabanc bodies in 1925, but no more is known about the company or its work.

ROBSON

J.S. Robson Ltd built single-deck bodies for the smaller chassis in the 1920s and as late as 1931. The company premises were at Durham Road Coach Works, Blackhill, Consett, in County Durham. Robson built quite extensively for independent operators in the north-east before the outbreak of war in 1939, for example on Chevrolet chassis in the 1920s and on Dodge chassis in 1931. The company's eventual fate is not clear.

At least the advertising copywriter thought this eighteen- to twenty-seater body on Chevrolet chassis had graceful lines.

Built for Roe's own local municipality, Leeds Corporation, at the end of the 1920s, this 32-seater was on Crossley Eagle chassis.

ROE

The Leeds firm of Charles H. Roe Ltd was one of the major players on the British PSV bodybuilding scene from the 1920s until the 1980s. Although the company closed down in 1984, former staff and managers pooled their redundancy money and in 1985 returned to the old factory at Crossgates Carriage Works in Leeds with a new bus-building business under the name of Optare Ltd. This has gone on to become a major player in its own right.

Charles Roe served his apprenticeship with the carriage works of the North Eastern Railway and later worked as a draughtsman in the railway works of Roberts of Wakefield (*q.v.*) and then at RET in Hunslet, who as Railless Electric Traction were pioneer trolleybus builders. His design for a lightweight body with steel panels on a reinforced teak body frame entered production and sold well.

Exempt from war service by virtue of his job, Roe established his own company in 1917 next to the RET premises. He built trailers, mobile shops and charabanc bodies, but quickly outgrew the site and in 1920 moved into a former munitions factory at Crossgates in Leeds. Roe built bodies on Railless and Straker-Clough trolleybuses for the Birmingham, Rotherham and Teesside municipalities, while continuing to build charabancs as well. However, trading difficulties in the early 1920s saw the company voluntarily wound up and then re-established as Charles H. Roe (1923) Ltd, still at Crossgates.

Bodies for motor buses gradually came to outnumber those for trolleybuses, with Roe obtaining a good number of orders from municipalities. Many of these remained firm Roe devotees for years afterwards. The first double-deckers were for Doncaster on AEC chassis in 1925 and a year or so later the company began rebuilding older charabancs with new enclosed coach bodywork. From

1928, Roe built double-deckers incorporating a new continuous waist-rail design that had been developed by its General Manager Bill Bramham and from 1930 introduced a central-entrance body with twin staircases to the upper deck. This became very popular and the design was licensed to other builders, including Burlingham; Roe built its last example in 1950. Many rear-entrance double-deckers of this period had a distinctive triangular staircase window.

By 1935, Roe was building single-deck bodies to BEF requirements, which of course widened its customer base. Roe bodies in this period were of composite construction, but were nevertheless respected for their sturdiness and durability. Much of this was attributable to the use of teak framing, which remained a Roe characteristic right into the 1960s. In 1937, the company showed a strikingly modern double-decker for Leeds on an AEC Regent chassis at the Commercial Motor Show; its four deep windows on each side of the lower deck were an acknowledged influence on the design of the London Transport RT class of two years later.

During the 1939–45 war, Roe built a variety of bodywork types for Government use, but the company was also chosen as a builder of 'utility' PSV bodywork. There were 240 single-deck bodies on Bedford OWB chassis and 400 double-deckers, mainly of lowbridge type, on Sunbeam trolleybus and Daimler and Guy motor-bus chassis.

The late 1940s brought changes in ownership. Park Royal Vehicles (*q.v.*) bought a controlling share in 1947, but in 1948 was itself taken over by ACV. This brought Roe into the same group as chassis builders AEC, Crossley and Maudslay. Meanwhile, Roe built a number of special bodies on Leyland Titan PD1 and PD1A chassis for East Yorkshire, with tapering top-deck pillars and an arched roof to allow the buses to negotiate the ancient Beverley Bar arch into the town of Beverley, Yorkshire.

There were still orders for trolleybuses and Roe also took on major repair programmes in the late 1940s, notably for Plymouth Corporation (for whom it rebuilt some 100 utility-bodied Guy Arabs) and BMMO (for whom in 1952–3 it also extended no fewer than 455 early postwar single-deckers to give extra seating capacity). In the 1950s and 1960s there were also some special single-deckers for Hansons of Huddersfield on reconditioned AEC chassis.

Double-deck bodies were always in the ascendant at Roe during the 1950s, however, and the company was a late entrant to the underfloor-engined single-decker business, waiting until 1953 to introduce its Dalesman

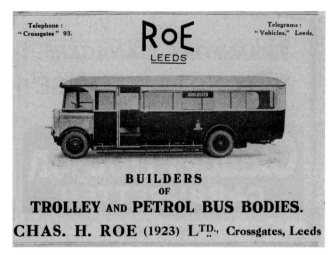

This time, the customer was Doncaster and the entrance was set back from the bulkhead by one bay.

This sixty-seat double-decker was one of a number supplied in 1930 to South Lancashire Transport on Guy trolleybus chassis.

This was Roe's patent centre-entrance body from 1934, with dual staircases. The bus was for West Riding, on a Leyland Titan chassis.

Big windows, just four bays and Roe's trademark staircase window; this was a pioneering style on a 1937 AEC Regent for Leeds City Transport.

Though the chassis dates from 1938, the body on this Keighley-West Yorkshire Bristol K5G dates from 1950.

coach body for AEC Reliance chassis. Unashamedly inspired by the Duple Elizabethan design, it sold just sixty-eight examples with periodic updates through to 1959, always on AEC Reliance chassis and mainly finding buyers among BET group operators rather than the fashion-conscious independent coach businesses. Roe was also a late entrant into the 36ft (11m) single-decker market, not beginning sales of service bus bodies until 1964. These were followed by standee types in 1967.

Meanwhile, the double-deck bodies were still of composite construction, but now with a new and even stronger waist rail featuring rolled steel plate over the teak structural member. Composite double-deck bodies remained in production until 1968, mainly for Daimler half-cab chassis and after 1957 featuring an aluminium top deck frame above the teak-framed lower deck.

Nevertheless, Roe also began to build metal-framed double-deck bodies to the new and rather severe Park Royal outline devised for the AEC Bridgemaster and later adapted for the Leyland Atlantean. These, sadly, became notorious for suffering from early corrosion. Roe also built bodywork for almost all the low-height Guy Wulfrunian chassis built between 1959 and 1965. More notably, it pioneered a more attractive shape with a peaked front dome for the double-deck bodies on rear-engined Leyland Atlantean and Daimler Fleetline chassis from 1962; with further modifications, this design

The famous Beverley Bar roof, designed to allow double-deckers to pass under a historic arch, is seen here on a 1952 East Yorkshire Titan. In this case, the Roe body had a full front.

This 1960 Leyland PD2/40 for West Hartlepool was pictured when new outside the Roe works where its H37/28R body was built.

The 1950s saw Roe fielding the Dalesman coach and a well-proportioned but rather square single-deck service bus body.

became the basis of the standard rear-engined double-decker style built by both Roe and Park Royal from 1968 to 1981. Roe began building 36ft single-deck buses in 1964, adding standee types from 1967.

Meanwhile, there had been further changes of ownership as ACV merged with Leyland in 1962 and in 1965 shares in Roe were exchanged with the Transport Holding Company (THC) for shares in Bristol and Eastern Coach Works (*q.v.*). When the THC was succeeded by the National Bus Company, Roe became one of the subsidiaries of the new Bus Manufacturers Holdings, owned equally by British Leyland and the National Bus Company. Roe was on a high in the early 1980s, with its 1981 production total being the best since 1966, and it developed body designs for the new Leyland Tiger and double-deck Olympian. However, Leyland assumed complete control of BMH in 1982 and the subsequent sales strategies and reorganizations made the Roe factory an unviable member of the Leyland empire.

ROGERSON

Robert Rogerson & Co. was at 1,214 South Street in Glasgow's Scotstoun district. This was next to the Albion Motors factory and the Rogerson company obtained all of its commercial and bus bodybuilding work from there between 1912 and 1930. Customers were not confined to Scotland, however, and included some abroad.

ROMILLY

The Romilly Motor Co. Ltd was based at 20 Romilly Crescent in Cardiff and became a registered company in February 1919. Its name was applied to some bus bodies built around 1930, but no further details of the company responsible have been discovered.

Roney's offered eight- to eleven-week turnarounds for coach bodies like this thirty-three seater on Commer chassis, which may nevertheless have been the only one they ever built.

RONEY

Roney's Coachbuilders Ltd was another one of the myriad companies that capitalized on the boom in demand for bus and coach bodywork in the late 1940s. The company was based at Leeds Road in Hull. An example of its work was a full-front 33-seat coach body on Commer chassis, which may have been the only body it actually built. (*See also* Runey.)

ROSSLEIGH

Rossleigh Ltd was established by Thomas Ross and William Sleigh at Kilmarnock in 1889. It became a limited company in 1907 and is thought to have bodied just one Dennis chassis as a single-decker in 1931 (although this is disputed).

Rossleigh was a car dealership by 1931, was sold to the Heron Corporation in 1972, to the Cowie Group in 1987, then to Reg Vardy plc in 2003.

ROUNDING

A company called Rounding based at Driffield in Yorkshire built at least one sixteen-seat coach body in 1949.

ROWE

M.G. Rowe was a Cornish bus operator from Liskeard whose proprietor developed bus and lorry chassis in the early 1950s specifically to suit the hilly Cornish roads. Just five Rowe Hillmaster coaches were built between 1953 and 1958, all with bodies by the chassis manufacturer. They found owners in the West Country and in Wales.

RUNEY

A company with this name may have built one bus body on a Bedford OB chassis in 1948 (for Conner & Graham of Easington). However, the attribution is questionable and a more plausible one is to Roney (*q.v.*), which was based in Hull and was served by Conner & Graham. A tenatative identification for the Runey company is H.G. Runey of Bootham Row in York.

RUSHWORTH

John Rushworth & Sons Ltd of Navine Street in Burnley built some coach bodywork in the early 1920s.

RUSSELL & PADDICK

Russell & Paddick were based at Reading and built some single-deck bus bodies in the early 1920s.

RUSTON & HORNSBY

Ruston & Hornsby of Lincoln was best known for its heavy engineering of such things as steam traction engines, railway locomotives and even tanks. However, it also turned its hand to bus bodywork, although the fourteen-seater built on Ford Model TT chassis for a Welshpool company in 1921 may have been a unique aberration. The company was associated with Ransomes, Sims & Jeffries (*q.v.*) from March 1919.

RUSTON & WILSON

This Birmingham company built some bus and coach bodies in the first half of the 1930s. Its premises were at Newton Road, Great Barr.

SALISBURY

The Salisbury Carriage Works operated from Wilton Road in Salisbury in the early 1920s. It built a range of bodies, including charabancs, single-deck buses and open-top double-deck types.

SAMLESBURY

Despite the pronunciation of 'Salmesbury', this is the correct spelling of the name. The Samlesbury Engineering Co. Ltd was named after the airfield where it was based – Samlesbury Airfield near Blackburn, Lancs. During the 1930s, the company had been in business as Lancashire Aircraft Ltd and, like so many other compa-nies of its type, had been involved in aircraft construction during World War II.

True to type, when the war was over, the company made use of its skilled workforce by getting into the bus bodywork business. There was repair work for municipal bus operators whose vehicles had suffered from lack of maintenance during the war years; many of these involved nothing less than complete body rebuilds. The company also took on some assembly work for Leyland, putting together a number of bodies from parts. From there, it was a short step into building its own bodies.

The 1946–7 bodies seem to have carried Lancashire Aircraft Ltd plates, but from 1948 the company was Samlesbury Engineering; consecutive deliveries on Leyland PD1A chassis for Isle of Man Road Services moved from one name to the other. The first body of

The ornate side flashes on this Foden PVD6 are an unusual feature of its Samlesbury L53R body. It was new in 1950 to Green Bus Company of Rugeley and Uttoxeter.

Samlesbury's own design was completed in 1949, a 53-seater double-decker on Foden chassis for Whieldons Green Bus Service of Rugeley in Staffordshire. This had a lowbridge layout, which Samlesbury called a 'lowhyte' design. It was jig-built with a largely metal frame, but used timber lower frame sections that were said to prevent distortion elsewhere in the body after accidents.

Samlesbury also built a number of full-front coach bodies over the next few years, as well as some bus trailers for export, but by the mid-1950s had returned to the aircraft business.

SANDERS

Ralph E. Sanders & Sons Ltd was at Walsworth Road, Hitchin, in Hertfordshire and was involved with single-deck bus bodywork in 1920.

SANDERSON & HOLMES

This company was based at London Road in Derby and built bus bodies in the 1920s and possibly beyond 1930. A late example was on a Maudslay chassis for Blue Bus in 1930. The company has sometimes been recorded under the name of Holmes.

SANDWELL

Sandwell was a West Bromwich maker responsible for some charabanc bodies in the early 1920s.

SANKEY

Joseph Sankey & Sons Ltd had existed since at least 1902 and was based at Albert Street, Bilston, in Staffordshire. The company built charabanc bodies in the period up to 1928.

SANTUS

Santus is a well-known name in Wigan, where William Santus & Co. Ltd is a major confectioner responsible for a range of sweets sold under the Uncle Joe's brand. The Santus Motor Bodyworks Ltd, also of Wigan (at 11 Powell Street) seems to have belonged to a different branch of the family. It came to prominence in the 1920s, building single-deck bodies on chassis such as Thornycroft.

By the 1930s, Santus was able to sell its bodywork to the local municipality and there were some Leyland Tiger buses for Wigan. Some stylish coach bodies followed, with Santus building for most of the Wigan area operators during the 1930s; later in the decade, the company was confident enough of sales to be able to order chassis and build vehicles for stock.

After the interruption of the war years, Santus was back in business in the late 1940s, building (for example) full-front coach bodywork on Seddon chassis for West Riding in 1949, but its designs were unoriginal, being largely inspired by pre-war Plaxton designs. They were also of poor quality, which contributed to the company's demise in the early 1950s.

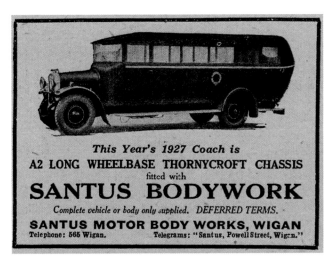

This Year's 1927 Coach is
A2 LONG WHEELBASE THORNYCROFT CHASSIS
fitted with
SANTUS BODYWORK
Complete vehicle or body only supplied. DEFERRED TERMS.
SANTUS MOTOR BODY WORKS, WIGAN
Telephone: 565 Wigan.   Telegrams: "Santus, Powell Street, Wigan."

The Wigan coachbuilder was offering this all-weather coach for 1927 on Thornycroft chassis.

From this angle, the Saunders-Roe body on 1948 London Transport RT1158 was indistinguishable from the standardized design also built by Park Royal and Weymann; there were subtle differences, however.

The Saunders-Roe lightweight service bus body on Leyland Tiger Cub chassis was a classic of its time. This example was one of many operated by Ribble.

SARO

See Saunders-Roe.

SAUNDERS-ROE

During the 1939–45 war, Saunders Engineering & Shipyard Ltd at Beaumaris on Anglesey was engaged on the maintenance of Catalina flying boats. Like so many other companies engaged on war work, it found itself without business, but with a skilled workforce, when the war ended, so the pent-up demand for bus bodywork offered a straightforward solution.

Saunders-Roe began by refurbishing worn-out coach and bus bodies and this work continued into 1948. However, it quickly moved into building its own all-new bodies, the first double-deckers appearing in mid-1947 and being based on a 1934 Short Bros design. Saunders-Roe's own single-deckers followed and by this time the company was busy with export orders. The company also picked up an order for 300 56-seat double-deck bodies for London Transport's new RT class of AEC Regents, building these between 1948 and 1951.

The company's familiarity with light-alloy fabrication in aircraft pointed the way ahead for its own designs. Jig-building and an imaginative quest for light weight became Saunders-Roe hallmarks. In 1949 it introduced its own Rivaloy single-deck body, so named because it was made up from aluminium alloy sections that were riveted together; this was followed with a double-deck version in 1950.

In 1951, the company was renamed as Saunders-Roe (Anglesey) Ltd. From 1952, it had an attractive single-deck bus body for underfloor-engined chassis, distinguished by a ribbed aluminium moulding around the body (which actually concealed a structural feature). This was generally known as the Saro type and large numbers were built for BET companies in 1953–4, mainly on Leyland Tiger Cub chassis. The same basic body was also used in 1953 for a prototype integral single-decker, to which Saunders-Roe fitted a Gardner engine.

Other interesting prototypes included a new lightweight double-deck body and, in 1953, the body for one of the Leyland Lowloader protoypes that eventually evolved into the Atlantean. Meanwhile, big export orders, including the body contract for the huge Cuban export order of 620 Leyland Royal Tigers, kept the company busy. However, by 1955 demand was falling and Saunders-Roe built the last bodies under its own name in 1956.

In 1959, the Beaumaris works was sold to aviation company Hawker Siddeley, later becoming part of the Laird Group. Laird also owned bodybuilders Metro-Cammell and in 1968–9 the Beaumaris plant returned briefly to bus bodybuilding on that company's behalf. It completed a batch of MCW Orion double-deckers from the recently closed Weymann plant, built ten Leyland Atlanteans to MCW design for Devon General and also assembled a small number of Superior PSV bodies imported as kits from the USA by Metro-Cammell.

SAVILLE

The company called Saville that built some coach body-work in 1929 is thought to have been Saville & Ezard Ltd of The Garage, Falconers Road, Scarborough, in Yorkshire.

SCOTT (1)

Archibald Scott was a joiner and vehicle bodybuilder at Bellshill in Lanarkshire. He built a single known bus body in 1926 on a Graham-Dodge chassis. Nearly sixty years later in 1984, and now known as Scott of Bellshill Ltd, the company re-entered the PSV market with mini-buses and small PSVs.

SCOTT (2)

M.J. Scott was the proprietor of Lambourn Racecourse Transport, which built horseboxes at Lambourn in Berkshire. In about 1931, the company put its name to a single-deck coach body as well.

SCOTTISH AVIATION

Scottish Aviation Ltd was one of the new bodybuilders that sprang up immediately after World War II. Located at Prestwick Airport in Ayrshire, the company had started out as a flying school, but diversified into aircraft maintenance in 1938 and during the war maintained and modified Liberator bomber aircraft.

During 1947, the company developed a light-alloy bus body with lightweight stressed-skin construction as used in aircraft. The first orders were fulfilled in 1948 and there was no shortage of demand from (mostly) Scottish operators – until the post-war shortage began to ease and the extra cost of these bodies made sales unviable.

The last Scottish Aviation bus bodies were built in 1952 and the company subsequently returned to aircraft work, but also undertook contract work on commercial bodies for companies such as Bonallack in the 1960s. It became part of British Aerospace in 1977.

SCOTTISH COMMERCIAL

Based in Glasgow, the Scottish Commercial Motor Co.

Ltd entered the PSV market in 1943 with some bodies on Austin chassis for operators in the Scottish Islands. It was an agent for Crossley and, not surprisingly, built several bodies on Crossley chassis in the 1940s. It also rebodied a solitary double-decker for Glasgow.

Scottish Commercial made no more bodies after December 1950, but continued to trade as a dealer until 1956.

SCOTTISH CO-OPERATIVE WHOLESALE SOCIETY

The Scottish Co-operative Wholesale Society (SCWS) had its own motor-bodybuilding department from 1911, but did not begin building bus bodies until 1948, after acquiring Cadogan (Perth) Ltd (q.v.) in 1946. SCWS also bought Walker's of Aberdeen (q.v.) in 1948, but retained the Walker name for bodies built there until mid-1949.

SCWS bodies were built on Albion and Bedford chassis for Scottish operators until 1950, when national demand lessened. There were also welfare-type bodies from the SCWS in the 1960s.

SCOTTISH MOTOR TRACTION

Scottish Motor Traction (SMT) was a Scottish operator, established in 1905. It began building bodies for its own vehicles in 1913 and by 1915 was building for other Scottish operators as well. From 1915, its workshops were at Valleyfield Street in Edinburgh. After a reorganization in 1929, bodybuilding became a task allocated to the SMT Car Sales and Service Department, with customers in both Scotland and Northern Ireland.

From 1942, SMT's bodyworks were at Marine Gardens in the Edinburgh district of Portobello. From 1943 until the end of the war in 1945, these workshops built large numbers of Duple-designed bodies on Bedford OWB chassis for operators in Scotland and the North, as well as the Royal Air Force. The company continued to build on Bedford chassis after the war, when it was able to serve more distant operators; examples were 29-seat coach bodies on OB chassis for Dove Coaches of Beer in Devon and Warburton of Bury, then in Lancashire, in 1947.

After a further reorganization in 1949, the body-building activities were separated from the bus operating business, which continued under private ownership as SMT Sales & Service. The company continued to build commercial bodies, now from 29 East Fountainbridge, and a few specialized bus bodies until 1985.

SCUNTHORPE

Scunthorpe Motors Ltd built bus, coach and welfare bus bodies between 1931 and 1951 from premises in Smith Street.

SEDDON

The chassis-maker Seddon of Oldham built a number of single-deck bodies for its own chassis in 1949. In later years, it established Pennine Coachcraft (q.v.) as a separate company for such work.

SENTINEL

The Shrewsbury firm of Sentinel built a number of rather undistinguished bodies for its own integral-construction single-deckers between late 1949 and 1952, basing the design on one drawn up by Beadle (q.v.) for the prototype in 1948.

SERVICE MOTOR WORKS

Service Motor Works Ltd was a Belfast company, apparently sometimes known as the Belfast Service Motor Works Ltd. It built single-deck bus bodies for local operators from 1929, but was wound up in 1936.

This 1920s Short Bros body for East Surrey Traction is notable for the absence of any weather protection for the driver.

SHEARING & CRABTREE

Shearing & Crabtree Ltd was one of the many companies in which Jack Crabtree was involved. This company built single-deck coach bodies between about 1931 and 1936 from Moorhey Works, Moorhey Street, off the Lees Road in Oldham. It was connected with Elite Bodies Ltd in nearby Heywood, Elite Coaches Ltd of Rochdale, Lewis & Crabtree (q.v.) of Heywood, Shearing & Crabtree of Oldham, Shearings of Oldham, Oldham Construction and Challengers Coachbuilders (q.q.v.).

SHEARINGS

Shearings of Oldham employed Jack Crabtree as their designer and manager from 1929 to 1939. For at least part of that period, Mr Crabtree was also working for Shearing & Crabtree Ltd (to 1936) (q.v.). Other companies in which Jack Crabtree featured were Elite Bodies Ltd of Heywood, Elite Coaches Ltd of Rochdale, Lewis & Crabtree, Oldham Construction and Challengers Coachbuilders (q.q.v.).

SHELVOKE & DREWRY

Shelvoke & Drewry Ltd was best known for its innovative refuse collection vehicles, constructed at its premises at Icknield Way in Letchworth, Hertfordshire. Its first product was the Freighter, designed as a flatbed truck and featuring tiny wheels and tiller-type steering. Between 1922 and 1926, the company bodied a number of these as toastracks for seaside resort use.

SHINNIE

R.J. Shinnie was an Aberdeen company that had built horse trams in the mid-1870s. From 1919 it was constructing charabancs and single-deck buses from its premises in Union Row, including many for the Aberdeen Corporation fleet. The last bodies were built in 1925, when the company was voluntarily wound up.

SHORT BROS

Short Bros (Rochester & Bedford) Ltd was an aircraft manufacturer with premises at Seaplane Works,

The Rochester firm supplied a number of these 52-seat open-staircase double-deckers to Sheffield Corporation on AEC Model 507 chassis in 1926.

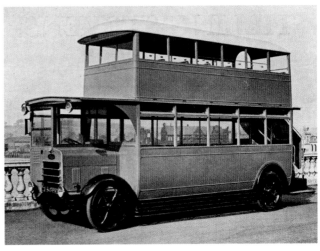

This one dates from 1927 and is another 52-seat open-staircase, covered-top body, this time on a Bristol chassis.

The 25-seat all-weather body on this Maudslay chassis for SMT had a Beatonson folding top.

The body on this Railless trolleybus looks curiously ungainly, even by the standards of the late 1920s.

Rochester. From 1919 it began building bus bodies and there were car bodies in the 1920s as well. By 1924, there were covered-top double-deckers for Birmingham and from around 1927 Shorts became one of the first companies to build all-metal single-deck bus bodies. That year, it also built the unique Crellin Highway Motor Yacht, described as a 'flat on wheels' and constructed on a six-wheel Guy chassis. (Its designer, George Crellin, designed the Crellin-Duplex bodies some twenty years later; *see* Lincs Trailer and Mann Egerton.)

It was Short Bros that picked up the contract to build the double-deck bodies for the first AEC Regents in 1928–9, using a body design drawn up by AEC under the supervision of that company's Chief Engineer, J.G. Rackham. This had a distinctive 'camel-back' roof design, low

Steel-framed, with fifty-four seats and a lowbridge design, this body was built on a Leyland Titan chassis in 1935 for Greenock Motor Services.

A double-decker on AEC chassis for Sheffield Corporation.

This 1926 Guy FCX was built for Morecambe Corporation Tramways.

The bodybuilder claimed that the rounded front corner on the nearside of this 1932 front-entrance body deflected air and prevented dust entering the vehicle.

The Shorts 'camel-back' design looked low from the sides but was really a highbridge type, with a hump in the roof to give headroom above the gangway. This one was new to Chester Corporation in 1930.

This 1934 body on a Sunbeam trolleybus chassis for Walsall still betrays signs of 1920s designs in the overhanging roof at the front and the shape of the cab.

at the sides but with a humped centre section over the centre gangway on the top deck. This reduced the apparent height, but in practice the humped centre meant that the design was a highbridge type. Several more of these camel-back bodies were built for a variety of operators.

Around 1930, Shorts was one of the companies contracted by Leyland to help out when its own body shops were under pressure and many bodies were built at the Rochester works to Leyland designs. The company was also a pioneer of aluminium construction in PSV bodywork, employing Max Meltz (*q.v.*) to assist in their development. For 1934, Shorts claimed to be drawing on aircraft construction methods for greater rigidity in their bodywork, but PSV bodywork activity ceased the following year as the company refocused on aircraft work. Nevertheless, the Short designs were not entirely lost; Saunders-Roe (*q.v.*) drew on them for its first postwar double-deck bodies.

SIMPSON (1)

A. Simpson & Son was a motor engineer at Brechin by 1920 and for a period during the following decade operated its own buses as well. In the second half of the 1920s, the company built some bus bodies for local operators alongside commercial bodywork.

SIMPSON (2)

Robert Simpson worked from 170 Millerfield Road at Bridgetown in Glasgow from at least 1914 and by 1919 he was building charabanc bodies as a subcontractor to Albion Motors. He built some bus bodies on Halley chassis for the Lanarkshire Tramways of Motherwell in 1923–4, but his last known bus body was in 1926 and the company closed soon afterwards.

SIMPSON (3)

The third Simpson was another Scottish concern and a second Robert. This one was a wheelwright and builder in Killearn, Dunbartonshire, who built at least one bus body on a Daimler lorry chassis in 1919.

SIMPSON & SLATER

Simpson & Slater Ltd built charabanc and single-deck bus bodies during the first half of the 1920s from premises at 92 Huntingdon Street in Nottingham.

SLOPE BROS

This company was based at Camberley in Surrey and was briefly involved with single-deck bus bodywork in 1919–20.

SMITH (1)

A.E. Smith & Son was an old-established commercial coachbuilders of Carrington Street in the Northamptonshire town of Kettering. In the late 1940s, it built some coach bodies, but then withdrew from the PSV market.

In the 1970s and 1980s, the company – by now A.E. Smith & Son (Kettering) Ltd – became heavily involved in converting Range Rovers for Middle Eastern markets.

SMITH (2)

In the early 1930s, A.F. Smith & Son (Coachbuilders) Ltd built single-deck bus bodies from premises at 9 Granville Street in Peterborough.

SMITH (3)

G.C. Smith (Coachworks) Ltd built bus and coach bodies, together with a range of horseboxes and mobile libraries. The company's works were at Ashby Road, Long Whatton, in Leicestershire. It may have been active as early as 1934; in the late 1940s the company built some single-deck bodywork on Bristol half-cab chassis, but by 1952 it was building caravans.

The company went into liquidation in 1999 and was dissolved in 2003.

SMITH (4)

H. Smith & Company was a coach and motor-body-builder at Langlands Brae in Kilmarnock between 1929 and 1931. The company built four single-deck bus bodies on AEC chassis for Ayr & District.

SMITH (5)

T.C. Smith & Company was a motor engineer in Aberdeen and by 1915 was also building motor vehicle bodies. More were built under subcontract from Albion Motors in 1919–20, but by 1928 the company had stopped building bodywork and was focusing on its garage activities.

SMITH (6)

Thomas Smith & Son was at Victoria Coach Works, Percy Street, in Larkhall, Lanarkshire. The company was building bus bodies as early as 1910, but its only known body in the period covered by this book was on a Leyland chassis in 1919.

SMITH (7)

With workshops in Millbank Road, Wishaw, Lanarkshire, Walter Smith set up in business as W. Smith & Sons in 1921 after experience with Pickering (*q.v.*). He built a handful of bus bodies for local operators between then and 1925, remained in business until the second half of the 1930s, then closed the business and went to work for Central SMT in Motherwell.

SMITH (8)

Between 1934 and 1936, W. David Smith & Co. Ltd built single-deck bus bodies from premises at 68–76 High Street, West Bromwich. The company always stressed the David element in its name, to distinguish it from W.J. Smith & Son who were at the other end of the High Street. Among its deliveries were some rebodies for Walsall Corporation.

In 1947, the company relocated to Fernhill Heath in Worcestershire, becoming operators and also continuing the dealership business they had started while at West Bromwich.

SMITH (9)

W.J. Smith & Son Ltd was a West Bromwich coach-builder that built single-deck buses and coaches from 1914 to 1934 on a wide range of chassis; in the 1920s, for example, Blue Bus Services took Smith bodies on Halley, Maudslay and Morris-Commercial chassis. The company had an address at 377c High Street, but its workshops were in nearby Shaftesbury Street; the premises were later described as at Carters Green (which is an extension of the High Street), but did not change location.

In 1931, the Jensen brothers bought the company, continuing with its original commercial, PSV and car-bodying business. In 1934, they changed its name to Jensen Motors and moved wholeheartedly into the car business.

This all-weather body was among the West Bromwich firm's 1928 products.

Front-entrance saloon bodywork was on the W.J. Smith menu by 1929.

A good story is told of the early days of Jensen ownership. A coach for a Leicester operator was completed and taken down to the offices where all new commercial vehicles had to be checked to see if they conformed to the length regulations then in force. This one turned out to be three inches too long because the front overhang of the chassis was greater than normal. As the customer wanted the coach in a hurry, the only solution was to take the vehicle back to the works and shorten it. 'We took three inches out at the rear, a section was removed from the body, and all the seats inside were shuffled forward,' explained one of the staff many years later. 'Needless to say, the customer never knew!'

SMT

See Scottish Motor Traction.

SOUTH WALES COMMERCIAL MOTORS

South Wales Commercial Motors Ltd was based at Penarth Road in Cardiff and had some involvement with PSV bodywork in 1928.

SOUTH WESTERN COACHBUILDERS

Some coach bodies were built in the 1950s by South Western Coachbuilders Ltd, of 33 Cannon Street in Taunton, Devon.

SPARSHATT

John Herbert Sparshatt of Portsmouth was involved in the construction of commercial vehicle bodywork as early as 1925, when he took out some design patents. He seems to have been associated with Portsmouth Commercial Motors and in 1942 took out more patents, this time relating to tubular construction for vehicle bodies.

Tubular Coach Bodies of Portsmouth may have been an early attempt by Sparshatt to set up on his own in the late 1940s. One way or another, he was in business as J.H. Sparshatt & Sons (Southampton) Ltd by July 1948, when that company advertised all-steel tubular-framed coach and bus bodies. This tubular construction was ideal for semi-integral construction, where the body had to bear some of the load, and Sparshatts consequently built the bodies on at least two of the semi-integral JNSN buses. The tubular framework also lent itself to jig-building and could be broken down into compact sections to reduce shipping costs for overseas assembly. Sparshatts also built bodies on Bedford OB chassis, including a number that were exported to Ceylon in 1949.

The company was initially based at The Causeway in Redbridge and later at Burfields Road in Copnor. It was still active in the 1960s, although by then was building school and works buses on chassis such as BMC. At some point, the company seems to have been split into two. Sparshatts (Coachbuilders) Ltd was absorbed by Wadham Stringer, the commercial vehicle and ambulance builders of Waterlooville, while Sparshatts (Metal Bodies) Ltd had become Steels (SMB) Ltd (q.v.) by 1971.

SPEN

In 1965, a single coach body is known to have come from Spen Coachworks Ltd of Station Road in Heckmondwike, Yorkshire. It appears that the Spenborough Engineering Co. Ltd of Valley Works, Union Road, in the same town was also involved with its construction.

SPICERS

Spicers Motors Ltd of Southport was also known as Spicers Coachworks and advertised itself as Spicers Luxury Coachbuilders. From late 1932 it became Ernest Spicer Ltd, trading from 141 Shakespeare Street. During the 1920s, the company was building on Dennis and Thornycroft chassis and in 1930–1 built on Leyland Lion and Leyland Tiger chassis for Scout of Preston. There was a Spicers body on a Commer Avenger chassis at Olympia in 1931. The roofs of some Spicers half-canopy single-deck bodies had a distinctive sloping forward section.

The company also acted as a dealership, remaining in business probably until the outbreak of war in 1939.

SPITE

This company was located at Bridge Street, Thrapston, in Northamptonshire, and built the coach body on a Maudslay chassis in 1934. Nothing further is known.

The Southport firm built this dual-entrance coach body for Gore's Pullman Safety Coaches on Leyland chassis.

SPURLING MOTOR BODIES LTD

Spurling Motor Bodies was active in the 1950s and 1960s as an occasional builder of PSV bodies, mainly, it seems, on Bedford chassis. The company had many other strings to its bow, building commercial bodies, military ambulance bodies and mail vans, and had aviation links as well, making airport steps, aircraft seating and supplying interior trim and soundproofing for airliners.

Always associated with Bedfords, Spurling built this rather odd-looking body on a truck chassis.

Founded in 1922, the company was for many years based in the Colindale area of north-west London, but also had premises in Colchester, Essex.

STAR

The Star Motor Company was a Wolverhampton company that had begun in the cycle business and moved on to cars and light commercials. It had earlier traded under other names.

From 1927, it also introduced a low-loading normal-control bus chassis intended for twenty-seat bodies, which developed into the Star Flyer, the company's most famous product. Around 1930, Star constructed some bodies for this chassis, but the company had already been sold to Guy Motors in 1928 and was liquidated in 1932.

STARTIN

Thomas Startin set up as a coachbuilder in 1840 and his business was continued into the twentieth century by members of his family. Based in Birmingham, the company built some charabanc bodies in the first years of the 1920s.

The company's modern descendants are the Startin Group, a car dealership chain with headquarters in Redditch.

STEANE

J. & A. Steane built some single-deck bus bodies in the second quarter of the 1920s.

STEANS

The Steans company constructed charabanc bodies in the 1920s.

STEELS

Steels (SMB) Ltd grew out of Sparshatts (Metal Bodies) Ltd (*q.v.*) in 1971. It had premises at Totton, near Southampton, and also at Ringwood, near Bournemouth. The company built some single-deck bus bodies in the 1970s.

STENNING

The name of Stenning is associated with some single-deck bus bodywork at the end of the 1930s. The company responsible may have been A. Stenning of Catford Wheel Works, London SE6.

STEWART

John Stewart owned a joinery and building construction business at Carluke, near Wishaw, Lanarkshire, specializing in pithead installations. In 1919, he set up a new firm, John Stewart and Company (Wishaw) Ltd, to take over the existing coachbuilding business of John Steel and Sons. The new company retained Steel's old premises at Coltness Coachworks, 180 Kirk Road, Wishaw.

The Stewart company built both commercial and bus bodywork, almost exclusively for local customers. Many of the chassis were locally built, too – such as Belhaven, Clyde and Halley – and from the mid-1920s a lucrative contract with Albion Motors saw the Stewart company building extensively on that manufacturer's chassis. As the business expanded, so did the premises, eventually taking over the whole of 138–180 Kirk Road.

Many of the Stewart body designs were distinctive, notably a 32-seater from the mid-1930s for Albion Victor chassis. However, there seems to have been no bus-body activity during the 1939–45 war and after that orders for buses became scarce. The last one was on an AEC Regal chassis in 1951. Stewart's had built somewhere around 275 bodies in all, the exact number being in dispute.

The company continued as a builder of commercial bodies, constructing large numbers of welfare vehicles and minibus conversions from the 1960s on and in 1979 merged with Hunter of Wishaw as a garage service business. This company in turn was liquidated in 2001.

ST HELIER

As the name suggests, St Helier Garages was a Jersey company. It made some bus bodywork during the boom period of the late 1940s.

STOKES & HOLT

See Willowbrook.

STRACHAN & BROWN

Strachan & Brown was active in the 1920s as a builder of single-deck bodies on both lightweight and heavyweight chassis. In 1894, Walter Brown had started a coachbuilding business in Shepherd's Bush, West London. With the addition of a partner in 1895, this became Brown & Hughes, and with the arrival of a third partner in 1907, it became Brown, Hughes & Strachan, with a new factory at Park Royal, London. Just before the Great War, Strachan and Brown both resigned and set up a new company in their own names in Kensington, West London.

During the war, Strachan & Brown, Coachbuilders, built ambulances and other vehicles for the military. This led the company to focus on bus bodywork from 1919 and in 1921 it built a new factory at Wales Farm Road, opposite London's North Acton station. From 1923 it moved out of the Kensington site and Acton became its headquarters. There were some car bodies as well as the charabancs and bus bodies, plus horseboxes in later years.

Typical examples of this company's work were B26D bodies on Guy B chassis for Colne Corporation (1923), B26F bodies on Leyland PLC1 for the same operator (1928), and 'super de luxe buffet coaches' on ADC 416A chassis in 1925 for the Bristol to London service run by Greyhound Motors. The company built double-deckers, too, including some on Dennis Lance chassis for Salford in 1932.

In 1928, Walter Brown left the firm to join Duple as a director and a year later James Strachan died. The company briefly became Strachans (Acton) Ltd in 1929, but seems to have run into financial difficulties and became Strachans (Successors) Ltd (*q.v.*) in 1934.

This forward-entrance 32-seater saloon coach was built on a Guy chassis in 1927.

STRACHANS

Strachans (Successors) Ltd grew out of Strachans (Acton) Ltd in 1934; before that, the company had been Strachan & Brown Ltd (*q.v.*), so it already had a reputation and a portfolio of clients by the mid-1930s. Prominent among those clients were Aldershot & District, who favoured Strachans with orders until the 1960s. Aldershot & District also favoured the local chassis builder Dennis and its Strachan-bodied half-cab Dennis single-deckers were always distinctive and readily identifiable. The company built double-deckers, too, including some on Dennis Lance chassis for Salford in 1932, and even built some Austin taxis in 1938. When Short Bros (*q.v.*) withdrew from the PSV market, metal-framing pioneer Max Meltz (*q.v.*) worked with the company on new designs.

During the war, Strachans was designated to build utility double-deckers, most of which were very austere-looking lowbridge types on Guy Arab chassis. When peace returned, the company built a number of single-deck bodies on front-engined chassis such as Commer,

This 32-seat rear-entrance saloon for the National Omnibus Co. Ltd dates from 1928 and must be one of the first bodies built by the new Strachans company.

Distinctly unusual was this sleeper coach on an AEC 426 chassis for the Irish Sleeper Omnibus Service in 1929.

This double-deck body was built for Western SMT in 1935.

This 1964 coach was built for Rickards, the London operator.

On Leyland PD2 chassis, this double-decker with platform doors was built for A1 Bus Service in Scotland.

Crossley, Leyland and Maudslay, some with full-fronts, and was still building this type of bodywork on Dennis Lancet chassis as late as 1953. There were double-deckers, too, but this was not a good time for Strachan quality and the metal-framed double-deckers for Western SMT on Leyland PD1 chassis in 1949 consequently had a very short service life. Aldershot & District remained committed customers in the 1950s and there were bodies on underfloor-engined Dennis chassis from 1952 and the centre-entrance Everest coach body on AEC Reliance chassis from 1956. The 1950s also saw Strachans building bus bodies for local and police authority users, plus there were also some Trojan minibuses.

By the early 1960s, the company was known as Strachans (Coachbuilders) Ltd. It kept up with the times by building on Bedford VAL three-axle chassis, but sold out to the Giltspur group in 1963 and moved to Hamble Lane, Hamble, in Hampshire. It continued to construct double-deck bodies (including some late half-cab Guy Arabs for Wolverhampton), built a number of early stan-

dee single-deckers on AEC Merlin chassis for London Transport and was active as a minibus converter until it finally closed its doors in 1974.

STRADLINGS

A company with this name built some single-deck bus bodies in the 1920s. It is thought to have been based at Newbury, Berkshire, with premises possibly at 79 North-brook Street.

STRAKER SQUIRE

Straker Squire Ltd was a chassis builder that had started out as the Straker Steam Vehicle Co. Ltd in 1901 and imported German Büssing motor-bus chassis in the first decade of the twentieth century. By 1912, it was also building trolleybuses (marketed as Straker-Clough or

Clough-Smith chassis). As late as 1920, it was constructing single-deck and open-top double-deck bodies for these and for its A-type motor-bus chassis, but it closed down in 1927.

STREET

Henry Street & Co. began as a wheelwrights business in Nottingham, but also built bus and coach bodies between 1925 and 1949. In the early 1930s it was at Orange Street, but thereafter its premises were at Arkwright Street.

STRUTHERS

R. Struthers & Sons was a motor bodybuilder in Larkhall, Lanarkshire. In 1925–7, it undertook some bodybuilding for Albion Motors, mainly of school buses for Glasgow, but also built at least one body for a Yorkshire operator.

STURDILUXE

Sturdiluxe Bus Bodies was a trading name of H. Young Motors Ltd (*q.v.*).

SUNSALOON

The name of Sunsaloon Bodies Ltd occurs quite often in relation to PSV bodywork in the 1920s, but the company was not in fact a bodybuilder. Based at Castleford Road, Sparkhill, in Birmingham, it was actually a constructor of sunshine roofs that it supplied for other firms to fit into their coach bodies.

SWANNICK

A company with this name was active as a builder of bus bodies in the mid-1920s, possibly from the Oswestry area in Shropshire.

TAYLOR (1)

See Eaton.

TAYLOR (2)

John Taylor, of Foundry Street in Barnsley, Yorkshire, built coach and single-deck bus bodies from 1924 until the middle of the 1930s. Many customers were local, a major one being County Motors of Lepton.

TAYLOR (3)

L. & L.W. Taylor Ltd was located at Park Lane, Fallings Park, Wolverhampton, adjacent to the Guy Motors

This Yorkshire coachbuilder displayed two different single-deck body types in a late 1920s advertisement. Both were for local operators: the upper one was a Reo Pullman for County Motors of Lepton; and the lower one was for T. Burrows & Son of Wombwell.

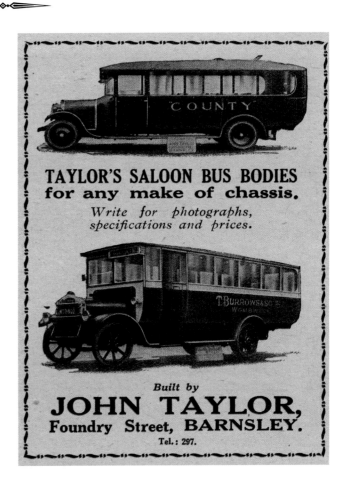

TAYLOR'S SALOON BUS BODIES for any make of chassis.
Write for photographs, specifications and prices.

Built by
JOHN TAYLOR,
Foundry Street, BARNSLEY.
Tel.: 297.

premises. The company is known to have built a sleeper coach on a Guy chassis in 1928. During the 1930s, the company became Holbrook & Taylors (*q.v.*).

THEALE

The Theale Motor & Engineering Works Ltd was based at 22–24 High Street in that Berkshire town. Between 1949 and 1950, it built some coach bodywork, apparently as part of the co-operative group that included Associated Deliveries, Dutfield, Longford and Hogger (*q.q.v.*).

THOMAS

W. Thomas & Son Ltd was established in 1877 at Great Bridge Street in West Bromwich. It built at least one 24-seat bus body in 1964 and remains in business as a vehicle sales and engineering company.

THOMPSON

F.M. Thompson & Sons, of Ramsgate Road in Louth, Lincolnshire, built both single-deck and double-deck bus bodies in the 1920s. Examples were a group of ten AEC 504 double-deckers for Birmingham in 1926.

THORNYCROFT

Thornycroft is best known as a chassis builder, but in fact started out as a constructor of steam launches at Chiswick in West London. It moved to Basingstoke in 1898, focusing initially on steam power, but by the time of the Great War was a leading motor-lorry builder.

From 1922, the company offered a range of PSV models, designing the single-deck bodywork for some of these, although the actual construction appears to have been subcontracted to others. However, by the 1930s the Thornycroft focus was firmly on chassis building and specifically on lorry types.

The company survived until 1970, latterly as part of the British Leyland empire.

THURGOOD

Thurgood's was a small but respected coachbuilder that operated from Ware in Hertfordshire between 1925 and 1967. It was founded by Walter Thurgood, who had been foreman of the Phoenix Coachworks (*q.v.*) and bought that company's Church Street premises when it closed. He built his first bus body on a Morris chassis in 1926; a second one on a Chevrolet chassis persuaded him to build a fleet of similar buses that he operated himself as People's Motor Services Ltd from 1928. This company was absorbed into the London Passenger Transport Board in 1933 after a period of interim ownership.

Meanwhile, the business expanded. A notable coup had been the contract to build a baggage van for King George V on a Leyland Lioness chassis in 1927. Thurgood bodies often had decorative 'flashes' on their sides and from early 1930 could be fitted with the company's own patented folding roof design called the Easiway; from

For the 1927 coaching season, Thurgood offered this sixteen-seat all-weather body on a Chevrolet chassis.

New in 1936 to Faichney's of Chester, this Thurgood-bodied Dennis Ace had C26R bodywork.

1932, Thurgood set up a separate company (Comfort-Travel Patents Ltd) to make this and a patented Non-Chafe Seat for other coachbuilders. A move to larger premises in Park Road followed, although the company was building only three bodies a month on average, on both small and full-size chassis. Most went to small independent operators.

During World War II, Thurgood's moved into timber supply work at first, although its factory was destroyed by bombing in October 1940 and the company subsequently switched to aircraft production work. The first post-war body swiftly followed the war's end, being completed in December 1945. It was one of many pre-war chassis sent to Thurgood's for rebodying; between 1947 and 1950 the company would also body more than 100 new Bedford OB chassis as well as others like the Albion Victor. The late 1940s were boom years for the company, but orders had dropped off by 1951, when Thurgood's constructed some bodies for Bedford SB chassis and also tried its hand on bodies for the underfloor-engined Leyland Royal Tiger. Despite the decline, the company was confident enough to buy new premises at Widbury Hill in 1953.

In the late 1950s, Thurgood's developed a 28-seat body called the Successor for the Bedford VAS. This was soon followed by a version called the Forerunner, available as either bus or coach for the competing Ford Thames FC chassis. In the meantime, the company had also diversified into dealing in second-hand PSVs. The Thurgood business was sold to Plaxton (q.v.) in June 1967, its Ware premises becoming Plaxton's southern area service depot. The final Thurgood body was a 29-seater on a VAS chassis for Elms of Kenton in Middlesex, completed in July that year.

TILLING

Thomas Tilling Ltd was formed in 1897 by the sons of Thomas Tilling, who had established a horse bus service in London in 1846. The new company continued to operate bus services in London, in 1909 reaching a joint agreement with the London General Omnibus Company that focused on co-operation, but restricted the Tilling company's growth in London. Keen to expand beyond its south London base, Thomas Tilling Ltd opened a subsidiary in Brighton after World War I and began to build its own bodies for this and other operators. The workshops were in Lewisham and Lee, in south-east London.

Tilling bodies were made into the mid-1930s and over the years included charabanc, service bus, coach and double-deck types, the latter with both open and closed tops. Notable among the closed-top designs was Tilling's 1930 ST on AEC Regent chassis. Some of its body designs were also built by Dodson (q.v.).

Tilling was also instrumental in the creation of the Tilling-Stevens petrol-electric bus, where a petrol engine drove a generator that in turn powered the traction motor. This grew out of an agreement between the operator and W.A. Stevens of Maidstone.

TIVERTON

Tiverton Coachbuilders Ltd was active in the PSV world between 1934 and 1951, building single-deck bus and coach bodies from premises at Blundells Road, Tiverton, in Devon. In the late 1940s, the company was best known for its work on Austin K and CX chassis.

The company still survives, as the Tiverton Body & Container Co. Ltd.

TODD

The bus, coach and charabanc bodies built by F.H. Todd & Sons are sometimes known as Triumph types, after the name of the independent operator for whom many were built (Darlington Triumph Services). However, the company also built bodywork for other operators from its premises at Oxford Street (and later also at Chestnut Street) in Darlington, County Durham, between 1920 and 1949.

TOLSONS

Tolsons Ltd was a Cockermouth, Cumbria, firm that built some single-deck bus bodywork between 1921 and 1936 at New Street and at Imperial Garage in Crown Street. Some of its late 1920s work was for Isle of Man Road Services.

TOOTH

Charles T.W. Tooth was a Wrexham company active between about 1921 and 1934. It built single-deck bodywork for local operators and also some bodies for Crosville on Leyland Cub chassis in 1933.

TORQUAY

A Torquay Motor Co. built coach bodywork in 1931, but nothing further is known.

TORQUAY CARRIAGE

The Torquay Carriage Co. constructed charabanc bodies between 1923 and 1928, probably only for local operators.

TOWER COACHWORKS

Tower Coachworks was a Leeds company that entered the PSV market in the late 1940s, although it seems to have been involved with commercial bodybuilding since the early 1930s. Its involvement with the PSV scene was short-lived. The company's address was in Woodhouse Street, Leeds 6.

TRANSUN

See Trans-United.

TRANS-UNITED

The Rochdale firm of Trans-United Coach-Craft Ltd (which sometimes called itself Transun) was actually a co-operative venture set up by a number of local coach operators, among whom the most prominent was Yelloway Motor Services of Rochdale. The company opened

for business in the first quarter of 1947 from premises at Oldham Road, initially building half-cab coaches on chassis such as the Leyland Tiger PS1.

Bodies for the new underfloor-engined chassis followed at the start of the 1950s and the early Yelloway examples on AEC Regal IV chassis with bulbous front wing projections were known to their drivers as Sabrinas after the popular film starlet of the period. The company remained in business until mid-1955, its last products being a pair of Commer Avengers for Johnston of Middleton.

TRICE

Bus bodywork came from the Cumberland Street, Ipswich, Suffolk, workshops of R. Trice in 1927.

TRIUMPH

See Todd.

TURNER

E.A. Turner was an independent operator at 163–165 London Road, Kingston, Surrey, which built the occasional coach body for other operators between 1930 and 1950.

Yelloway Motor Services of Rochdale was one of the operators behind Trans-United, whose bodywork is seen here on a 1951 Leyland Royal Tiger for that company.

TRANSUN spells QUALITY DIGNITY ECONOMY

BUILT TO BE FIRST AND BUILT TO LAST

LUXURY COACHWORK • STAGE CARRIAGE • STAGE CARRIAGE WITH LUXURY APPOINTMENTS • SPECIAL TYPES OF PASSENGER VEHICLES

If you need a single deck passenger carriage, you need a Transun Specification

TRANS-UNITED COACH-CRAFT LTD., ROCHDALE

The company claimed to stand for quality, dignity and economy, although the 1949 AEC Regal for Yelloway had few special design features – unless the projection of the body alongside the bonnet is counted.

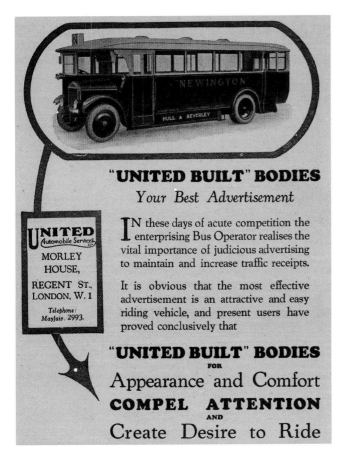

Though its workshops were in Lowestoft, United had offices in London and, in this case, was building for a Yorkshire operator in 1926.

UNDERHILL

Underhill & Sons Ltd was a Jersey company that built single-deck bus bodywork in the 1920s, probably only for local operators and possibly only for their own use.

UNION CONSTRUCTION CO.

The Union Construction Co. was based at Feltham in Middlesex and was established in 1901 as part of the Underground group. From 1925, it was busy renovating older London Underground trains and from 1927 built new rolling stock for that company. It also rebuilt a large number of trams for the Metropolitan Electric Tramways and then from 1929 constructed the famous Feltham trams operated by London United Tramways and by Metropolitan.

The company was renamed the Union & Finance Construction Co. Ltd in 1929. It built the distinctive bodies for the first sixty London United 'Diddler' trol-

leybuses on AEC 663T chassis that began to replace trams from 1931. However, when the London Passenger Transport Board was created in 1933 to absorb the myriad operators working in and around the metropolis, the new company was forbidden to build its own vehicles directly. The Union company was therefore wound up in 1934.

UNITED

A Sunderland-based company called United built a 33-seat forward-entrance coach body on a Daimler CVD6 chassis in 1951, but this vehicle was not for PSV use.

UNITED AUTOMOBILE SERVICES

United Automobile Services was an operator that built several hundred bodies for its own use in its Lowestoft workshops in the 1920s. It later became Eastern Coach Works or ECW (*q.v.*). However, the company also built bodywork for other operators, including some double-deck bodies on Guy FCX and AEC Regent chassis for Great Yarmouth Corporation. Its head office was in London's Regent Street.

UPFIELDS

A Hastings company with this name built some single-deck bus bodywork in 1919.

The bunting was not standard ... these were two of the first Union 'Diddler' trolleybuses on special duties prior to tram replacement in 1931. The front canopy recalled tram practice.

VAN HOOL McARDLE

Van Hool was a long-established bus-body manufacturer in Belgium, with a factory at Koningshooikt. However, it had no impact on the British market until the 1970s — even though in 1966 it touted a pair of special continental touring coaches based on Leyland Olympic underframes.

The Irish state-owned bus operator Córas Iompair Éireann (CIE) had its own workshops at Spa Road in Dublin, but by the early 1970s was looking for a joint-venture arrangement with a bus manufacturer that would provide it with the new buses it needed. In 1973 it reached agreement with Van Hool, which set up a joint venture with Thomas McArdle Ltd of Dundalk and took over the lease of the CIE workshops.

The plan was to satisfy CIE requirements and to build for export as well, but Van Hool soon found that production was too small for profitability. Other problems arose. Poor reliability of the Leyland Atlantean chassis on which the first Van Hool McArdle bodies were constructed led CIE to look for a contract with a different chassis manufacturer. The company was also dissatisfied with the 'cost-plus' nature of its agreement with Van Hool McArdle. So the Van Hool McArdle operation gave way in 1980 to a new venture, jointly run by the Canadian company Bombardier (*q.v.*) and by the General Automotive Corporation.

VICKERS

Vickers (Crayford) Ltd was an engineering company at Crayford in Kent founded in 1888 to manufacture the Maxim machine gun for the British armed forces. Between 1907 and 1910 the company also built cars for the Siddeley Autocar Company of Coventry. Vickers

redesigned the Maxim gun in 1912 and its main activity during the Great War was the manufacture of these weapons under its own name. There was also aircraft manufacture, of the FB5 fighter and Vimy bomber.

Wartime expansion made Vickers the most important firm ever to operate in the Crayford area and other factories were opened in Erith and Dartford. After the war, the Crayford factory began making motor-car parts,

The chassis is a Tilling-Stevens B10B and this three-seater saloon body was built for Stoke-on-Trent Motors in 1927.

A thirty-seat front-entrance saloon body on Maudslay ML3A chassis for Church's Safety Coaches of Leicester in 1928.

This 32-seat rear entrance saloon was on a 1929 Tilling-Stevens B10A2 chassis, for Mr W. Ll Davies of Swansea.

This Thornycroft was bodied by Vickers as a twenty-seater for a Cornwall operator in 1926.

This was a 51-seat Vickers body on a 1929 Leyland Titan chassis for Bradford Corporation.

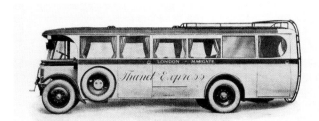

1929 again, and this time a repeat-order 32-seat coach body on Tilling-Stevens chassis for the Thanet Express company of A.W. Bangham. The spare-wheel mounting is especially interesting.

sewing machines, sporting guns (from 1921) and bus bodies. Known examples include a double-deck trolley-bus for Birmingham on AEC 607 chassis in 1926, another trolleybus body on a Clough, Smith chassis in 1927 and single-deck bus bodies the same year on Guy FBB and Tilling-Stevens B101B chassis.

In 1927, Vickers Ltd merged with the Armstrong Whitworth engineering company and the joint Vickers-Armstrongs concern made armaments, trains, aircraft and cars. An advertisement that year described Vickers as 'England's largest motor bodyworks', but bus-body manufacture seems to have ceased a few years later, although Vickers was among the companies that built bodies under contract to Leyland when that company's body shops came under pressure around 1930; some of these used Leyland designs.

From 1929, Vickers-Armstrongs merged its railway business with that of Cammell Laird in the Metropolitan-Cammell Carriage and Wagon Company (q.v.).

VINCENT

Vincent's of Reading enjoyed a brief career as a builder

of bus bodies in the 1940s and 1950s, but the company could trace its origins back to 1805. William Vincent Ltd was building car bodies by the end of the century, going on to become an important provincial coachbuilder in the 1920s. It became best known for its horseboxes, a field in which it was a pioneer from 1912. As demand for car bodies dropped during the 1930s, the company turned increasingly to commercial bodywork.

Vincent's capitalized on the demand for new bus bodies in the late 1940s and among its contracts was one to rebody a number of Dennis Lancet chassis for Aldershot & District. There were some rebuilds for Reading Corporation in 1946, Glenton Tours of London took some luxurious coach bodies on Dennis Lancet chassis and local operator Smith's Luxury Coaches took a full-front coach on a Lancet chassis in 1950. However, the company gave up all coachbuilding activities in the mid-1950s and today survives as a chain of car dealerships.

VINCENTS

Vincents Motor Works, later Vincents of Yeovil Ltd, traces its origins to the wheelwright business founded by John Vincent in the 1840s. The Yeovil business was established by 1900 and it built single-deck bus bodywork in the 1920s from premises at 23–26 Market Street.

From 1954, the company owned the operator Hutchings & Cornelius of South Petherton and rebodied some vehicles for them in the 1950s. Vincents of Yeovil is today a car dealership.

This is a 1949 forward-entrance Vincent coach body on Dennis Lancet chassis for Glenton Tours of London.

VULCAN

The Vulcan Motor and Engineering Co. of Crossens, Southport, was founded in 1902 and focused on car manufacture up to 1928. Thereafter, it switched to commercial vehicles. The first buses were built in 1922 and in the second half of the 1920s the company built single-deck bodies for its own PSV chassis, adding the double-deck Emperor in 1930. Southport Corporation was one customer. There were bodies for Manchester Corporation on Leyland chassis in the late 1920s and Vulcan built the frames for more Manchester Leyland single-deckers in 1932, although the bodies were finished by the Corporation. Birmingham also took some Vulcan-bodied AEC Regents in 1930.

Vulcan went into receivership in 1930, but remained active until 1937 when it was sold to Tilling-Stevens. That company sold out to the Rootes Group in 1950 and the Vulcan name disappeared in 1953.

WADHAM

The Wadham concern has had many different incarnations, but started life in 1919 as Wadham Bros (Coachbuilders) Ltd with premises at 97–99 London Road in Waterlooville, Hampshire. By 1965, it had additional premises in Portsmouth; from 1970 it was Wadham Stringer (Coachbuilders) Ltd; and there were further changes after 1981.

The company was best known before World War II for its ambulance bodies, but had built PSV bodies as well. These included examples on Albion, Leyland Cheetah and Thornycroft chassis, some double-deckers for Portsmouth and an eighteen-seater on Morris-Commercial chassis in 1938 for the GPO.

After the war, examples included 27-seaters on Morris-Commercial chassis and a 29-seater on a Guy Vixen chassis for a Devon operator. Welfare coaches and minibuses formed much of the Wadham Stringer repertoire, but the company later developed designs for chassis such as the Leyland Swift.

WADHAM STRINGER

See Wadham.

WALKER

William Walker set up his coachbuilding business at Ashgrove Road in Aberdeen in 1919. For a brief period, he operated as Moir & Walker, but was working on his own by 1923. He built both commercial and PSV bodywork and in the 1920s and 1930s was the largest bus bodybuilder in the Aberdeen area. His major customer in the 1930s was Aberdeen Corporation Transport, one reason being the Corporation's concern about unemployment locally. Some of these bodies in the early 1930s were overweight when delivered and the Walker company eventually lost the Corporation's business.

Walker's was nevertheless chosen in 1943 to provide bus repair facilities for the area during the war period. There were a few post-war bodies as well, but in 1948 the company was sold to SCWS (*q.v.*) and the last Walker bodies were built in 1949.

WALTER ALEXANDER

See Alexander.

WALTON

I.E. Walton & Co. Ltd, of Crescent Garage, High West Street, in Gateshead, built charabanc and single-deck bus bodies in the early 1920s, trading as the Crescent Bus Co. The company was taken over by the operator Northern General in January 1924, but continued in business as bodybuilders and as agents for Reo chassis.

WARDS

James Wards was a joiner of South Ronaldsay in the Orkneys who built some bus bodywork for local operators in the 1920s.

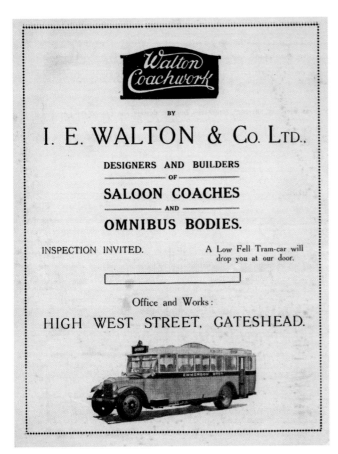

This late 1920s advertisement shows a rear-entrance single-deck body for Emmerson Bros.

WARWICK

The Warwick Motor Bodyworks built charabanc and single-deck bus bodies in the second half of the 1920s. It was named after the Warwick Mews in south London where A.F. Moore and H.W. Durling had set up their car bodyworks in 1919. The company had moved to Croydon by 1922 and was still building PSV bodywork on Overland and Tilling-Stevens chassis as late as 1929–30.

The company went on to become a builder of commercial bodies and undertook conversion work during the 1939–45 war. It closed down in 1972.

WATSON (1)

P.W. Watson & Sons Ltd was at North End Garage, High Street, in Lowestoft, Suffolk. From about 1922, it constructed bodies for its own coach fleet and in the 1930s built some stylish bodies for other operators over quite a wide area.

The company resumed coachbuilding activity after the 1939–45 war, building just two coach bodies, both on AEC Regal chassis for Moore (Viceroy) of Saffron Walden, Essex.

WATSON (2)

W.M. Watson & Sons Ltd was a car dealer in Liverpool that also built some car bodies. In the 1930s, it supplied some local independent operators with PSV bodies.

WAVENEY

The Waveney Co. Ltd was a small but well-respected Lowestoft coachbuilder based at Oulton Broad in that town. It was founded in 1924 by Thomas G. Betts and built both commercial and PSV bodies until 1940, when the war put an end to its activities. Betts subsequently worked for Commer.

Early bodies were on Bedford, Chevrolet and Commer chassis, and there were some Guy BB single-deckers for

Waveney called this fourteen- to sixteen-seater its Hendon body. It is seen here mounted on a Chevrolet chassis.

This was a 1929 body for Imperial Pullman's express service from Luton to London via St Albans.

R.L. Orsborn of Kettering bought this Waveney C20F body on Commer PN3 chassis in 1938.

Lowestoft Corporation. Llandudno Corporation was another customer, taking twenty-seat Waveney bodies on Commer and Guy chassis in 1937–8. There were also three double-deckers for the Warrington operator, Pusill (Suburban) of Penketh.

WELSH METAL INDUSTRIES

Welsh Metal Industries Ltd (WMI) was one of the many new entrants to the PSV bodywork business after the 1939–45 war. Based at Caerphilly in Glamorgan, the company had been caught up in wartime aircraft production work and found itself with a skilled workforce and no work when hostilities ended. It became involved with repair and reconditioning work, built a first prototype of its own on a pre-war Rhondda Transport AEC Regent, then went into production. Key characteristics were unit fabrication and the extensive use of aluminium, which resulted in a very light body. 'A WMI double-decker bus

WMI built a number of bodies on Foden PVD6 chassis for local operators. This one was for Merthyr Tydfil Corporation.

is approximately a ton lighter than one with a body made of wood and steel,' the company claimed. However, the WMI bodies were not known for their durability.

WMI built some double-deck bodywork for local operators on Foden chassis and also supplied components to chassis maker Sentinel (*q.v.*), which built them into its integral single-deckers. However, WMI faded from the scene in the early 1950s.

WENSLEY

Charles Wensley & Sons was a Yorkshire builder of charabanc bodies in the early 1920s. The company operated from 60–68 Ings Road in Wakefield.

WESTCOTT

Westcott Brothers was an Exeter coachbuilder that

A Foden again, this time for the West Wales fleet. WMI made much of its use of aircraft construction techniques.

constructed coach and charabanc bodies between 1922 and 1931.

WESTMINSTER

Westminster Coach Works Ltd was a London constructor of charabanc bodies at the start of the 1920s.

WESTMORLAND

Single-deck bus bodies made in the mid-1920s by Westmorland are thought to have been built by a Wakefield company of that name. Based at Alverthorpe Road, that company became part of the Bonallack bodybuilding group (as Bonallack Wakefield) in the 1960s. The factory was closed in June 1984.

WEST-NOR

C. & F. Bovey established the West-Nor Aircraft Sheet Metal Works at West Norwood in south-east London (hence the name) and from 1947 the company turned its skills to PSV bodywork as well. The venture lasted just a couple of years and customers for West-Nor coach bodies seem to have been in the London area.

One 33-seat forward-entrance example built in 1947 on a Maudslay chassis suffered from its poor-quality timber framework and had to be rebodied (by Metalcraft, *q.v.*) as early as 1952.

WESTWOOD & SMITH

Westwood & Smith Ltd was formed in 1921 as a motor-engineering partnership at Gorgie Road in Edinburgh, with bus manufacture as one of its aims. The company also ran Royal Blue Coaches, for which it built a number of bodies from 1926, but it made several other bodies for local operators up to 1934.

In 1935, the company became a subsidiary of Scottish Motor Traction, but was wound up in 1937.

WEST YORKSHIRE

The West Yorkshire Equipment Co. seems to have been the same company as the Yorkshire Equipment Co. (*q.v.*),

which eventually became part of East Lancs (*q.v.*). The company's name is associated with some double-deck bodywork in 1949.

WEYBRIDGE

The Weybridge Motor Engineering Co. Ltd was active as a PSV bodybuilder in the mid-1920s. The company was based at Black Boy Works in Weybridge, Surrey.

This 31-seater dual-entrance service bus body was on a Maudslay ML3 chassis and dated from 1928.

WEYMANN

Weymann was one of the big names in the British bus-bodying industry from the early 1930s to the mid-1960s. It had earlier made its name in the car-bodying business with lightweight bodywork, which used fabric skin panels and mountings that allowed the body to flex with the chassis, so reducing wear and the squeaks and rattles that were characteristic of early car bodies.

Charles Terres Weymann was a Frenchman whose background in aviation had inspired him to look for lightweight construction methods. He brought his patented construction system to Britain in 1923, initially selling

For the London to Glasgow service run by Orange Bros of Bedlington, Weymann constructed this dual-entrance body in 1930.

Constructed on Gilford chassis, this 1930 26-seat coach was for Olympic Coaches of Southsea, Hampshire, and used Weymann patent construction.

Although marketed as an MCW product, this 1933 double-decker on an AEC Regent chassis for Mansfield was built by Weymann at Addlestone.

The outward curve of the lower skirt panels was characteristic of Weymann bodies in the late 1940s. This 1946 H30/26R example was on an AEC Regent II chassis and was unique in the Eastbourne fleet.

This 1930 advertisement marks a turning-point for Weymann, when the company began to make orthodox PSV bodies alongside the fabric-panelled Weymann-patent type.

licences for its use; however, in 1925 he bought the old Cunard coachbuilding company of Putney and established Weymann's Motor Bodies in its workshops. Rapid expansion followed and Weymann moved to a former aircraft factory at Station Road, Addlestone, Surrey, in 1928. By then, however, the fashion for Weymann-style bodies was on the decline and the company needed new business.

By 1931 it had already begun to build bus bodies, some of them incorporating the Weymann construction patents. From 1932 the company became part of the new Metro-Cammell-Weymann (MCW) sales organization. It retained its own identity, although in later years some of the bodies from the Addlestone factory carried MCW plates. When Weymann's bank failed in 1937, the company was sold to the Prudential Assurance Company, which sold it on again in 1942 to United Molasses from the Tate & Lyle group.

The long-serving Fanfare coach body from the Addlestone factory is seen here on a 1956 AEC Reliance of the Yorkshire Woollen District fleet. CHRIS ASTON/OMNICOLOUR

This Leyland PD2 was bodied by Weymann in 1957 for J. Fishwick & Sons of Leyland.

Though bodied by Weymann for South Wales in 1958, these two AEC Regent Vs have the dome ventilator common to Metro-Cammell products.

This is a 1960 Leyland PD2 with Weymann body for St Helens Corporation.

In 1963, partner Metro-Cammell bought the Weymann company, but in 1964 a 21-week strike at the Addlestone factory marked the beginning of the end. Plans for closure were announced in 1965 and in 1966 the deed was done. All bodies from the surviving elements of the joint sales organization were then branded as MCW types. A year later, the old Weymann buildings passed to Plessey Radar, which became Marconi in 1990. The site of the former Weymann factory is now known as Aviator Park.

From 1933, Weymann had begun to build metal-framed bodies, although both Weymann-patent 'flexible' bodies and orthodox composite bodies also came from Addlestone right through the decade. By the end of the 1930s, Weymann was a very successful company. The company's double-deck types were popular with municipal buyers and there were single-deck service buses, too, but the company generally preferred to leave the coach market to others. Its largest pre-war order was for double-deck trolleybuses for London in 1936. Characteristics of Weymann bodies in this period included a pronounced 'shoulder' feature below the windscreen, outswept skirt panels and, on double-deckers, a convex frontal outline, a falling line for the top-deck guttering on the sides of the rear dome and a pair of narrow air-intake slots above the top-deck front windows. Nevertheless, these characteristics were not invariable.

Like other bus factories the Weymann works was subject to Ministry of Supply (MoS) requirements during the 1939–45 war. From 1942, the company built over 700 bodies to the MoS utility design, but its war work also included nearly 9,000 bodies for a variety of military vehicles. When peacetime production resumed, Weymann was one of the companies that picked up a

Virtually indistinguishable from the Metro-Cammell version is this Weymann body on a Leyland Atlantean for Ribble's long-distance express work.

contract for double-deck bodies to a standardized design for London Transport's RT class, and between 1946 and 1953 it built a total of 2,138. Meanwhile, double-deckers to its own design found a ready market all over Britain. Many of these, and the half-cab single-deck bus bodies of the time, had elegantly outswept skirt panels. By 1949, Weymann was at its peak, employing nearly 1,500 staff and achieving an output that year of 972 buses.

The Weymann works also built all the home-market bodies for the Leyland Olympic integral-construction single-deck bus between 1949 and 1951, plus did inspection and finishing work on those built by Metro-Cammell in Birmingham in later years. Weymann also built all sixty-six Leyland Olympians, the lightweight version of the Olympic built from 1954. Like the Olympic, this was always marketed as an MCW vehicle. There were many more businesslike single-deck bus bodies on underfloor-engined chassis over the next few years, many of which were bought by municipalities.

Weymann was never a mainstream coach manufacturer, but it did produce a number of designs in the 1950s that found most of their buyers within the BET fleets. The company's first underfloor-engined coach design was the Fanfare, introduced in 1954 and (unusually for the time) of all-metal construction. This was built almost without change right through until 1962, by which time it had begun to look rather dated; 144

were made. Its replacement was the Castilian – in effect an update of the original design for 36ft (11m) chassis, showing influence from the latest Harrington coaches. This was built only for Southdown, which bought two batches on Leyland Leopard chassis. The Fanfare was developed as an export design called the Arcadian in 1956, with a high floor and extra length, but only one was ever built. Then in 1960 came a special, unnamed coach design for Western Welsh that featured an unusual four-piece windscreen. An early 1960s attempt to break into the lightweight coach market failed, the bodies being marketed as MCW types.

From 1952, Weymann's version of the lightweight MCW Orion body became available as the Aurora. The company's 1957 prototype for the London Transport Routemaster class was passed over in favour of the Park Royal version. In 1962, Weymann built Britain's last new trolleybus, on a Sunbeam MF2B chassis for Bournemouth. Although there were many single-deck coach bodies in the early 1960s for BET group companies, these were to that group's standardized design.

WHITE

Graham White built charabanc bodies in the 1920s from an unknown address.

WHITEHORNS

This was a Bristol company that built bus, coach and other bodywork in the late 1940s. Nothing further is known about it, although it may be associated with A.C. Whitehorn Ltd, a precision-engineering company now in the Temple Meads area of the city.

WHITSON

Whitson was one of the more interesting small coach-builders that sprang up in the buyer's market of the late 1940s. Its founder was Alfred Ernest Whittit, who had been a foreman with Northern Counties (*q.v.*) immediately after the Great War, but moved on to the Riley car company in the 1920s. He was with the Dennis coachworks department in the 1930s and subsequently became Works Director at Strachans (*q.v.*) from 1938 to 1940.

Nevertheless, Whittit did not give his own name to the company he founded, which became James Whitson & Co. Ltd and was initially at Sipson Works, Sipson, in West Drayton, Middlesex. As early as 1946, the company was building single-deck coach bodies and over the next few years these were mounted on a variety of chassis – Crossley, Leyland and Maudslay among them. Some had full-front coachwork; most had thirty-three seats and a forward entrance.

From 1949, Whitson's branched out with a new venture. This was the half-deck or observation coach, an idea that had been seen before, but which took on a new elegance in Whitson guise. The company had a virtual monopoly of the type for about three years, building them on AEC, Leyland, Foden and Maudslay chassis.

Work on underfloor-engined types began indirectly, as the company is believed to have assembled some bodies

Whitson bodies were never conventional, as this example shows. It is a 35-seater coach built on reconditioned AEC Regal chassis.

for the Sentinel integral single-decker, using panels supplied by Sentinel. Its own flamboyant Grand Prix 41-seat central-entrance coach body appeared in 1952, with the protruding front styling adopted by some others at the time, allied to multiple side styling strips. The company hedged its bets by making preparations to body rear-engined chassis, taking out a patent for engine-cover support struts in June 1951.

From 1952, Whitson's moved to High Street in nearby Yiewsley and began to build fire engine and other commercial bodywork rather than PSV types. It moved into the GRP field from about 1956 and secured the contract for the first 250 Peerless car GRP bodies in 1957–9. At its peak, the company employed 350 people, but the PSV business had stopped by the mid-1950s. The company remained active, building GRP components for commercial vehicles.

WICKS

The Wicks company that built coach bodywork in the early 1920s is thought to have been based in Cambridgeshire.

WIDDISON

Widdison built single-deck bus bodies in the 1920s from premises at Pudsey, Leeds. Among the chassis it bodied were Overland types.

WIDNEY

The Widney company was established as a manufacturer of components for horse-drawn carriages and seems to have progressed into commercial vehicle bodywork. In the late 1930s it built some coach bodywork, probably only on smaller chassis.

The company is still in the PSV bodywork business, as a supplier of window frames and other coachwork fittings.

WILKINSON (1)

George Wilkinson was a joiner from Elston, near Newark, Nottinghamshire, who constructed some single-deck bus bodies in the early 1920s.

WILKINSON (2)

Active during the 1920s from about 1923, I. Wilkinson & Son Ltd was based at Stafford Street in Derby. The company built several bodies for Blue Bus Services of Repton, including a fourteen-seat body for an ex-Italian Army Fiat. In 1929–30 it built some 32-seaters on Maudslay chassis.

WILKINSON (3)

Joseph Wilkinson was a motor engineer based at Broughton in Edinburgh from about 1919. The company held a Leyland franchise and is believed to have built the bodies on a pair of Lioness chassis in 1928. In the 1930s it established a separate bodyworks at McDonald Road Coach Works. Among its final PSV bodies were some Leyland Tigers for Boyd of Bo'ness in 1938–9, which unusually had convertible coach and commercial vehicle bodies.

The company merged with Milburn Motors in 1972, subsequently becoming part of the Rossleigh group and then the Heron Corporation.

WILKS & MEADE

The name of this coachbuilder is commonly spelt incorrectly as Wilkes & Meade; it appears that the form without the 'e' is correct. The company was established in Leeds and in 1946 became part of the Wallace Arnold coach-operating group.

However, its coach and double-deck bodies were not confined to that operator. It built a number of single-deck bodies in the late 1940s and also three double-deck coach bodies on Daimler CVD6 chassis for Premier Travel of Cambridge in 1950. These bodies, which were the company's last, were lowbridge 53-seat full-front types very similar in concept and design to the Ribble 'White Ladies' of the time on Leyland PD2 chassis. They unfortunately did not last well, and had to be rebuilt by the operator quite early on.

WILLENHALL

Willenhall Coachcraft was established in the 1930s as a car body repair and garage business, and in the early 1950s became a Volkswagen franchised dealer. In the boom years of the late 1940s, it turned a portion of its workshops (County Bridge Works at Willenhall in Staffordshire) over to constructing coach bodywork. There were not many Willenhall bodies in this period, and part of the company later became the Willenhall Motor Radiator Co. Ltd (subsequently Willenhall Radiators Ltd).

WILLETT

Colchester, Essex, was the home town of Harold J. Willett Ltd, which operated from premises in the High Street from the mid-1920s until the end of the 1940s. The company had started out as ironmongers and may also have owned a local paint shop.

The company bodied only Ford chassis, such as a twenty-seater in 1929, and by 1937 had also become a Ford dealership.

WILLMOTT'S

Willmott's Motors Ltd was active as a PSV bodybuilder for most of the 1920s and until 1939. The company built

This was a 1932 body by Willmott's on Dennis Lancet chassis, for Slatter's Saloon Coaches.

In 1927, Willmott's advertised this 'semi all-weather' design for Chevrolet chassis.

both coach and single-deck bodywork from its London premises, initially at Woodger Road, Shepherd's Bush, London W12, and later from 50 Ravenscroft Gardens, London W6.

Willmott's 1930s bodies included a 1932 Dennis single-decker and, in 1939, a twenty-seat forward-entrance coach body on Bedford WTB chassis for Vincent of Thorncombe.

WILLOWBROOK

Willowbrook was a highly respected and successful bus bodybuilder between 1927 and the early 1980s, and one of the major players on the British scene. The company had begun in 1900 as Stokes & Holt Ltd, basket-makers at Belgrave Gate in Leicester. It moved into car-body construction in 1910 and by 1925 had established Willowbrook as a subsidiary at the same address to take over the company's bus and car building activities. Willowbrook Ltd was subsequently formed in January 1927 with new premises at Derby Road in Loughborough.

In the beginning, the company conformed to type by building single-deck bodies on chassis such as Chevrolets and the small Bedfords, but by the middle of the 1930s it was bodying full-size single-deck chassis as coaches and had moved into the double-decker market as well. There were even some bodies on the AEC Q chassis. Most of its customers were independent operators and almost all of its bodies were coach types.

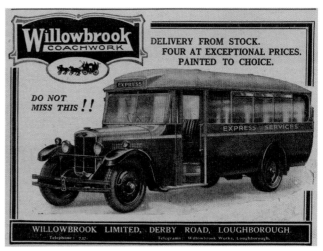

On AJS chassis, this body dates from 1930.

This Willowbrook service bus body on a Bedford chassis dates from 1969.

Pictured in June 1927, these Chevrolets for Allen's in Loughborough were among the coachbuilder's earliest products.

Again dating from 1930, this forward-entrance bus was for a municipal operator.

The end user of this AEC Regent is unclear, but it may have been Hants & Dorset. The vehicle was built in 1934.

During the 1939–45 war, Willowbrook was one of the companies designated to construct utility-pattern double-deck bodies and the ones it built were readily recognizable by a top deck that looked wider than the lower deck. There were some rebodies of older chassis, too, both single-deck and double-deck types, and these continued into the early 1950s.

After the war, Willowbrook built a standard design, but with minor variations to suit customer requirements. Among the more unusual commissions was one from Birch Bros, for whom the company built four full-front, forward-entrance highbridge double-deckers on Leyland Tiger PS1/4 chassis. The company took over the Brush (q.v.) metal-framed body patents in 1952. Although in this period it was largely a builder of bus bodywork, including many lowbridge double-deck types, Willowbrook also built some coaches. Notable were the special centre-entrance bodies for BMMO's operator-built C3 class. The rest was mainly for the BET fleets; an early style bought on underfloor-engined Guy chassis by Black & White had paired windows, a curved waist rail and a centre entrance.

The metal-framed Viking coach had a front entrance and was supposedly 'in the Continental style', with plenty of horizontal beading and twin stacked vertical lamps; fewer than forty were made in all, most going to fleets like Grey Cars (the Devon General subsidiary) and Northern General. The company joined Alexander, Park Royal and Weymann (q.q.v.) in building the standard BET-pattern single-deck service bus body from

The Loughborough company did its fair share of
rebodying after the 1939–45 war. This Bristol K5G was
new to North Western in 1939, but was rebodied in 1951.

Walsall Corporation took this forward-entrance body on a Dennis
Loline chassis in 1958.

This was the service bus body of the 1950s, seen here on a 1959 Leyland Tiger Cub for Soudley Valley Coaches of Littledean
in DP41F form.

A 1974 service bus body for Hedingham Omnibuses on a Leyland Leopard chassis.

LEFT: **This one on AEC Regent V chassis was for City of Oxford Motor Services and had an H37/26F configuration.**

BELOW: **The Viking coach body was neat and elegant. Here it is on a 1958 AEC Reliance for Northern General.**

the late 1950s, but also supplied these to independent operators.

Willowbrook's focus on bus bodywork made it an ideal fit with the Duple business, which depended on coach bodies. So, when Duple was looking to expand, it made a bid to take over Willowbrook. The deal was done in September 1958 and the Duple Midland operation (formerly Nudd Bros & Lockyer) moved to Loughborough. From 1960, the two Duple subsidiaries were merged, then from 1963 the Yeates (*q.v.*) coachbuilding premises adjacent to the old Willowbrook operation were used in conjunction with the existing Willowbrook factory.

Willowbrook continued with its own distinctive designs for a time, replacing its Viking coach body with the Viscount at the end of the 1950s, although its gaping grille and optional reverse-rake rear window did not help it to sell, with the result that fewer than thirty were made. The early 1960s saw the Willowbrook name on standardized coach and bus bodies for the BET group of operators; from 1963, it became Duple policy to badge all double-deck bodies and all single-deckers on 'heavy-weight' chassis as Willowbrook products. Single-deckers on lightweight Bedford and Ford chassis were meanwhile badged as Duple Midland. However, the policy was not entirely consistent and some lightweight single-deck chassis had Willowbrook bodies.

Willowbrook was sold in 1971 to George Hughes, who renamed it Willowbrook International. Hughes was at this stage a co-owner of Duple. A year later, the company launched its new Expressway or '002' coach with modern, European looks; most of the 150 or so built were equipped as dual-purpose bodies. Hughes himself did the first styling sketches for the Spacecar, or '008' design, that was announced at the 1974 Earls Court Commercial Motor Show on Bedford YRT chassis. The Spacecar was available for the latest 10m, 11m or 12m (metric measurements now being used) chassis and attracted a great deal of attention, although this did not lead to great success. Only ninety-three examples were built in four years of production, on AEC, Bedford, Leyland, Seddon and Volvo chassis.

Willowbrook ceased trading in 1984, but re-emerged a year later in new premises at Royal Way, Belton Road West, Loughborough, and with new Crusader coach and Warrior single-deck bus designs intended to secure the company a place in the rebodying market. Its activities ceased in 1993 and its premises are now the garage of a successful local bus operator, Paul S. Winson of Loughborough.

WILSDON

Wilsdon & Co. Ltd was a coachbuilder from Solihull in Warwickshire, with premises at Park Road and in Lode Lane. The company was primarily a commercial body-builder, but also built some coach bodies in the 1960s.

In 1968 the company acquired the Manhire Chandler (*q.v.*) business, but closed down in 1975.

WILTON

The Wilton Carriage Company was active from 107 Waddon New Road in Croydon, Surrey, by 1916. Later becoming a limited company, it moved in January 1921 to a new factory at 244 London Road, although the Waddon Road address seems to have remained current in 1924. By 1929 it had moved further down the London Road to number 470.

Dating from 1924, these are examples of bodies built by the Wilton Carriage Company in Croydon.

The company built both car and PSV bodies in the 1920s and was still active into the 1930s.

WINDOVER

The Windover company was new to the luxury coach-building scene in the late 1940s, building up a strong reputation in that period and the first half of the 1950s. Windover bodies were always known for their high standard of finish, which some described as better than Duple's.

Windover Ltd was established in 1856 in Huntingdon, Cambridgeshire, and was well established as a car body-builder before the Great War. In the inter-war years, it built bodies for prestige car chassis such as Daimler and Rolls-Royce and in 1924 relocated to Colindale in north-west London. After the Second World War, the focus of the business changed as the market for car bodies almost disappeared. There were bodies for Beardmore taxis and hearses, and in the 1950s for some of the Green Goddess fire engines built for Civil Defence. However, the main focus of Windover's activities from 1947 was on passenger-coach types.

Although half-cab coaches were being built as late as 1951, Windover moved into the underfloor-engined market that year with the Queensway, a competent but rather undistinguished style for which the only major customer was Yorkshire Woollen District, which had six. Much better known today is the Kingsway that replaced it, characterized by a reverse rake to its front panels and by full-length lower side trims and forward-projecting 'wings'. Several BET companies favoured this design, and

the best-known examples were probably those bought by Sheffield United Transport. The last example was built in 1955, featuring the unusual rear entrance that Windover offered as an alternative to a central entrance.

In 1956, Windover sold out to the London car dealer Henly's, and coachbuilding work ceased that year.

WISE

Wise (Coachbuilders) Ltd briefly built coach bodywork from premises at London Road in Staines, Middlesex, in the late 1930s. It was notable for some very stylish bodies, some with the full-front style that was not very common at the time. The company ceased PSV activity around the start of the 1939–45 war.

WITHNELL

Withnell was a bodybuilding company in the north Wales town of Shotton, Flint. The company constructed some coach bodywork in 1948–9, including several on Crossley chassis and one 35-seat forward-entrance type on an ex-Bolton 1942 Leyland Titan TD7c for an Anglesey independent operator.

WOODALL NICHOLSON

Woodall Nicholson is a Halifax company best known today as a builder of hearses. It was established in 1873 when Thomas Woodall Nicholson took over Piercey's, a coachbuilding firm. Initially building hansom cabs and horse carriages, the company was building car bodywork by the 1920s and during the following decade moved into hearse work.

During the post-war era of heavy demand, it became associated with single-deck PSV bodies briefly, building on Commer Q4 chassis among others in 1948–9.

WOODISS

So little is known about Woodiss that it is not even clear if the company was called that, or was actually Woodwis. Essentially, Mr W. was the local carpenter in the Derbyshire town of Bakewell. He built just one known body, a single-decker on Ford Model T chassis, for Hulleys of Baslow in 1921.

The Windover Kingsway was a distinctive style from the early 1950s. This example was on AEC Reliance chassis and was delivered to Hudson's Bus Company of Horncastle, Lincolnshire, in 1955.

WRAY

Wray's Motor & Body Co. Ltd built PSV bodies in the late 1920s from premises at 40 Waterford Road, Walham Green, London SW6. The company sold both bus and coach types to independent operators, building on chassis that included Daimler, Gilford, Leyland Lioness, Reo and Sunbeam (SMC). By 1929, it had moved into all-steel construction. It also had a second identity, as Wray's Motor & Accessories Company, which seems to have been the dealership side of the business.

One story told about the company, and verified by surviving photographs, is that it photographed most new vehicles at The Boltons, an oval of expensive Victorian houses just south of the Old Brompton Road in Kensington. The place took its name from the church of St Mary the Boltons, in the middle of the oval.

WYCOMBE

Wycombe Motor Bodies Ltd was established in 1927 as a subsidiary of the chassis-builder Gilford and its bodies are particularly associated with that make of chassis. In the early days, the Petty brothers (*q.v.*) acted as consultants to the firm, which had its works at Hughenden Avenue in High Wycombe, Buckinghamshire.

Wycombe's construction methods were interesting – the company made jigs from prototype bodies to ensure standardized sizes, which enabled the bodies to be built independently of the chassis and stored until needed. It was also a pioneer of cellulose paint finishes.

Wycombe normally employed wooden frames, but also built the all-metal bodies for two radical front-wheel drive prototypes from Gilford in 1931, using an integral structure. One was a double-decker. However, neither attracted any customers and the huge cost of this venture began the gradual decline of Gilford, which also took Wycombe with it. In 1934, the company moved into smaller premises at Brentside Works in NW10 on London's North Circular Road, but at the end of 1935 Gilford went bankrupt and Wycombe was voluntarily wound up in March 1936. Unfinished bodies in the works were completed by Burtonwoods Garage of Woodchurch Lane, Reigate, in Surrey.

WYLIE & LOCHHEAD

Wylie & Lochhead was running horse-drawn buses in Glasgow by about 1837, but was better known in the cabinet-making, furnishings and funeral trades. Coach-building began around 1902 and there were many commercial vehicle bodies from the company's premises at 113 Berkeley Street. In 1929–30, the company built some bus bodywork, the majority being school buses for Glasgow Corporation.

The remains of the Wylie & Lochhead business empire were sold to House of Fraser in 1957 and the motor department was eventually closed in 1991.

—⟫◆⟪—

YEATES

William Stanley Yeates spent some time as Gilford's sales manager before establishing his own business as the company's Midlands agent at Hallowstone, Nottingham, in October 1928. Business clearly went well, as by 1931 W.S. Yeates & Co. was able to move into larger premises, buying a site next to the Willowbrook (*q.v.*) works on Derby Road in Loughborough. A year later, it took on agencies for Bedford and Dennis chassis as well.

By 1934, Yeates had also begun to overhaul and repaint PSVs and goods vehicles. The company expanded further over the next five years and during the 1939–45 war became a repair and reconditioning centre for military vehicles. Though W.S. Yeates himself died in an accident in 1943, the company had sufficient depth in its management to carry on and in 1944 it restarted its coachbuilding activities.

Free to build commercially again by 1946, Yeates began with a fire engine for the local corporation and then rebodied an earlier Thornycroft Cygnet chassis as a coach. In October 1946, the company opened a new coachbuilding department on Byron Street, which began by refurbishing pre-war buses and soon moved on to building its own bodies as well. There were bodies on Bedford OB, Crossley and Dennis Lancet chassis; around 1949 there were some rebodies on ex-military Commer Q4s as well. The three styles offered in the late 1940s all had a strong resemblance to pre-war Duple products, but Yeates also created full-front versions, some of which were used on pre-war chassis lengthened to take advantage of the latest regulations. The company's bodies

W. S. YEATES LIMITED

Coachbuilders — Passenger Vehicle Specialists

41-seater de luxe Leyland Royal Tiger/YEATES Coach.

As coachbuilders of many years experience of building fine coaches, we know the appeal of style, when this is coupled with passenger comfort. We can offer you these features, and shall be pleased to quote for coachwork on customers' own chassis, and consider reasonable part exchange against complete vehicles. May we have your enquiries?

DERBY ROAD, LOUGHBOROUGH
Phone: Loughborough 4321 (4 lines)

This 1951 advertisement shows a Yeates 41-seat coach body on a Leyland Royal Tiger chassis.

gained a reputation for solid construction and ensured the survival of its coachbuilding activities into the underfloor-engined era.

The 39-seat centre-entrance body introduced in 1951 was certainly more attractive than many offerings by others new to underfloor-engine designs and an update of the original design in 1952 was named the Sherwood. Then from 1953, Yeates created its own very distinctive style for front-engined chassis (mainly the Bedford SB) with the Riviera, its sides wearing flamboyant aluminium beading.

Although 1957 saw a downturn in sales, the company bounced back with its new Europa body, adaptable to chassis with either front or underfloor engines. As its name suggested, this was heavily inspired by continental European designs of the period, but it was a strikingly

To make room for a front entrance, Yeates moved the axle of the Bedford SB chassis back; this was the company's Pegasus bus body, in this case seating fifty-three passengers thanks to 3+2 seating. PEP 380 was an SB5 chassis, new in 1963 to Mid Wales Motorways of Newtown.

Typical of the later, flamboyant Yeates designs is this 1960 Fiesta coach body on a Ford Thames chassis.

different style in the British market. It was replaced in 1962 by the further-evolved Fiesta design, also available for the latest 36ft (11m) chassis.

From 1960, Yeates also had its own conversion for the Bedford SB chassis, which moved the front axle back to create room for a front entrance. Initially available with a version of the Europa body, this was bodied from 1962 as a Fiesta FE44 type, while there was also a service bus or dual-purpose version called Pegasus. Though Yeates normally built only single-deck bodies, 1960 also brought a pair of double-deckers for Delaine of Bourne, built on Leyland PD3 chassis using Metal Sections (*q.v.*) frames.

However, Yeates bodies were not cheap; the later ones were jig-built with extensive use of aluminium. The company's last new design was a simplified Fiesta in 1963, but it was unable to compete against the volume-produced designs from Duple and Plaxton. The Yeates coachworks was sold to Duple in November 1963 and that company completed the last Yeates body at Byron Street in June the following year. The Yeates factory went to Willowbrook, which used it for repair and rebuilding work, and Yeates continued in business as a bus and coach dealer. Surviving records suggest that there had been just over 1,000 Yeates bodies in all since the beginning.

YORKSHIRE EQUIPMENT

The Yorkshire Equipment Co. Ltd is thought to have been the same company as the West Yorkshire Equipment Co. Ltd (*q.v.*). It was based at Bridlington in Yorkshire, seems to have built some PSV bodywork in 1949 and subsequently became East Lancashire Coach Builders (*q.v.*).

YORKSHIRE YACHT

Apparently capitalizing on the boom years after the 1939–45 war, the Yorkshire Yacht Building & Engineering Co. Ltd of Bridlington turned its hand to coach bodywork between 1947 and 1949.

YORK, WARD & ROWLATT

This company built single-deck bus bodywork in 1924, probably from an address in Wellingborough, Northamptonshire. By 1933 it was located at 8 Oxford Street in that town, but it is not clear if it was still active as a bus bodybuilder.

YOUNG

Young's seems to have been primarily a chain of car dealers, first registered as H. Young (Motors) Ltd in January 1924. It had branches at Darlington, Easington, Newcastle and Sunderland, but the headquarters was at 150 Front Street, in Chester-le-Street, County Durham.

The company's PSV bodywork was probably only a sideline, conducted from Chester-le-Street, and may have prompted its acquisition of additional premises in that town at Foundry Lane. These premises were called the Sturdiluxe Works, a name which presumably inspired Young's PSV trading name of Sturdiluxe Bus Bodies. The company was active as a builder of PSV bodies in the later 1920s and into the 1930s.

APPENDIX

OPERATOR-BUILT BODYWORK

Many bus operators, both large and small, constructed bodywork for their own vehicles in their own workshops. Sometimes the body would be on a new chassis and sometimes it would be a replacement for a damaged or worn-out body on an existing chassis.

This Appendix lists those operators that are known to have constructed, as distinct from merely repaired, their own motor-bus or trolleybus bodywork in the period 1919–75. Those who also constructed bodies for others feature in the main lists.

Abbey Lane Motor Services Ltd	Sheffield
Aldershot & District Traction Co. Ltd	Aldershot, Hampshire
Allchin (William Allchin Ltd)	Northampton
Ashton-under-Lyne Corporation	Ashton, Lancashire (to 1972)/Greater Manchester
Bailey	Bracknell, Berkshire
Barnes	Clacton-on-Sea, Essex
Barnsley British Co-Operative Society Ltd	Barnsley, Yorkshire
Barton	Chilwell, Nottinghamshire
Belfast Omnibus Co. Ltd	Belfast, Northern Ireland
Black & White Coaches Ltd	London
Blackpool Corporation Transport	Blackpool, Lancashire
Blair & Palmer	Carlisle, Cumbria
Bolton Corporation Transport	Bolton, Greater Manchester
Boyer (H. Boyer & Son)	Rothley, Leicestershire
Bradley & Lane (S.J. Bradley & OCW Lane)	Newcastle, Shropshire
Brighton, Hove & District Omnibus Co.	Brighton, East Sussex
Bristol Tramways & Carriage Co.	Bristol
British	London
British Railways Board (Eastern Region)	London
Broughton (Harry Broughton & Sons)	Barnoldswick, Lancashire
Brown (A.T. Brown)	Trench, Shropshire
Buckmaster Coaches Ltd	Leighton Buzzard, Bedfordshire
Bullock (J. Bullock & Sons Ltd; B. & S. Motor Services)	Featherstone, Yorkshire
Campbell Bros (Coaches) Ltd	Whitburn, West Lothian
Castle Motor Services	Forest Hall, Tyne and Wear
Catherwood (HMS Catherwood Ltd)	Belfast, Northern Ireland
City Coach Co.	London
City of Oxford Motor Services Ltd	Oxford
Collenette Bros (t/a Shamrock)	St Sampson, Guernsey
Creeth (A.H. Creeth & Sons, Premier Motors)	Nettlestone, Isle of Wight
Crosville Motor Services	Chester

Cumberland Motor Services Ltd	Whitehaven, Cumbria
Davies (Sydney J. Davies)	Penygraig, Glamorgan
Davies (W.J. Davies; Merthyr Motor Services)	Merthyr Tydfil, Glamorgan
Dowell	Exeter, Devon
Down	Ottery St Mary, Devon
Dublin United Tramways	Dublin, Ireland
Dunn (E.J. Dunn)	Taunton, Somerset
Eastbourne Corporation Transport	Eastbourne, East Sussex
East Kent Road Car Co. Ltd	Canterbury, Kent
Elliott Bros (t/a Royal Blue)	Bournemouth, Dorset
Embankment Motor Co. (Plymouth) Ltd	Plymouth, Devon
Everall (Don Everall)	Wolverhampton, West Midlands
Fleetwood & Knott End Motor Services Ltd	Fleetwood, Lancashire
Gaudy (James Gaudy)	Netherskail, Orkney
Gelligaer Urban District Council	Gelligaer, Caerphilly
Glasgow Corporation Transport	Glasgow
Glasgow General Omnibus Co. Ltd	Hamilton, Glasgow
Goodall (J. Goodall)	Echt, Abderdeenshire
Great Eastern Railway Co.	London
Great North of Scotland Railway	Kittybrewster, Abedeen
Great Southern Railway	Irish Republic
Great Western Railway	Swindon, Wiltshire
Guernsey Motors Ltd	St Peter Port, Guernsey
Guernsey Railway Co. Ltd	St Peter Port, Guernsey
Gunn (Herbert L. Gunn, Gunn's Tours)	Rackenford, Devon
Halifax Corporation Tramways	Halifax, Yorkshire
Hall Bros (t/a Invincible Bus Co.)	Seaham Harbour, Co. Durham
Hants & Dorset Motor Services Ltd	Bournemouth, Dorset
Harper Bros (Heath Hayes) Ltd	Heath Hayes, Staffordshire
Harvey (William S. Harvey)	Stromness, Orkney
H.C. Motor Works (Kingston) Ltd (t/a Kingston Services)	Kingston-upon-Hull, Yorkshire
Hedon Motor Coaches (R.A. Johnson)	Hedon, Yorkshire
Hire Cars (Market Weighton) Ltd	Market Weighton, Yorkshire
Huddersfield Corporation	Huddersfield, Yorkshire
Hutchins (Frank Hutchins; Yellow Bus Services)	Stourton, Surrey
Irvine (Peter Irvine & Sons, t/a Golden Eagle Coaches)	Salsburgh, Lanarkshire
Jersey Motor Transport	St Helier, Jersey
Jones (T. Jones & Sons)	Menai Bridge, Anglesey
Ledgard (Samuel Ledgard)	Leeds, Yorkshire
Leeds City Tramways	Leeds, Yorkshire
Leeds Industrial Co-Operative Society Ltd	Leeds, Yorkshire
Leicester Corporation Tramways	Leicester

Liverpool Corporation Passenger Transport	Liverpool
London & North Western Railways	Wolverton, Buckinghamshire
London General Omnibus Co. Ltd	London
London Midland & Scottish Railway Ltd	Derby
London Passenger Transport Board	London
London Transport Executive	London
MacRae & Dick Ltd	Inverness, Highland
Manchester Corporation Transport Dept	Manchester
Mansfield District Traction Co.	Mansfield, Nottinghamshire
Marsh (A.E. Marsh, t/a Black & White Coaches)	Harvington, Worcestershire
Martindale (G.E. Martindale)	Ferryhill, Co. Durham
Massey (Robert B. Massey & Co. Ltd)	Market Weighton, Yorkshire
Mathews (A. Mathews or W. Mathews)	Whitbourne, Herefordshire
Matthews (A. Matthews & Sons, t/a Greyfriars Coaches)	Winchester, Hampshire
McLennan (A. & C. McLennan)	Spittlefield, Perthshire
Mid Cheshire Motor Bus Co. Ltd	Northwich, Cheshire
Midland Bus Service Ltd	Airdrie, Lanarkshire
Neath & Cardiff Luxury Coaches Ltd	Neath, Glamorgan
North Eastern Railway	York
Northern General Transport Co. Ltd	Gateshead, Tyne and Wear
Northern Ireland Road Transport Board	Belfast, Northern Ireland
North Western Road Car Co. Ltd	Stockport, Merseyside
Owen (P. Owen & Sons Ltd)	Abberley, Worcestershire
Parfit (Edward James Parfit)	Rhymney Bridge, Caerphilly
Pass & Co.	Newbury, Berkshire
Pitcher (Arthur A. Pitcher, t/a Tantivy)	St Helier, Cornwall
Plymouth City Transport	Plymouth, Devon
Potteries Electric Traction Co. Ltd	Stoke, Staffordshire
Preston Corporation	Preston, Lancashire
Priory Garage & Coaches Ltd	Leamington Spa, Warwickshire
Reading Corporation Transport	Reading, Berkshire
Rich (J.A. Rich)	Cardiff, Glamorgan
Rochdale Corporation	Rochdale, Greater Manchester
Rotherham Corporation	Rotherham, Yorkshire
Rugg (W.J. Rugg, t/a Wayfarer Bus Services)	St Sampson, Guernsey
Salford City Transport	Salford, Greater Manchester
Sheffield Corporation Transport	Sheffield, Yorkshire
Shutt Bros	Burnley, Lancashire
Silcox Motor Coach Co. Ltd	Pembroke Dock, Pembrokeshire
Southampton Corporation	Southampton, Hampshire
Southdown Motor Services Ltd	Brighton, East Sussex
Southern Traction	Southampton, Hampshire
Southport Corporation Transport	Southport, Merseyside
Stocker (Harry Stocker Ltd)	St Margarets, Hertfordshire

Tiverton Motor Co.	Tiverton, Devon
Ulster Transport Authority	Belfast, Northen Ireland
United Counties Omnibus Co. Ltd	Desborough, Northampsonshire
Walsall Corporation	Walsall, West Midlands
Watts	Lydney, Gloucestershire
Wells (E. Wells)	Biddulph, Staffordshire
Wessex Coaches	Bristol
West Bromwich Corporation	West Bromwich, West Midlands
Westwood & Smith Ltd	Edinburgh
White Heather Transport Ltd	Southsea, Hampshire
Wilts & Dorset Motor Services Ltd	Salisbury, Wiltshire
Worthing Motor Services Ltd	Worthing, West Sussex
Yarranton Bros	Eardiston, Worcestershire
Yeadon Transport Co.	Yeadon, Yorkshire
Yeoman	Canon Pyon, Herefordshire

INDEX